Cottar & Croft to Fermtoun

Autobiography of Mary Michie

ARDO PUBLISHING COMPANY

*My thanks are due to Mrs Duguid, Aberdour and my neice Agnes
for their help in typing, my granddaughter Aileen for taking
photographs, and last but not least the Reverend Charles Birnie
without whose encouragement the book could not have been
written.*

Published by Ardo Publishing Company, Buchan
Printed in Great Britain by BPC-AUP Aberdeen Ltd

Contents

EDITORIAL NOTE

I often hear people bemoaning the fact that there is no farming ladder any more. Certainly there was a time when poor folk could work hard and save and invest wisely, and graduate to a big farm. Mary and Ivan Michie did it and this is their story.

Mrs Michie's book is also remarkable in that it is written by a woman; there is plenty written about this period by men but, as part of the little written by the other half, Mary Michie's book is precious.

Charlie Allan

Ardo Publishing Company would like to acknowledge the work put in by Banff and Buchan District's Department of Leisure and Recreation in preparing this volume for publication. In particular they undertook the lengthy task of transcribing the text.

This book is dedicated to Sandy

Foreword *by Rev. Charles Birnie*

Burns said that he wanted to make *"some usefu'plan or beuk"* for dear Auld Scotland's sake. This is exactly what Mary Michie has done.

She takes us through a period of social evolution. She gives us a picture of the Buchan way of life during what can now be seen as the last days of the great farm-servant class. Farming was labour-intensive then with a vengeance. But on the other hand it was still possible for a weel-doing chiel to make his way by the sweat of his brow, especially if his wife was a managing deem. To her it fell to ring the changes with the staple diet of meal and milk and tatties; to arrange and rearrange the few bits of plenishing as they loaded up yet again at the term for yet another tied house. And it was her grit and industry that enabled her man to make the quantum leap from cottaringto the self-employment of crofting and jobbing. For this meant exchanging the assured cash flow, meagre admittedly though it was, for the uncertainties of independence. The womenfolk were right behind their menfolk in their dream to be their own boss.

So then, with their experience both of service and initiative, the eident couple eventually graduate to the ferm-toun with its horseman, baillie and loon. And still it devolves on the guidwife to "maet the men". It's the belly that hauds up the back.

Mary Michie tells her story with an unaffected simplicity. Most of us have story material in our life experience and pretend we could write a book. Few of us exert the discipline and reslive to put it into practice. But the guidwife of Bankhead of Aberdour has done it and paid the reader the compliment of sharing a countrywoman's throughbearing, loyalties and aspirations.

This is good plain honest writing about good plain honest folk and we should all be grateful that it is now presented in "guid black print".

CHAPTER ONE

COURTSHIP

MORMOND - THAT place of a thousand memories is where my story will and must begin. Throughout my school years I had but one object in view - to pass my exams, go to university and then take the road that led over Mormond to distant lands. I did pass my exams but, quite suddenly, my dreams and whole life plan disappeared and I was left wandering in a sort of no-man's-land.

Mormond as it used to be with the old lodge and the White Horse

Then, one day at harvest in September when the golden sheaves were being brought in, I found the road that fate decreed I would follow. It was 1930 and it had been a good summer ending in a bumper harvest. All through the day the horses and heavy-laden carts had made their way to the back of the farm steading where the sheaves were being built by expert hands into a symmetrical line of rucks awaiting the thrashing mill.

This harvest day I had been sent to help out a neighbour - new arrivals. There were three boys in the family and I, who had never been interested in the opposite sex, began to feel an attraction to the middle one, Ivan.

All day I had been in the field tossing the rustling sheaves on to the carts. There was plenty of teasing and banter and, if I got too saucy, a sheaf would be thrown back at me, either to miss or give me a clout. Ivan was so very quiet and shy, but I teased him a lot, trying to draw him out. In the act of catching one of the sheaves, he looked down and I looked up, our eyes met and something happened between us - from that moment our fate was sealed.

When the gloaming came down and it was too dark to work we adjourned to the farm kitchen for a meal. When I left for home, it was no surprise to find Ivan loitering by the roadside. We did not talk a lot, just about this or that. What it consisted of I've little memory, but I do remember being greeted at home with the words, "You've surely been workin affa late." That was how the love affair began. It progressed slowly with casual meetings, meetings that sometimes Ivan contrived and other times I did. Although he was in partnership with his two brothers, there was not a livelihood for all three on the farm and Ivan had taken a horseman's job at Blairfowl in the Lonmay district.

There was little time for courting - holidays were never thought of. In the summer, when the horse were out at grass, he had most Sundays free, but in the winter only a Sunday once a fortnight. There were no free Saturday afternoons and Ivan would only have a day off for a Games or a Ploughing Match (he competed at quite a few). Sometimes he managed an evening meeting, though in the winter he had to attend to his horses: supper time was six o'clock. Then, between nine and ten o'clock they had to be taken out for a drink and given some feed.

They say that opposites attract and it was thus with Ivan and me, for two people could not have been less alike. He was slow and I was quick. I spent half of my time reading, but a newspaper was all he ever read. We often quarrelled and many a time I left him vowing never to

8

Ivan's family with Ivan on his mother's knee

see or speak to him again. Yet, when Sunday afternoon came around, I would be off to the hill, our unspoken trysting place. In the delight of being together our quarrel was forgotten.

Our romance was no fairytale and I was not very romantically minded. It was not love stories or books of that sort I read. I knew all about the birds and the bees, and I had been around with boyfriends and knew where their interests lay. But the tumult that sex could cause had as yet not touched me. I resented and rebelled against the attraction I felt for Ivan. I had a lot of ideas of what I would do with my life and marriage was not one of them. Ivan had no great ambitions, but his dream was to have a croft of his own. Often he talked of it, but the annoying part was that he never included me in his plans.

Shortly after we began to meet, his mother died. This was indeed a grievous blow - he had been very close to her and loved her very much. In the short time I knew her, I came to like and respect her. She really was a remarkable woman to have brought up thirteen of a family. Ivan was the eleventh son and her second daughter was born two years later, but died when only a few months old. Her last child, Cecil, was not born until five years later and this made Ivan her baby for much longer than the others.

Ivan and I played around for almost two years, but I think both of us were finding it more difficult to part and I know that at the back of my mind I was beginning to think more about marriage.

Then, one night, when we had lingered lovingly, finding good-bye difficult, he held me close and began to whisper, "This canna go on lassie; I want ye. We'll hae tae dae something about it or else I'll jist hae tae stop comin tae see ye." I said nothing but just snuggled a little closer. Then suddenly he left me and I was desolate. If he had come back then, I am of a mind he would have had little difficulty in persuading me to do something I had always vowed I would never do.

It was a fortnight before he had a day off, but the next week I got a letter from him. It was not a very well-written letter and it was one that only I could understand. He just could not keep on coming to see me the way he had been doing, but there was a croft to let quite near. He would put in an offer for the tenancy and, if he got it, would I come with him? If the answer was "no", he wasn't coming back.

I did not answer the letter but, when Sunday came around, I made my way to our usual trysting place with somewhat mixed feelings, hardly knowing what I was to say. Funny people that we were, although the letter was uppermost in both our thoughts, it took us some time to mention it. He was still of the same mind, and I still hesitated. But knowing he might go, that I might never see him again, filled me with despair. Yet the way he sat there saying so little - he had a sprig of heather in his hands which he was slowly pulling to pieces, showing no emotion whatsoever - exasperated me. I felt I was going to cry and said I was going home. With that he grabbed hold of me and said, "No ye winna, ye'll gie me yer answer first". I struggled for a few minutes and kept my face hidden against him, but the feeling of his arms around me was, I felt, all I had ever wanted. My doubts vanished, I snuggled closer and with my arms creeping up around his neck I whispered that I would come with him to his croft. From that moment I said goodbye to many a dream, for deep down in my heart I knew that this was meant to be. The tiny flame of the faith which I had lost might flicker anew and be rekindled in the new life before me.

All Ivan's plans were for the croft, and I often used to think it meant more to him than I did. My people had half expected our engagement so no objections were put in our way. My mother had been planning to give up her work and come to look after my grandmother. I was brought up by grandparents. My grandfather, whom I dearly loved, died when I was ten years old. By the time I finished my secondary education and was planning to go to college, my grandmother was getting on in years and needed someone to stay with her. This I had agreed to do, somewhat against my will. She was very demanding and my biggest fault was that I was always deep in a book. Many a time she would say, "Lassie you'll never mak a livin wi yer heid in a book."

During that winter Ivan had begun to come to the house and he got on very well with my grandmother. She liked company and Ivan was better at talking to old ladies than he was to young ones. Now and then he brought her (never me) a bag of sweets and this certainly put him into her good graces. It was usually half a pound of pandrops or mints he brought, but sometimes it would be a quarter pound of chocolates. Ivan was a canny lad with his money, never spending it on trifles, but

11

there were times throughout our life together when he quite surprised me. The first was about a week after I gave him my promise. Very shyly, he took a small box from his pocket and offered it to me. I was thrilled to find a gold ring in that box. He had known my favourite colour was green and no, it was not an emerald, but a tiny piece of jade. I was overjoyed with this present, for I had given him no hints, and having an engagement ring in those times was not at all common. The ring became very precious to me. Unfortunately, 25 years later I lost it. I just laid it down somewhere and, although I hunted high and low, I never found it. Not so long ago I saw an exact replica of my ring in a jeweller's shop in Aberdeen. How I was tempted to go in and buy it, but I knew it could not possibly be the one I had lost, so I was able to resist. Today I think, if I had purchased it, it might have been some comfort just having it to look at.

For a short time all was well, but our hopes and plans were shattered when Ivan was told that a neighbouring farmer had won the tenancy of the croft. This man was quite a big farmer, but getting on in years. He had decided to pass his farm on to a son and thought the croft ideal to retire to. He knew the factor and perhaps the laird too, so he had little difficulty in acquiring it. This was mostly the way things were done; it was all the easier if you knew someone to put in a good word for you, or someone who knew someone else. Another croft came on to the market and, once again, our hopes were raised. But the same thing happened again and someone else got it.

Ivan was bitterly disappointed, he got moody and tension again arose between us. We could have been married I expect with me staying on at home, but I had no intention of doing this. He never spoke of it himself, but I could not understand why he would not take a job with a house. Most of the larger farms had cottages for their workers. Some even had five or six houses.

One evening as we sat by the fire, he in the armchair and I on a stool beside him, I brought the subject up. Immediately, I sensed he was against this cottaring business. I had no idea what I was up against in Ivan's nature. He had been brought up on a three horse farm (a pair and an orra beast) and, although not in the class of the larger farms, it was superior to a croft where they had only one horse and sometimes not even that. Cottars again were on a much lower scale, and I think they gave themselves a bad name by the way some of them carried on. Most had large families and, when a few houses were huddled together, they were inclined to quarrel, usually over their children. Some of them were very poor managers and poverty was prevalent. I had led a sheltered life and was a stranger to their ways.

Ivan would not tie himself up in a cottar house. I could not understand this nor yet his resentment at taking orders. This never left him; his longing for a croft of his own was about being his own master and taking orders from no man. I got nowhere with him that night - arguing with Ivan was like knocking your head against a granite wall and expecting it to crumble. When he left, there were no lingering goodbyes and, as I shut the door on him with a bang, I felt I never wanted to see him again.

The mood did not last long. I was unhappy, hurt and bewildered and could not understand his reasoning. But I had little thought of what it meant to him, for I had never taken an order from anyone, nor worked for a wage. The nagging thought at the back of my mind, though, was that he cared a lot more for that blasted croft than he did for me. One evening, about a week later, he appeared unexpectedly. No, he was not coming in, but would I come out as he had something to tell me. I turned and got my coat and we made our way to the end of the garden, crossed the ditch and sat ourselves on the grassy bank. He began by asking if I was still mad at him and I said, "Nae really." That was a relief as he had gone back wondering if I would ever speak to him again. He was so disappointed at not getting the lease of the croft, the idea of cottaring had never entered his head. He just thought that surely I deserved something better. This line of argument had never struck me, for I was not then and never have been class conscious, so all I said in return was: "Ye hinna come back tae jist say that an start fechtin a ower again?"

No, no, there would be no argument this time but whether I'd be happy about it he just did not know. He was not too happy himself but the deed was done - then I got the story.

The day or so after our quarrel he had been looking through the paper and his interest was drawn to an advert requiring a married foreman for the farm of Fridayhill, Strichen, only a few miles distant. He thought about it all afternoon and, once his work was over, he cycled up to Fridayhill to see the farmer, a Mr Forman. After some negotiation a start was agreed for the 28th of May - the working of the first pair of horse was Ivan's along with a cottage.

After all our arguments, I could hardly believe it, but it was true. Ivan, who never did anything in a hurry, had left us just about three weeks to get married and have everything ready.

We talked a lot, or at least I did, but our talk mostly went in circles. As little money as possible was to be spent, for a croft was still his main objective and he was sure we would get one within the year. We both wanted a quiet wedding, so no argument there. He favoured a registry office wedding but I was all for a church one. This was decided in my favour. Ivan was working in the Leeds parish and I was in Rathen. Banns, therefore, would have to be called in both parishes. Ivan knew the routine as his brother had married the week before.

Darkness came down and it was getting colder, but we lingered on, loath to part. I was glad to snuggle closer and wrap my coat around him. The lights in the house had gone out and I knew my grandmother was in bed. Our talking had almost ceased, only a murmured word now and again. I knew if I gave him any encouragement he would have slipped into the house and thence to bed. I was full of a bubbly joy and felt no need for sleep. Yet when my head touched the pillow, it only took minutes to reach the land of nod. My last waking thought was not of Ivan or marriage, but of something I had almost forgotten. Tomorrow would be my birthday: I would be 22 years old.

The day of our wedding was fixed for the 24th of May and this time arrangements went according to plan.

The other day I was reading about wedding arrangements; I am afraid no girl of today would comprehend the marriage and start I had. The paper stated it would take at least £4,500 to cover a wedding, but ours cost less than £30.

All the new clothes Ivan got were the new shirt and tie I bought him. He had had a new suit made just six months before, so there was no need to get another. I did have a new dress, but not a white one. At that time, it was only wealthy people like big farmers who could afford to have their daughters married in white. I bought a piece of blue material and a friend made up the dress from a paper pattern I had chosen. I got a new coat, hat and shoes, and a handbag, and with some new underwear, that was my complete trousseau.

I already had quite a good stock of nice clothes. My mother had been cook to a titled lady who had three daughters, all older than me. Most of their cast-offs were given to my mother and she altered them to fit me. I was spoiled in this respect, and I acquired a taste for really good clothes, which was often a disadvantage in later years. I was also lucky to get all my mother's linen, blankets and towels.

Our furniture was just bits and pieces that Ivan got his brother Gordon to buy at a roup; no carpets or cookers or washing machines in those days. We had no wedding reception, no invitations sent out, but we did get a lot of useful gifts from relations and friends, especially from Ivan's brothers, six of whom were abroad in South Africa and Canada. He also had a canteen of cutlery given him by his workmates after a feet-washing spree. Ivan was working at Black-slack, a farm near the village of New Leeds, where there were five other workers and a maid. One worker was single and slept with Ivan in the chaumer, the other four were cottared. Here in the North-East the tradition of feet washing before a wedding lingers on, but in a much more refined and sedate manner than in those days of the 1920s and 1930s. In a way these farm workers were a rough lot, but it was all good natured fun and teasing that went on. Boot polish, black-lead, black treacle and soot were all used to some purpose. Today few people would know what black-lead looks like. At that time all fireplaces, grates and stoves in farm houses were black-leaded - the women folk really prided themselves in having a grand polish with black-lead. It was a different matter getting it off your clothes, especially if mixed with treacle, and there was a barrel of treacle to be found in most farm 'toons'.

Ivan had hoped to keep the wedding a secret from his fellow workers, but news of this sort has a way of getting around and, when it did, there was no escape from some fun and games and the usual 'dookin'. Not only his work mates but others from the neighbouring farms took part and I believe it turned out to be a right royal occasion. Once they had him properly blackened, someone started up with a melodion and another with a fiddle and the rest of the night was spent in song and music, drink and dancing. They knew how to enjoy themselves those lads, and a dram or two was grand for putting

15

everyone in a happy mood. If I had stayed nearer, there is little doubt I too would have been made to join them and get my feet washed and blackened but, as it was, I was a stranger to them and too far away to be fetched; there were no cars to run around with in those days. Both the trousers and the shirt Ivan wore that night had to be burned.

In the run-up to the wedding we had one slight hitch. My cousin, who was to be bridesmaid, took ill a few days before the wedding, but another friend from a neighbouring farm filled her place.

Ivan's brother Gordon, the one who had got married recently, kept Ivan right on matters of procedure and I stayed in the background being, I think, only out with him twice, once to Fridayhill and once to Fraserburgh, where we went to buy the wedding ring. Most shops then kept open until nine o'clock. The shop we visited, right on the corner of Broad Street across from the Royal Hotel, is still a jeweller's, a Mr. Buchan. Once the ring was purchased, the shop-keeper brought out some lockets and necklaces. I was very surprised when the he was able to persuade Ivan to buy a string of pearls. As I said before, Ivan did do unexpected little deeds. The pearls did not cost a great deal of money, about seven pounds, but in those days that was a great deal to spend on luxuries. I wore them on my wedding day and still have them.

On the 24th of May 1932, at a simple ceremony in Rathen Church, Ivan and I took our marriage vows; vows we both kept till death parted us almost fifty-four years later. Afterwards, we had a meal at home. Although we had no honeymoon - for Ivan's start at Fridayhill was imminent - we did manage to escape for one night.

My grandmother was brought up on a croft near Lonmay, a small place quite near to the big house of Corties. In later years, after she returned to Mormond, she had got acquainted with the people who had moved into her old home - the McKessors. When I came on the scene only the unmarried daughter, Jeannie McKessor, remained on the croft. It took almost an hour to walk from our place to Jeannie's croft and, when Granny's old legs got too tired to climb the hill, I was sent on my own. On the Sunday before our wedding, I decided to visit Jeannie and Ivan came with me. As usual, Jeannie made us welcome;: it was unthinkable that we should leave without tea. Naturally, the conversation worked round to the wedding. It ended with her offering us 'bed and breakfast' on our wedding night. When I accepted, Ivan gave me a funny look, but said nothing. On the way back, he admitted that Jeannie's croft would be the perfect hideout. He was certain we would be able to slip away into Corties Wood and make our way to the croft house unseen.

My mother prepared a tea for a few guests after the wedding, but we did not linger long over this ritual. Somebody suggested we should all go to the pictures. If it had been a Friday, a local dance would have been the obvious choice for a night out. We announced that we had our own plans and there was a great deal of teasing before we got on our bicycles to escape. We did not change our clothes and took nothing with us, except a nightie which I had managed to slip into my bag. Ivan had a bottle of sherry for Jeannie which he secreted in his pocket. No-one knew our plans except my mother and she was forbidden to tell the guests. In those days, people would get up to awful capers and 'bedding' pranks on a wedding night. Though it was all done in good spirit, we wished to avoid it.

It was only a short run down to Rathen and then up the main road to Corties Wood. A lake lies at the entrance to the wood and I can never pass it without recalling a story about two local farmers who had been out celebrating late into the night. They both stopped beside

Rathen Church where we were married

17

the lake. It was a lovely clear night and a full moon was reflected in the still waters of the lake. One turned to the other and said, "Gosh man, that's the meen doon there, but far the hell can we be?"

We went through the wood until we joined a track which Jeannie trod on her way to work. Ivan found a place to hide our bikes and we quickly made our way to the croft house. The door was opened immediately by Jeannie. She was radiant. "Come awa ben," she said, and we were ushered into a combined kitchen, living room and bedroom. It was a lovely warm evening, yet she still had a welcoming fire ablaze on the hearth. We made small-talk about the wedding for a while. Ivan seemed content to talk through the night, but I got restless. So, we both made a visit to the 'wee hoosie', left our shoes by the fire and made our way to her room 'ben the hoose'. She had looked after our comforts well. The bed covers were turned down to reveal lovely white linen sheets. It was one of those bedsteads that, today, antique dealers would give a fortune to possess - ornamented with brass fittings. Soft, fluffy towels were laid on a chair beside a stand with a lovely big basin and ewer filled with a kettle of hot water. Bidding us goodnight, Jeannie slipped out of the bedroom, gently closing the door behind her.

I took off my coat and dress and hung them up on a home-made coat hook. Our clothes had to be kept neat, for the next day we had to attend church. A couple was not considered properly married until the two had gone to the church the Sunday after the wedding to be 'kirkit'.

Ivan sat in a chair playing with the coat hanger and I went and washed myself and unpinned my hair, which I wore in two plaits coiled and braided on either side of my head - they were called headphones. Suddenly, Ivan appeared behind me. He took the brush which belonged to Jeannie and began to brush my hair. It was not long before I was in his arms and back in the armchair. He got very amorous and I tried to wriggle free. "Come on. Let's awa tae wir bed," he whispered. He lifted me up and dumped me right into the middle of the softest bed I have ever lain on. I had always slept on chaff but this was a luxurious bed filled with feathers. Somehow, I got into my nightie and a sweet contentment swept over me. It was dark now and the room was filled with soft shadows. The sheets smelt of roses and lavender and I thought the comfort of Ivan's arms around me was all

I would ever need. And then, strangely, we both fell sound asleep.

I awoke next morning still heavy with sleep and it took me some time to realise where I was and to remember the events of the previous day. Trying to free one of my arms, which was trapped below Ivan, I awoke him too.

"You didna even kiss me guidnicht," I teased him.

"Oh, but we'll seen sort that oot," was the reply.

With that, there was a timid knock at the door and Jeannie appeared. "Guid mornin ma dears. I'm thinkin if it's the kirk ye're meaning tae ging til, ye'll need tae rise."

Ivan was very unwilling to let me go. The kirk could wait, he said. But he was mollified and we were soon up and dressed. I was ashamed to find both our pairs of shoes, cleaned and polished to perfection, waiting for us. Ivan had a couple of eggs for breakfast; I had some bread which I toasted over the open fire on a long handled fork. All Jeannie's food was good to eat. Her oatcakes, wafer thin, spread with fresh butter, melted in your mouth. But, oh dear, I did not like her tea. The little brown teapot was kept constantly by the fire with more tea and boiling water added as required. The brew that poured forth from the pot was black and the only way that I could drink it was barely to cover the bottom of the cup and fill it with milk.

Before we left, Jeannie gave us some bowls and plates carefully wrapped in newspaper and parcelled up. With many thanks for all her kindness, we affectionately said good-bye to Jeannie. It was a lovely May morning. We recovered our bikes, fastened our parcel on to the carrier and headed off in the direction of the Church bells. Ivan had wanted to go to his own church at Old Deer, but I insisted we attend at Rathen for I knew it might be a long time before I returned, and it is strange now to recall that, since that day, I have been in the churchyard several times but never in the church.

Soon we were on our bikes and making for Old Deer. In the village's only hotel we had our midday meal. I expected we would head for Stuartfield and then up to the Hill o' Dens where Ivan was born and brought up, and we would have a walk, visit old haunts and have tea with his sister and family. But our conversation turned to Cruden Bay and a farm Ivan had worked on. "Fit aboot going there?" he said.

Soon we were heading for the coast and Cruden Bay. Nearing our destination, Ivan was suddenly hailed by a man leaning on his garden fence. The man shouted, "Jean, come out and see fa's here." A woman appeared in the doorway and she too seemed delighted to see Ivan. Later, they were introduced as Mr and Mrs Cadger. He was the grieve at Earlston. Ivan was persuaded to stay for his tea and afterwards the two men left for a walk around the farm and I was left with Mrs Cadger. I was inclined to be shy with strangers and I did not make much headway in conversation with her.

The journey back seemed to me much longer. There was little conversation and I constantly lagged behind. When we eventually arrived home, it was much later than we had intended and I was bone weary.

We were never able to go back to Jeannie's croft, nor did we ever see Jeannie again, for in the out-turn of the year she died. Some sixty years have passed me by and I wonder if her croft has disappeared like so many others. Perhaps a new bungalow for incomers has sprung up in place of the croft house, but I will always remember our wedding night and her kindness.

It was a long, long time ago, yet it seems like yesterday. Ivan and I had our ups and downs, our days of sorrow with many a tear, and our days of gladness when the birds sang, the flowers bloomed and our small world was a paradise. Through it all, looking back, I never once regretted it. I loved him that day, through all our 'trauchles' and I loved him the same the day he died.

CHAPTER TWO

COTTARS at FRIDAYHILL

FRIDAYHILL, THAT surely was an unusual name for a farm, but in those days I never gave it a thought.

Ivan left his old employment on the morning of the Saturday we got married. We had Sunday together, then on Monday morning it was pack up and go, for he had only a couple of days to get settled in before starting work at Fridayhill. All our goods and chattels were stored at Ivan's home ready to be collected and moved.

Ivan's brother Gordon had his shelt Polly harnessed to a small lorry - a float they called it - and our belongings were loaded on to this to be taken to the cottage. How little there was, but to us it was ample. I think I can remember most of our possessions. First, there was a large chest of drawers, a handsome piece of furniture Ivan's father had given us. Then there was a dresser, or sideboard, Ivan's brother bought at a sale, along with a table and four chairs. We had a wash stand and two iron bedsteads with wire springs and a mattress filled with chaff. We were to get the other bed when more chaff was available. The chaff-filled beds were all folk in the countryside ever slept on and soft and cosy they were. The biggest drawback with these beds was mice; often they decided to make a home in the mattress and tipped the chaff out. That was a real embarrassment and nuisance. Why two beds? Well you had to be prepared to offer a visitor a bed for the night. That time was not like now, when you have a car to take you home quickly; then you had either to walk or cycle, or take a train. Often it was not possible to return from a visit the same day. Present day visitors coming and staying the night might be considered a nuisance, but at that time you were indeed very inhospitable if you could not provide a bed.

Polly waited patiently at Waughtonhill close for the loading to be completed. There was really little more to add to the furniture: some boxes packed with crockery, pots and pans and sundries, among them a box of groceries from my mother and a box of books. There was a zinc bath with two enamelled basins for washing and bathing. Topping the pile were two pails for water and two smaller ones for slops and washing-up, and a washing-stool. Tucked away somewhere was Granny's old nursing stool. It had always been my favourite seat, so I was given it with her blessing; though badly the worse for wear, I still have it.

Amongst our possessions was Ivan's 'kist' packed with his clothes. A very dainty rosebud china tea set, which he had at one time given his mother and which I now inherited, was packed in amongst the clothes. Another large chest with blankets, two complete sets of bed covers and linen and several pairs of towels, most of which had been my mother's, was also loaded up.

While we were having tea, Polly was given a feed of oats out of a nose bag. Afterwards, Ivan found himself a seat on one of the boxes and, just as he moved off, Ina, my sister-in-law, threw him a large cushion. With lots of waving and a good deal of banter, Polly disappeared around the corner. I was to follow with my bike, but I lingered a while as my two wheels could cover the distance much faster than Polly's four legs.

Then a fish van called with fresh herring. Ina bought me some and I put them on top of a carrier bag I had filled with odds and ends. With a case strapped on the carrier of my cycle, I was off. It was one of those lovely late spring mornings when nature bestows all the shades of green on the trees, plants and grass and you can see, in the gentle heat, dewdrops glistening in the sun. On top of the world, I hummed a tune as I covered the miles. I must have passed Ivan somewhere but I cannot remember where. It is strange how some things come to mind while others have completely disappeared. One thing I do remember: on the brewery road out of Strichen I was startled by a strange noise, so much so that I lost my balance and came off my bike. I wondered if it was a bell of some sort ringing in the brewery. In a few moments I realised that it was coming from my suitcase. I sat down on the bank by the roadside helpless with laughter; Ivan's alarm clock was telling me it was time to get up.

Soon I arrived at the approach to the farm. The cottage, a sturdy three-roomed granite building, stood half way up the road on a slight incline. A small patch of garden stretched down to the road. As I came in sight of the house, I was surprised to see smoke rising from the chimney and to find a fire burning brightly in the living room. On the window-sill sat a flagon of milk, along with a basket full of fresh baked pancakes wrapped in a towel. Someone indeed had gone to some effort to make me welcome. I fetched in my bag and case, and took the clock and set it on the mantelpiece. Then I went exploring my domain, which did not take very long - three empty rooms, all spotlessly clean.

The living room occupied one half of the house and the other half was divided into two rooms, one very small - just big enough to hold a bed and chair. The small room had a tiny window looking out to the back of the house, but the other two rooms had large windows - much bigger than I had been accustomed to - opening out on to the front of the house. In those days windows were generally very small; you would have thought light had to be paid for. Perhaps glass was very expensive.

Outside I found a small shed with a bag of coal and a box with some potatoes, one spade and a fork with a prong missing. Next to the shed was the little 'hoosie' - our toilet - and the ash pit or midden.

The garden was surrounded by a broken-down rickety old fence, and what had once been the garden gate lay buried deep in grass. Except for one small patch, which Ivan had dug and planted with potatoes, it was a wilderness. One big patch of buttercups gave a pleasing splash of colour. At the foot of the garden, lying close to the road, were a few stunted willow trees. Nearby was the well. I did not like it. The well water was still whereas at home I had been accustomed to water running clear and fresh from a 'spootie'. Here we had either to dip the pail in or use a ladle. Another thing I disliked was the film of dead flies that covered the water in summer. Some people kept a trout in the well to catch the flies, but I found later that a puddock did the trick.

Walking up to the cottage at Fridayhill today

I thought I might as well read the *People's Friend* and fill in the time till Ivan arrived. I had been so busy getting married, I had had no time to read my stories. But I knew I would have to get a meal ready after Ivan arrived. The herring would be nice, but first they had to be cleaned, a job I hated. I remembered I had seen an enamelled basin lying in the old ash pit. I fetched the basin and found it had only a small hole and was sure if I tilted the basin on its side it might hold water. Next, I retrieved a small pair of scissors and a fruit knife from my handbag. Armed with these, I took the fish down to the well and in no time had them ready for frying. After this success, my mind turned to the potatoes which I had seen in the shed. They were a wee thing soft but the knife did the job reasonably well. I covered the peeled potatoes with water and left the basin beside the well, lying on its side. The herrings I took to the house and put in a wall cupboard next to the fireplace.

Now I was ready to tackle my *People's Friend*, but I was just getting settled on the doorstep when I spied Ivan and Polly turning into the road. The promise of the morning had been fulfilled; it was a gorgeous day, and both Ivan and the mare were hot and sweating. Poor Polly had quite a haul getting the load off the road and up the brae to the house. I fussed her a bit and fetched her one of the pancakes which she ate with relish. Ivan said he would have to leave me with her and go to the farm to find someone to help with the lifting, but with that Mr Forman appeared. The unloading did not take long and since Polly would need a rest and food before she tackled the return journey, they unhitched her from the cart. Mr Forman said he would take her back to the farm and put her in the stable, and Ivan could fetch her when he was ready.

It was now twelve o'clock, dinner hour for most country folk, time for the main meal of the day. Ivan carried a pail of water and the potatoes to the house. I had unpacked the essentials but I only knew one way of cooking herring, frying them in oatmeal. Inside the oven which was attached to the fire, I found a baking tray. This got a good scrub and the herrings, rolled in oatmeal, were laid on it. The tray was placed on top of the coals, cooking the herring beautifully in some butter. With potatoes, and followed by a glass of milk, this was a meal fit to set before the Queen. I think this particular way of cooking herring is typical in Buchan. When Robert Boothby came to Buchan, fried herring covered in oatmeal was his delight, so much so, that he went back to London and got some of the high-class restaurants to put them on the menu as Hareng a la Boothby. Many more meals were cooked on that fire. Just give me a whiff or a taste of herring and the memory of that first meal comes flooding back.

Before Ivan left to take Polly back to Waughtonhill, he helped me put up our bed in the living-room recess. This one room served as kitchen, living-room and bedroom - the norm for most cottages and small croft houses. In fact the cottage was just slightly more modern than some, for box beds were still common.

Ivan was full of fun and a terrible tease. Something set us off and the bed making ended in a pillow fight with blankets and covers in a shambles. However, in the long afternoon, I soon put things to rights. I black-leaded and polished the fireplace and put down a rug I had made from strips of cloth out of the rag-bag. I found a cover for the table and I even placed a vase of the flowers I had picked in the morning, from the garden at home, on the sideboard. All my life I have loved flowers in the house and have seldom been without them.

It was well past supper time when Ivan returned, but I had the table set for tea with plenty of oatcakes, scones and pancakes, and had boiled an egg. Those we ate with teaspoons out of saucers, for I had neither egg spoons nor egg cups. It had been a long day and on the morrow we planned a trip to Aberdeen. We were both glad to retire early to bed for the day in Aberdeen meant getting up before six to catch the first train from Strichen at about 6.45am.

When we left the train, we made our way up King Street on a tram to where a cousin of Ivan's stayed. She gave us lunch and, as neither Ivan nor I knew a lot about finding our way around the city, she came out with us to help with the shopping. First on Ivan's list was a pair of heavy boots for his work; I needed some net for curtains. Then we went to the Castlegate and Cocky Hunter's. Everybody knew of Cocky Hunter. He kept everything from a needle to an anchor, new and second-hand. Ivan found himself a wooden armchair which I am sure only cost shillings. I badly wanted a dressing-table with a mirror but, as it did not suit Ivan, he did not find one. We did buy an iron poker and tongs, a bellows and a hanging paraffin lamp. That pair of tongs did valiant service ending its life years later at Redbriggs.

We arrived back at Strichen just after 9 o'clock. The local shops were still open and we did some more shopping. Ivan fancied some sausages from the butcher and I visited the grocer, whom I knew quite well, and bought a frying pan and a bread bin. Those two articles are both still in service.

Our flitting was not yet complete. A wooden hen-house with a dozen and a half birds had still to come from Waughtonhill. Next day, which Ivan still had free, he arranged to borrow Polly again and bring them up. Keeping a few chickens was a privilege which was mostly conferred on single cottar houses for, if two or three cottages were together, it would have been another cause for quarrels. In the early 1930s poultry-keeping was just beginning to come into its own. Before that era, some farmers would have housed a few hens in some old shed and the hens would peck a living around the steading, supplying the household with a few eggs. Now, among the smaller farms, the sale of eggs was becoming quite a lucrative source of income for the farmer's wife. Later on they really did come to be big business.

The hens were kept in colonies of wooden houses, which were

rotated around the corners of the farm fields. A year or two before, Ivan had bought his mother a small wooden house and this I filled with a few hens from my grandmother's flock and chickens I had reared with a 'clockin' hen. Some of them were pullets but the majority were cocks and these made a few Sunday dinners. To save Ivan a double journey and help with the unloading, his brother came back with him to take Polly home.

This completed our flitting and next morning Ivan started work. There followed a time full of happy days. It was not possible that two people like Ivan and me with such different natures could live together and not have arguments, but I cannot recall any angry words. My way of life had changed little and adjusting was not difficult. At home I had done most of the cooking and I budgeted my grand-mother's ten shillings pension, a sum which was little different to Ivan's weekly income. Every four weeks Ivan was paid £2 and the rest - an extra ten shillings a week - at the end of his six month term of employment. A grocer and a baker's van called weekly. If we were in

need of meat, we had to visit the butcher's shop in Strichen. This had been the usual run of things at home.

One thing I did miss, and miss badly, was my walks and rambles on Mormond. I had moods when I felt I had to get out into the open and Mormond had provided me with this sense of freedom in abundance. In Fridayhill I was surrounded by open fields and all I could do was go up into the field at the back of the house and gaze longingly into the distance where I could see the outline of that beloved hill.

Ivan seemed well content at the farm and often spoke of his

Cecil Michie, Ina Simpson, me and Ivan

27

pair of Clydesdales. One night, when he knew the other horseman was away, Ivan took me with him when he went to 'supper' the horses and introduced me to his bonny pair, Clyde and Bess. What magnificent animals they were, those gentle giants, so quiet and docile. I do not think that you would have found more faithful, intelligent and loveable animals anywhere, and what sadness fills my heart when I think of them and those worthy sons of the soil who attended them, now vanished.

It was strange living in a community and not knowing your neighbours. The people in the next farm had made themselves known to us, but this was only because they were related. Once a week, I was able to buy butter from the farm and I was also given buttermilk to bake with. This gave me an opportunity to get acquainted with Miss Forman who kept house for her father. I was asked to come into the kitchen and this led us into conversation, and we found we had a lot in common. Although she was a little older, we had been to the same school and I really began to enjoy my visits until one day Ivan found out. He was very displeased and I was told in no uncertain manner that I was forgetting my place. She was the mistress and I the cottar wife. I did not understand his attitude and resented it, but I gave way, though I am sure a flowering friendship was nipped in the bud. She never came to visit me, so I suppose although I did not know my place, she knew hers.

Suddenly all changed and our happy way of life came to an end. For a few days I had been feeling unwell and one night before bed I was violently sick. The sickness continued through the night and by morning my temperature had gone up and I was slightly delirious. This got Ivan alarmed and he went down to Strichen for the doctor (there was no telephone in those days). I do not think the doctor knew what to make of me, but I was given some horrible medicine which just came back up again. The sickness took more than a week to settle, leaving me very weak and listless and it was decided I should go home for a short time. It was then I realised I was pregnant. It seems strange now that the doctor never even suggested that this might be the cause. Such a thing happening so quickly had not crossed our minds. If I had tackled the problem differently, the months that followed might not have been so unhappy. Some people in this situation enjoy better health, but the bouts of sickness and depression continued and in a way I must have resented the pregnancy. Ivan persuaded me to go and see the doctor, but all he did was confirm that I was three months pregnant and might expect my baby about the middle of March. No advice was given nor any future visits planned.

I lost interest in the house, took to reading a lot and, although I usually got up and made breakfast, Ivan often came home at midday to find me in bed and no meal ready. We did not quarrel, but all the companionship and enchantment of being together had vanished. I withdrew into a world of my own. Often I spent hours during the day in bed feeling sick and sorry for myself and when night came, instead of going to bed to sleep, I had other things to do.

One day, rummaging among my books for something to read, I found one of my school text books and a half-written essay on Jews and the Hebrew nation. This rekindled my enthusiasm and I decided to try and finish it. Pregnant women often take queer fancies but, looking back, I think this must have been one of the daftest. Here was I at midnight in a cottar house, with a candle for a light, trying to solve the ills of the wandering Jews.

Poor Ivan must have been hurt and bewildered but he never complained, only retreated into himself, putting up a wall of silence between us and for days hardly a word passed either of our lips. At that time I did not care but in later years, when he was still subject to those moods, it caused me much unhappiness.

Although I still felt far from well and the sickness lasted right up to the last two months, we did gradually return to a more pleasing routine. During the late summer, on a Sunday when the horses were out in the fields and I was in the mood, we would go visiting: mostly back to Waughtonhill, but sometimes to other relations. We visited James Laird, Ivan's cousin. He had a small farm called Woodside just outside the village of New Pitsligo. He spoke a lot about his father's farm, Bankhead, where he was brought up. I had also heard someone else say of Bankhead: "That was the place where the Lairds made all their money," fairly giving me the impression that it was indeed a very fine farm. Mrs Laird gave me my first kitten, a fluffy little creature I called Sammy. It was a very dark tortoiseshell with just the merest spot of white and I am afraid I gave that cat a lot more attention that

I did Ivan.

Old habits die hard and once or twice I made the effort and went to the Strichen church service. All my life, as far as I can think back, had centred round the Church. At one time I taught a class in the Sunday School but a tragedy in the family caused a change in my life. Those Christian beliefs I had held dear were gone, yet the principles remained.

The minister, the Rev Charles MacGlashan, had come from St Machar's Cathedral in Aberdeen to Strichen - on the orders of his doctor to take a less demanding post. He may have been a good and sincere man, but I found him remote and his ramblings on Christian psychology far removed from the common people. He had what we would have called an educated Cambridge voice. I still remember my rebellious thoughts when I heard him say, "Bless all our superiors, our equals and our inferiors." Surely, here in God's house we were all equals. I did not return.

I cannot recall our first Christmas and New Year together. Most likely we went home, but I do remember that, after this, I began to feel much better. I can also remember being teased by Ivan when I found my clothes were not fitting. We seldom spoke of the baby and it was about this time my mother took me to task and said it was time I was preparing a welcome for the coming stranger. Oddly, I had never given it a thought. With no great enthusiasm, I began to knit some tiny garments. Ivan was not very liberal with money and wool did not grow on bushes. Some material was purchased and my mother made this up into various gowns and dresses. She also gave me a lovely Shetland shawl left over from my own babyhood. Prams and cots were never thought of but great store was set by an old cradle.

One weekend towards the end of February, Ivan had the Sunday free and on the Saturday night we cycled down to Waughtonhill. My baby was due in about three weeks, but I had only seen the doctor that one time and the district nurse had never paid me a visit. During the Sunday snow came on and, since it looked as if it was to be a bad night, instead of waiting until evening, we left in the afternoon. Once we left Strichen, the wind and the snow were in our faces and we practically had to walk pushing our bikes. When we arrived at the cottage I was utterly exhausted and Ivan had to help me to bed. But he was so kind, making up a fire to boil a kettle for a hot drink and a hot water bottle. I did not sleep much and by morning my pains began. All through the night it had snowed and, by morning, the road was blocked. How he got word to the doctor, I cannot remember, but both doctor and nurse arrived after battling their way through snow drifts. They did not stay long, but promised to come back later in the day. It had been a difficult pregnancy and it was to end that way. Ivan's Auntie Maggie, who lived in Mintlaw, was to come and stay but that day it was impossible for her to travel. So Mrs Morrison on the next farm came to my aid.

The doctor and nurse returned in the evening striking across two fields to reach the house. It was an all-night vigil. About six o'clock on Tuesday morning, 28th February, my daughter made her entry into this world. I was told I was lucky she was a small baby or it might have been another day's wait, but all I wanted was sleep and still more sleep. The snow had eased off, but we were completely blocked in. They kept you in bed much longer then than they do now. For more than a week the nurse made her daily trek across the fields. Fully a week after the birth, Mr Forman had cattle ready for the sale at Maud. He put his men to work with shovel and spade to clear the road for the float and that day for the first time the nurse was able to bring her car to the house. She remarked that cattle were more important than folk.

My daughter was a lovely child with Ivan's deep blue eyes. Most babies are born bald, but she had a head of lovely golden curls also inherited from her father. We argued about most things but about a name for our child there was no argument. I had wanted a boy and a name was all ready - David, after my beloved grandfather. The choice was Ivan's for a girl. He had not given it any thought and was slow in making up his mind. One night, sitting around the fire, his aunt tried to help out. She pointed out that, although Ivan's father had a lot of children, none were named after him and she suggested Georgina. I did not like the name nor did I think it suitable, but next day Ivan went off and registered her Georgina Mary Michie. My little golden-haired angel Georgina . . . never! Usually it becomes Ina, but I chose Ena. About this time the Queen of Spain, Princess Eugenie, the grand-daughter of Queen Victoria, was in the news. She was known as Queen Ena and the name appealed to me. Ivan adored his little daugh-

31

ter and to him she was always his little Princess. Miss Bruce, Ivan's aunt, stayed three weeks. She was retired but had been in service for a long time with the gentry. First, she was a lady's maid then, when she was older, she took up the post of nanny to the lady's grandchildren. She was very kind, but I often got the feeling she disapproved of me.

Our own problems seemed to dissolve and vanish. One night, just before Aunt Maggie left, Ivan and I slipped out for a walk. We climbed the brae at the back of the house and crossed the field towards a 'funn' - gorse - dyke, the march between Fridayhill and another farm. Except for small patches of snow lying here and there, all traces of the recent storm had gone. Some blades of fresh green grass could be seen peeping through the soil and a few buds on the gorse bushes were making a splash of yellow. Both were signs that the earth was awakening from its winter sleep. I slipped my hand into Ivan's and, as we walked slowly towards the top of the old dyke, riddled with rabbit burrows, we caught a glimpse now and then of a little white tail disappearing underground. It was the gloaming hour, the hour I loved best, and as darkness came slowly down we lingered on, loath to leave this magic place. His arm came around me holding me close and, although not a word was spoken, much was conveyed. We returned to the house content and from that moment, although troubles did not altogether vanish, we were again together.

I wonder what a young mother would think and say today if her new baby was put to sleep in an old clothes basket. This is where the nurse placed baby Ena, and for weeks this was all the cot or crib she had until I got my fine new pram. I had not dared suggest to Ivan we might get one, but here again was one of the times he surprised me. On his own, he had been in touch with his cousin in Aberdeen and it was a complete surprise when the pram was delivered. It was a Pedigree baby carriage, one of the best makes. The chrome shine and the cream leather work and brown paint were immaculate. I loved the pram and began to go out in the afternoons just to show it off.

About that time a sad event occurred. Mr Forman was an elder of the Strichen church and word was sent to me that on a certain afternoon I might have a visit from the minister. I could not say I was madly thrilled; I had gone to the church once or twice and he had not impressed me.

Our living room got an extra dust and polish, the bairn was dressed in her best bib and tucker. I put on a clean, flower-patterned overall - at home we always dressed in cotton overalls. All afternoon we waited, but our visitor did not appear. I had noticed extra traffic on the road, but took no particular notice. When 6 o'clock came and went and Ivan had not appeared, I began to think something must be wrong. When he did arrive, a good half hour later, he gave me the news that the Rev MacGlashan was dead.

Up from Fridayhill, on the edge of the moss, was a croft where a family called Crawford lived. After he paid his visit to the farm the minister left his car and walked up the narrow road to the croft. The approach to the house was very steep and, though it was still only April, the weather was very warm. It proved too much for him and, as he entered the cottage, he collapsed. Mrs Crawford was able to get assistance quickly as the workers from the farm were casting peats in the moss near the croft. The doctor was called and, with all the procedures attending a sudden death, it took some time before Ivan and one of the other men could carry the body down to the farm.

I felt regret that I had been unable to meet him. Perhaps, in the few times I listened to him speaking from the pulpit, I got a wrong impression. Yet, he seemed so far removed from the common people and I felt it ironic that he died in so humble a home, one of the few houses left with an earthen floor.

Ivan had just a year's contract with Mr Forman and it came time for renewal or otherwise; 'biddin time' they called it. I knew Ivan had not forgotten about his croft, for I had seen him scanning the columns of the *Press and Journal*. We must have been about the only cottar family to have a daily newspaper delivered by post. Some of the farmers got them but it was extraordinary that a cottar did. Ivan was no great reader, but he did like his paper and indulged himself with this luxury. The only other papers we bought were the weekenders - the *People's Journal*, the *People's Friend* and the *Woman's Weekly*. As Ivan seemed content and there were no complaints about his work, it had not crossed our minds that we might have to leave Fridayhill. Therefore it was quite a shock when Mr Forman approached Ivan and said that, before we had come, a cattleman had occupied the house and he found it more convenient to return to this arrangement.

Another job and another home had to be found. It was hard to think of having to pack up and go and I began to appreciate some of Ivan's feelings about cottaring. No horseman's job came up and, rather against his will, he settled this time for a cattleman's job at Royston, a farm between New Deer and Cuminestown. Again luck favoured us, for it was a single cottar house, once a croft. Thank goodness there was little time to brood. Three weeks or, at best a month, was all the time that was given.

We had no more furniture; I still did not have my dressing-table. I was using Ivan's shaving mirror hanging above the wash-hand basin. But it was surprising how much more there was to load up compared with what Polly had taken on that small cart. This time a motor lorry came for us, sent by our new employer. The day we were to move, Ivan's father decided to come for a visit and help with the flitting. Knowing that my cat might go berserk I took Sammy (he was a she) and, with no basket or box to transport her, tied her in a sack and deposited her in a cardboard box in the back bedroom out of harm's way. Everything was just about loaded when Granda appeared carrying the sack with the cat, determined to throw it on the lorry. I would not hear of it and we had quite a set-to before I was able to rescue my poor cat. The last rope was secured, the driver got into his seat and Ivan climbed into the cabin beside him. The vehicle moved away down the Howe road with all the goods and chattels which, only a year before, Polly had so gallantly pulled up the hill. The hired car was waiting and inside was a very impatient Granda. The key was in the door, but I only pulled it gently shut and, with my baby daughter in my arms, I stood a moment on the step, full of sadness, saying a silent goodbye. There had been bad days, but oh so many good and happy ones. I bent down, picked up the bag with the wriggling cat and took my seat in the back of the car. As it moved off, I did not look back for my eyes were filled with tears.

CHAPTER THREE

COTTARS AT ROYSTON

ANOTHER HOME and still the croft was a far distant dream. The lorry with our goods moved down the New Deer High Street and turned into the road to Cuminestown.

Up and over Bruce Hill it rolled where, long ago, Edward, brother of Robert the Bruce, fought a battle with the Comyns before vanquishing the proud Earl of Buchan and razing the Abbey of Deer in retribution. The people of that time held no romantic notions of Robert Bruce, for he plundered the Buchan countryside and reduced to ashes their homes and buildings in a terrible rampage known as the Harrying of Buchan. Somewhere on Bruce Hill our car overtook the lorry and, in a short while, we came to Gillybrae, where we turned into the entrance for the farm of Royston. Only part of the house was visible; all else was surrounded and hidden by trees. We stopped to collect the key, which was handed over with neither comment nor welcome. Nearby, in the howe of Allathan, nestling in the side of the brae, was the croft house that was to be ours for the next three years. Its name was Braeside. As we turned in by the gable end of the house, my attention was drawn to a small clump of trees and a feeling of delight passed through me. But that was dispelled when I caught a glimpse of the wooden pump, one of those you primed and pumped. I wondered, could this be our water supply?

Ena was fast asleep when we arrived and the taxi driver said he would wait, as the lorry was on its way and he backed the car further up the close. I laid Ena on the back seat, rescued my cat and followed

Granda to the front door. When I arrived at Fridayhill, a fire was lit and there were other things to hand. But there was no welcome here, just an empty house and an empty grate. Our first priority was to get a fire going. Here I was back to the open hearth with a few bars and binks, and a swey for hanging pots and pans.

Granda said he would go to the shed, which we noticed as we arrived, to find some firewood. Still carrying the sack with the cat, I went exploring. Behold my delight when, in the back pantry be-

The house at Royston in 1934

side the staircase, I found a sink and a small iron pump. When I cranked the handle, water ran. At the top of the stair, I found two fair sized rooms with dormer windows. In one of them, after some soothing words, I left the cat, making sure the door was shut. I knew she would be safe there until the 'steer' had passed. Granda found nothing to build a fire with, so we had just to wait till the lorry arrived.

As I lifted my little bundle of joy from the back of the car, she awoke and was determined she would have some attention. Before we left Fridayhill I had the foresight to mix her a feed. She was soon fed and changed and her basket was lifted off the lorry. I placed it out of the hurry and scurry in the scullery and, for once, she proved very accommodating and fell asleep. The living room seemed much smaller than the one at Fridayhill and I wondered where we would put all our furniture. Then I spied, not altogether to my joy, that we had a box bed. I slept in one for most of my young life, but it was not my favourite. I did not enjoy the feeling of being confined. I remember my grandparents had a shelf in the bottom of their box bed where they kept some of their valuables: one item was a hat box with granny's best Sunday bonnet, a little round black straw hat covered in veiling with two strings which she tied in a bow below her chin. Another was leather covered and filled with silver cutlery and of course the big family Bible, which my grandfather took down on a Sunday night. Much later, when I fell in love with the works of Robbie Burns, I came to know that lovely poem 'The Cottar's Saturday Night' and I associate it with that time. To me the man that Burns was describing was my grandfather.

I reminded Ivan that we had a bedroom upstairs, but we both agreed that, at least for the time being, it would be easier to use the box bed. Ivan's father liked to retire early and soon after supper his bed had to be got ready. Upstairs it had to be, for the front room was full of boxes and the big chest of drawers. Ivan's father was a very impatient man and when he needed something done you had to jump to attention. Ivan, on the other hand, was never in a hurry and I was caught between the two of them. One of the rooms was already occupied by my cat which I fed but kept shut in. The cat was only let out once Granda was gone, for he disliked cats and sometimes was not very kind to them. We were relieved to get him settled for the night and, not long afterwards, we too were glad to crawl into our box bed for the first night in our new home. The long day and the changing about had also tired our wee lamb and she too was sound asleep in her basket which rested on two chairs by our bedside.

Just one more day for Ivan and then back into chains and a new regime. The night before, I boiled the last of my milk for the baby's morning feed so when morning came around, I persuaded Ivan to go up to the farm. The house, fire, milk, potatoes and meal were all part of the wages and about £54 per year - barely a pound per week. Ivan came back with his pail only half full. He was told he would get his full supply when he began work the following day. A fleeting disquiet passed through my mind, not a happy omen for the future I thought. None of our other perquisites, as they were called, were to hand, but all we were short of was firewood. Among the trees Ivan and his father eventually found part of a tree which the old man chopped down.

After he came back with the milk, Ivan set off with his bike to New Deer for one or two messages. He came back with a grin on his face and a tin of Nestle's Full Cream Milk, the first tin of milk I had ever seen. Ena was a 'Sister Laura's' bonny baby - her baby food had to be mixed with full cream milk. I had been diluting my milk supply with water to eke it out until the next day when we would have our full pail. I used the Nestle's in the same way and no ill befell the child. I tried it in our tea but none of us liked it. I cannot remember using it again until years later, and that was to make a trifle.

In the afternoon Ivan's brother Alex arrived. He was an agricultural salesman and had to attend Maud cattle sale every Wednesday. It had been arranged that he would call on his way home to Huntly and take his father back to stay with him for a few days. Bedtime came and still no sight of the farm folk. Morning came before we were ready; Ena had kept us both awake during the night and we slept in, but worse was to follow.

Peat fires can usually be rekindled easily - all you need is some kindling. I found the hearth completely cold but, as I had plenty of dry kindling to hand, I thought I would soon have a fire and a kettle of boiling water. I reached up to the mantelpiece for my box of matches but my groping fingers could find none. Then I remembered. Ivan's father was a heavy smoker, seldom without his pipe and forever striking matches to light it. Vaguely, I could recall, just before he left, seeing him fumble in his waistcoat pocket. Failing to find his box of matches, he had reached up to the mantelpiece and used my one. Then I knew that instead of replacing the matchbox on the shelf, it had gone into his pocket.

Somewhere in the next room, perhaps in the bottom of one of the unpacked boxes, there may have been a packet of matches, perhaps not. No match, no fire, no hot water, and no breakfast. Go to work on an egg? I could not even boil one. So, Ivan had a prisoner's breakfast that morning, two slices of bread spread with syrup and a drink of cold water.

A match - a 'spunk' - had to be got, for a slice of bread and water would not satisfy Ena. Ivan did not have time to go up to the farm and come back, so I had no choice but to go with him. Surely the farm folk would supply the matches. I waited outside, around the corner from the kitchen door, and I can still recall the relief I felt when my fingers closed over that box of matches. Today with all our modern facilities for cooking and heating it is difficult to understand what one small box of matches meant to me.

It was thus in the year 1933 that Ivan began his working days with the Mitchell family on the farm of Royston, New Deer. They were not altogether happy days. I think he missed his bonny pair - he had no horses to yoke and lowse. He began work in June, the season for sowing turnips. How easy this is today. Then, cultivating took weeks of back-breaking toil, whereas today it is completed in days.

In the 1930s and much later the ground was ploughed with a pair of horses pulling a single furrow plough. The ground was broken with a grubber, a miniature of the cultivators of today and followed by a harrow to make a smooth tilth. Back-breaking days followed, with the men pulling weeds, string grass, couch and knot grass and piling them up to be burnt. Next the drills were put up. These had to be filled with dung, all carted by horse from the midden. There were no mechanical loaders then and this was one of the hardest jobs on the farm; graip and man-power. Someone followed the cart, breaking the dung and spreading it evenly. The drills were split by horse and plough covering the dung, and the turnip seed was then sown. Once the plants were big enough, they had to be singled - another tough task which took weeks to accomplish. In late June or early July squads of men were strung across the turnip field, their arms swinging in rhythmic precision, an art in itself. The grieve took the first drill followed by the horsemen and the cattlemen and, bringing up the rear, the 'orra loon'. You had to keep up your pride by not falling behind. Away in a corner, or well behind the others was a lone figure - the farmer himself.

Women were often glad of a day's work hoeing - I recall the pay was about five shillings per day. It was one job around the farm I never succeeded in accomplishing: leaving the single plant with a hoe was beyond me. I had to single by hand and sometimes even then the lot came out. My efforts to transplant the plants were not successful either and, on my last attempt to hoe turnips, I was chased back to the house. Ivan was strong and hard work never got him down. It was his habit of resenting orders that did him most damage and at Royston he found someone who delighted in giving them.

The boss, Mr Mitchell senior, was a nice old man and he and Ivan got on very well, but alas there was Bob the son. He liked to override his father's authority and often countermanded the orders his father gave. This caused friction amongst the workers, particularly Ivan. The pair hated the sight of each other and many a day Ivan came home vowing vengeance. The Mitchell family was seven strong. Bob, the youngest son, had stayed at home. Two older sons were in farms nearby and a daughter was married to a local farmer. The other three daughters were at home; one was a visiting-out teacher at local schools. We were three years at the farm but I never spoke to Mrs Mitchell. She was a strange person and only at odd times did I catch a glimpse of her. If she was alone in the house, she would never answer the door. Instead she had the irritating habit of watching from a side window.

I had my abode, my bairn and Ivan, a little Eden - a world all my own. This home of mine, surrounded by green fields, stood on the brae side within a hollow, completely isolated. To our right were the Watts of Allathan. On the left lay Royston, but all you could see were the tops of the trees which surrounded it. I had little contact with people and saw none of the comings or goings of the neighbouring farms. Living in the farm bothy were other two or three men, single workers. Theirs were six month engagements. In the three years we were there, there were numerous changes in personnel, though I met but a few of the workers or their families.

Lying to the north was my favourite place, a long narrow strip of wood. Ever since I was a child, I liked to have somewhere, a secret place, where I could be alone. At Fridayhill there was nowhere, but here I found a quiet spot inside the wood - a perch on top of an old stone dyke where I could sit and gaze across to my beloved Mormond Hill.

In this world of my own, I was happy and contented. I liked being alone, I liked my house and I had found a way of earning a little more money to supplement Ivan's meagre wages. We had brought with us our hen-house, but there was also already ra shed fitted up with roosts. I filled both houses with birds as no limit had been stipulated. The hens could do no harm to crops for all around the fields were in grass. We also found an old chicken coop abandoned by previous tenants. I set eggs under broody hens and soon I had hatched out quite a number of cockerels. A grocer's van, G. Watson & Son, New Deer, called once a week and often I had enough eggs for sale to cover my grocery bill. I never knew the eggs to exceed one shilling per dozen; the lowest I can recall was seven pence. On this income, I was able to save and I collected quite a few things for the house.

The grocer was a man of many talents. Forbye being a grocer, he sold new and second-hand furniture, ironmongery, clothing, and food for the hens and much, much more. From him I was able to get lino for the upstairs bedrooms, some chairs and other knick-knacks. In the early spring after our arrival, we forsook our box bed and moved upstairs. I was also able to furnish the other front room as a spare bedroom. Ena was promoted from her basket to a small cot. About this time I won a rug in a raffle, my first shop one. How grand it looked beside my home-made 'clootie' rugs.

Through the howe ran the Burn of Allathan. Of a winter evening, a few of the lads did a bit of fishing in the burn. Some would, perhaps, call it poaching. Two or three lads from the farm began to come down to the cottar house with their catch, which I would cook for them - we had some scrumptious suppers together. I remember one night they came very late and Ivan was fast asleep in his bed. It was my habit to sit up late and read, so I welcomed them in. But this night they wanted to waken up the sleeping Ivan. I tried to do so but failed, then one of the lads, to my annoyance, went up and put a fish in the bed beside Ivan. What a fright he got. He really was furious but it all ended in a good laugh, though they had to wait till the next night for me to cook their supper. Some years ago, one of the same lads called at Bankhead with a lorry load of fertiliser and another had a grand-daughter working as a nurse with Ena in an Aberdeen hospital.

At Fridayhill Ivan had found fault with me for being too friendly with the farm folk, but here I had no opportunity to overstep my station. I cannot recall ever speaking to Mrs Mitchell or the youngest daughter Bella. The other two, Anne and Margaret, I did occasionally see but the meetings were few and far between. Bob I only saw from a distance. There was no butter, no extra milk, no extra anything. In fact, I had the impression that everything was grudgingly given. There was one member of the family I came to know very well, Mr Mitchell himself.

Our croft house home was surrounded by fields where ewes and lambs were put out to graze. That first summer the weather was particularly good, for I remember the nappies got dried every day. The warmth and sunshine may have contributed to the problem which afflicted the sheep. They became badly infected with maggots and Mr Mitchell had to attend to them and clean them daily. For this chore, he had a pen built against the wall of the ruined steading. One lamb was particularly badly infected; I often noticed the poor thing taking shelter among the ruins trying, I suppose, to get into the shade.

One day, answering a knock at the door, I found Mr Mitchell on the doorstep. I knew him by sight but, up to this time, I had not spoken to him. He apologised for bothering me, explained about the ewes and asked if he could have some water to mix the disinfectant solution. I am a bit daft on animals, especially ill ones, and I had to offer my assistance. Even though I got little encouragement, I accompanied him around the back of the sheep pen, where he held the infected lamb and I washed and cleaned it. It took several dressings to get the lamb cleared of the horrid things, and later there were others who needed attention. Always, I was there, and a friendship struck up between us. Occasionally, he came to the house for a chat and a rest; he was well into his seventies. Like most older folk he liked to talk of bygone days. He had been brought up in a worker's cottage and it was by his own efforts that he became a landowner.

One time I was able to offer real help and gained his gratitude. A black mare, of whom he was very fond and proud and who was expecting a foal, had been put down to graze in one of the fields beside our house. He paid her numerous visits but one day, when no one was about, I noticed she was in distress and went to fetch him down. There were no complications and she delivered a fine colt foal, the first and only time I have seen a mare giving birth. For the rest of the summer, she and the foal stayed in the field beside us. I got a lot of enjoyment watching them. They became quite tame and I fed them titbits though I believe Mr Mitchell did not approve. He sometimes popped in to see me and although there were often months in between those visits, they continued until Ivan's employment ended.

Ena was three months old when we went to Royston, but we had been unable to get her baptised. When we married, I transferred my church membership to Old Deer and I went several times with Ivan

42

to worship there. He wouldn't consider changing his membership. He had been brought up under the minister, Dr Kemp, a family friend who baptised most of the Michie children. At that time, the custom of baptising babies in church was not common. Not many people had cars and it would have been necessary to hire one to get to the church, something cottar folk were seldom able to afford. Most baptisms were carried out at home. Discussing the project of Ena's baptism, Ivan decided he would go and see Dr Neilson, the New Deer minister. Dr Neilson did not refuse us but, as we were not members of his church, he said he would have to consult with our own minister. At that juncture, Dr Kemp offered to come and baptise the child himself. This he did, cycling the fifteen miles between his manse at Old Deer and our cottage at Braeside. He was a grand old man and served the parish of Old Deer for about 50 years. He baptised all our children, but the youngest two were taken to Old Deer Church for we could afford to have a car by then. For years after Dr Kemp died, we regularly went to Communion at Old Deer.

Our first year at Royston slipped past for me quite happily, but I cannot say the same for Ivan. He often came home from work looking dour and unhappy. The ambition to have his own croft was still burning, though seldom voiced. A twist in his nature began to show - a dark cloud floating across my blue sky, a cloud that in later years got bigger and blacker and caused me much unhappiness. These black moods manifested themselves for no apparent reason. Sometimes they lasted for only a day, but at other times they continued for two days. I learned with time to adjust and they did leave him in his later years.

My life was far removed from what a short time before I had dreamed and planned for. It was a narrow and isolated world that I inhabited, but I was content. I had books, I read a lot and my wants were few. There were no holidays, no shopping sprees. The baker's and butcher's vans called once a week along with the grocer and they supplied a kaleidoscope of goods. That little extra money I made from the poultry made all the difference to my self-esteem, giving me the satisfaction of contributing towards our livelihood.

It was July of our second year at Braeside when my grandmother died, and I went back to my old home and stayed a couple of weeks with my mother. At that time, Ena was a lovely little imp of eighteen months. For her transport, we acquired a basket seat and fitted it to my bicycle. When I set out to cycle the twenty miles back to Mormond she was strapped into this seat. On the return leg to New Deer, I attempted to do the same but I encountered a a strong head wind and it was also much more uphill. I gave up at Strichen and hired a car from there. Later that summer my mother gave up her old home. It was a sad day for me for I loved that old place dearly and, although there had been sadness, there had been so much that was good. Still the memories were there to hold and treasure.

Another incident that summer, which caused quite a stir, was the murder in Aberdeen of a small girl called Helen Priestly (aged eight). I can still see the bold black headlines in the daily newspaper. It was quite a sensation, but today a murder is a commonplace event and affords but a small caption, so much have our values changed. I recall how I sat in the hen house and read the story one Sunday night. Ivan had gone to see our visitors to their bus. I had taken the pram and gone with them up past the farm. Returning, I encountered one of the Mitchell daughters, Maggie I think it was. We talked of the murder and she gave me a Sunday paper to read. Reaching home, I realised Ivan had gone off with the house key and the bairn and I were securely locked out. The only shelter I could find was in the hen house. I passed the time in there and for almost the next two hours I sat on a roost and read all about Helen Priestly.

At the end of that summer I realised that, if all was well ere another came around, Ena would have a playmate. At first, I was somewhat dismayed but I was reassured when none of my previous symptoms developed. That same year Bob Mitchell got married. Quite near to the farm lay Manor House of Allathan estate. Mr Mitchell bought this land and the newlyweds set up house there. I envied them for it was a beautiful old house surrounded by a large garden with lovely trees and shrubs. Bob's marriage did not ease the dislike and animosity between Bob and Ivan however. Finally, a full blown quarrel broke out with Bob accusing Ivan of stealing. Every few weeks Ivan brought home corn which he paid for out of his wages. The corn, supplemented with mash I bought from the grocer, fed the hens. Bob was ploughing near the house and he spent some time counting my flock of poultry. He went straight to his father and, in Ivan's hearing, suggested that the corn Ivan bought could not possibly feed the number of hens we kept. Therefore he must have been stealing. Today, petty thieving is common and, in fact, many think that anything is there for the taking. But then theft was a very serious matter, to Ivan in particular, and it took a lot, both on my part and on Mr Mitchell's, to soothe him. It took much longer for the effects of that dispute to wear off.

At the beginning of our third year in Royston, fate was unkind; our lives seem to sail into troubles. I had a cold water tap, but hot water had to be heated in a pot hung from a swey over the open fire. One day I had been cleaning, scrubbing down the white wood of the stair case. It was almost dinner time and I had to get the potatoes on to boil; they were also cooked on the fire. I lifted the big pot down - it was half full of very hot water - and I placed it on the floor at my feet. At that precise moment, Ena came running towards me demanding a 'mummy', her name for sweets. I reached up and gave her one from a tin on the mantelpiece and, as she put it into her mouth, she stepped back and fell into the pot.

Acting on instinct I got her undressed, applied some powder and bicarbonate of soda, wrapped her in a blanket and nursed her. Almost immediately she went quiet. I laid her in her cot, but anxiety was beginning to mount in me, for I knew she was ill and a doctor would need to be fetched. The nearest help was two fields away across at the farm of Allathan. There was no telephone near. Someone would have to go on a bicycle to fetch the doctor from New Deer. These thoughts were racing through my mind when Ivan arrived. Instantly, he returned to the farm and got one of the lads who had a motor bike to go for the doctor. Of what followed I have no clear picture. I cannot remember crying; I must have gone partially into shock. My little girl was very ill, so much so that, almost immediately, she was taken by the district nurse to the Sick Children's Hospital in Aberdeen, Dr Crombie providing his chauffeur and car for the journey. What a long night of heartache and desolation Ivan and I put in. Aberdeen was 'hine, hine awa' and we had no communication with the hospital, no telephone and no car.

The doctor and nurse were concerned about me and both expected my child would be born, as I was very near my time. But they did allow me to go to Aberdeen next day - it was better that way than sitting at home fretting alone. We left early next morning and went to Ivan's cousin, the lady who had got our pram, and she took us up to the Sick Children's near Westburn Park. There was no change in our little one. She was just holding on, still very ill, and they would not say how it might go. Ivan had to return to Royston, but I stayed for another week. Ivan's cousin lived in Old Aberdeen near King's College and St Machar's Cathedral, and I came to know the district between Old Aberdeen and the hospital very well. Each day I walked one way and took the tram the other. Sometimes I arrived when the doctors were on their rounds and had to sit and wait. The lilies were in bloom and, to this day, their sweet-scented smell brings back to me the memory of those anxious times. But God was good and our beloved daughter was given back to us.

Ivan came in to Aberdeen again and took me home. In those days, the hospital rules were very strict. Once Ena came off the danger list, we were allowed only one visit per month. Visiting mothers were regarded as a nuisance, upsetting the children and the nursing routine.

When I arrived back, Maggie, Ivan's Auntie, came to stay. I was still causing the doctor concern for I was now two weeks overdue. I do not think I gave much thought to the coming baby. The night I came home I went into labour. They say trouble never comes in single file and everything that could go wrong did so that night. I was still in shock and incapable of doing anything myself. When morning came, Ivan had a badly-battered nine and a half pound son, just alive, and a wife much the same. The first thing I can recall when I came back to this world was Dr Crombie looking down on the baby in his basket and saying, "It's such a pity about the baby. He is such a nice wee chap, but it just isn't possible for him to live." But it was possible and he did live. Within a week of his birth, however, our son David had joined his sister in hospital and, although he did not need an operation as they had first feared, he was kept under observation for almost three months, until the end of September.

It was such a delight to have our little girl back. She was away four weeks and in that short time she had forgotten how to walk and needed a lot of encouragement to begin again. She was no great talker and had words of her own. The word she used for a hat or a bonnet embarrassed us on one occasion. We had gone on a Sunday run with Ena strapped into the basket on my bike. We went as far as Turriff, the very first time for both of us. It was a lovely day and the High Street was full of people, all dressed in their Sunday best. In those days most ladies wore a hat. One lady, who was walking in front of Ivan, wore an exceptionally extravagant one. Ena, perched on her Dad's shoulders, called out suddenly in a very loud voice, "Dad, Dad! Look at that lady's pappie." Ivan and I knew immediately what she meant but others were not quite so sure. Amongst several amused grins, Ivan very quickly moved off.

The summer of 1935 was strange. Sometimes, I could hardly believe I had another child; I had never held him and Auntie Maggie had cleared all the baby paraphernalia away. Only twice were we able to visit him in Aberdeen. Maggie visited the hospital and usually wrote once a week to give a report.

During the summer I made friends with our nearest neighbours, the Watt family, a father and daughter, who lived in the farm of Mains of Allathan. At the beginning of June, Margaret Watt got married. It was on the evening before David was born that they came home from their honeymoon. They noticed the doctor's and nurse's cars standing at the gable of our house. When they got up in the morning and saw the cars were still there, they knew that something was not quite right. Margaret walked across to the house and we became friends.

Towards the end of September, my small stranger came home and, of course, had to be fed. He needed a fresh supply of milk each day. There was none to spare at the farm but Margaret, now Anderson, came to my rescue. From then until we left the following year, I had a pail of milk each day. In the spring of the following year, I was able to repay some of her kindness. She had confided in me that a happy event was to take place and one night, very late, Alex, her husband, came knocking at my door. He was on his way to New Deer to fetch the doctor and asked if I would go across and keep her company. Hospital confinements were not considered necessary in those days; most babies were born at home. It was standard practice to engage a woman for a couple of weeks to nurse mother and baby and to help with the running of the household. Mrs Anderson had had a woman organised but she had withdrawn at the very last moment.

All went well that night. They had a lovely baby girl and I offered my help. For the next two weeks or so, I went across each morning, staying until late afternoon. I left some sort of meal at home for Ivan to take at midday. They had no cottar folk at Mains of Allathan, but Margaret had her husband and father and three men to feed - far too many for the young servant girl to cope with. It made me feel good to run the household. I felt I was walking ten feet tall. The bond of friendship formed between Margaret and me in those early days has stood the test of time.

Recently, when I was browsing through the pages of Jack Webster's book 'Another Grain of Truth', I came across a photo of Mrs Webster, his grandmother and was reminded of an incident.

Unbeknown to me, Jack Webster's grandmother and his brother lived quite near in a farm which stood out of sight beyond the wood to the north of our house. We were awakened one night in the winter of 1935/36, by someone knocking on our door. It was James Webster, Jack Webster's brother, seeking help. That night their servant girl, to their surprise and consternation, had given birth to a baby. Could I come and help, and bring with me some clothes for the child. I can still recall the midnight walk through the wood and entering the farm kitchen, all cosy with a flickering glow from the fire and the oil lamp. There I encountered a small grey-haired lady, neatly dressed in a long black skirt, a blouse fastened high at the neck and, over that, a spotless flowered cotton 'pinny' and black stockings, home knitted I expect. She greeted me quietly, but appeared rather bewildered, bemoaning the dreadful happening and wondering what she was going to do. I hardly knew what to do either, but knew we had better get the mother and child seen to. She agreed and I was taken upstairs to a small attic bedroom where the girl and baby were in bed. The girl would hardly answer me when I spoke to her. She looked so resentful and sullen, but she did let me take the baby and have him washed and dressed. He was a beautiful well-formed boy and, for such a small child, he made quite a noise.

Mrs Webster had found an old grey shawl and, once I was finished, she wrapped him in this and sat down near the fire to nurse him.

48

Meanwhile, I went upstairs and made the mother comfortable. Later we had tea and for a little while we sat discussing the problem. It was decided to leave matters until morning, when the Websters would contact the girl's parents and call the doctor or nurse. I left and I have never seen or spoken to any of them since. But one day a young lad came to our door and handed me a small parcelwhich he said was from Mrs Webster. Enclosed was a home-made cheese and a note thanking me for my assistance - signed Jeannie Webster.

We knew that when Whitsun came we would again be on the move. A rumour had been current for some time that Mr Mitchell senior was retiring and his son Bob would take over the management of the farm. When this handover took place, there would be little prospect of Ivan being asked to stay on. I hated the constant moving from place to place and saw no sense in it. Like Ivan, I longed for a place of our own and I often saw him scanning the newspaper for a croft. Although a few possibilities did come up, they led nowhere.

David had grown into a big hefty boy, as dark as his sister was fair. He was quiet and placid but Ena, now quite recovered, was completely the opposite, habitually up to some mischief. Two escapades of hers come to mind which can still raise a smile. Somehow she managed to crawl in below the box-bed in the kitchen where her Dad kept a box of seed potatoes stored ready for planting. In a very short time those small hands had removed every one of the sprouts.

The other incident gave me quite a bit of bother. Mr Mitchell came down one day, a few weeks before we were due to leave and dug and planted the garden for the new tenant. Ena, of course, was in attendance and I think he allowed her to help in her way to plant some shallots. After he went home, she went back to the garden and appeared later with those shallots in her own small pail. I really was in trouble, for I had no idea where they had been planted.

Then it was official that Mr Mitchell was moving to Allathan House and Bob was coming to the farm. Ivan had been so unhappy in his work that in a way I was not so disappointed at the thought of moving as I had been at Fridayhill. I was always afraid that the tension between the two men might erupt into something serious. One day it very nearly did.

Twice a week the threshing mill was put on. This work required all the farm hands to help Ivan to get quickly through the job. An argument arose between the two over straw, which Bob had put in the wrong place. Very much to the others' amusement, Ivan picked Bob up and threw him onto the midden among the cow dung. Bob was taken by surprise and in the hurry to get the work going, the incident was passed over, but there is little doubt that, on Bob's part, a smouldering resentment remained.

Another situation had to be secured. We were lucky to find that

Braeside today

our new home was to be a croft house, but we were not so lucky work-wise for the job was again amongst cattle and Ivan dearly loved his horses.

On Whitsun in the year of 1936 we moved to the farm of Littleton, Millbrex, Fyvie.

CHAPTER FOUR

COTTARS AT LITTLETON

WE DID a moonlit flit.

The 28th of May was term day and all cottar folk who were on the move had to be out of their house that day by twelve noon.

This time our goods and chattels were to be conveyed to Littleton by motor lorry rather than horse and cart. There were far fewer lorries about in those days and the queue of farm workers aiming to move on the 28th May often overstretched the motor pool. Our lorry driver, a Mr Chapman, understood that our new house would be empty and asked if we would be willing to move the night before. He assured us that the previous tenants would be out that night around six o'clock. This time Ivan's youngest brother Cecil came to help. It was late in the evening before everything was loaded up, for our numbers had doubled and so had our goods and livestock. Ivan and Cecil went with the furniture but the children and I, with a few of our more personal items, were bundled into a car we had hired from the lorry driver.

It was almost midnight and I vividly recall watching the red tail-light of the lorry as it bumped its way up the rough road leading to the farm of Littleton and the croft house beyond. The lorry drew into a close at the gable end of the house and the remains of the small steading. There was no space left for the car, so we had to park on a grassy piece of ground at the end of a hedge which partially sur-rounded the garden. There was no moon but it was a dry night with a sky like dark velvet full of sparkling stars. As I slipped out of the car with David asleep in my arms my feet encountered what I thought

All that is left of Littleton

were rhubarb leaves. I was so pleased, for rhubarb was a favourite
with both Ivan and me. At home it had been in plentiful supply but
I had had none in either of our last two gardens. You can imagine my
disappointment when I later learned I was standing amongst tobacco
plants, which I had never seen before. Strange to say, I have not seen
tobacco plants since except on a sentimental journey back to Littleton where I found them still flourishing.

We had arrived, but we were in for quite a shock: the house we
had been led to believe would be empty was occupied by a family all
sound asleep. Littleton was one of several farms which belonged to
a Mr Frank Beaton and he had grieves in most of them. These people
were only moving from one of his farms to another and were being
taken with a pair of carts and horses from Littleton to their new home
near Auchterless. I do not know which of us was more distressed.
They had intended moving during that day but were delayed. They
were all packed ready to move out early in the morning - a man and
woman with three children asleep on mattresses lying on the floor.

Ivan got rather annoyed with the lorry driver who had landed us
in this mess but everyone else seemed quite good natured about it.
The man put on some clothes and gave us a helping hand, and in no

time our furniture and goods were unloaded and dumped in the garden - the close had to be kept clear for loading up the other family. Thank goodness it was a dry night. Tea was even made and, once the lorry departed, Cecil and Ivan and Ena slept like the others on a mattress on the floor. David was in his pram, I snuggled up in an armchair by the fire and we all had a few hours sleep.

It was a hectic morning but we had a pleasant breakfast, all of us together and, with everyone helping out, the other family were soon on their way. We had met and then we parted and I never saw or heard of them again.

After such an inauspicious start, things settled smoothly into a pattern. The farm setup was completely different from Royston. The farm grieve, a Mr Thomson, and his wife stayed in the farm house. Three men stayed in the farm bothy - two horsemen and a young lad who helped Ivan in the byre. Mr Thomson was a small, quiet man. His wife was much larger, still quiet but dour, and I think it was she who 'wore the breeks'. I only spoke to her once or twice on the farmhouse doorstep. I couldn't say she was friendly.

Throughout that summer Ivan seemed content. Again, there was the rush to get the turnips in, followed by the hoeing. Hay was cut and coled and put into stacks. The peats were cut and carted home from the moss. Other jobs were ever-present: fencing, repair work around the steading, cleaning ditches and the odd jobs leading up to harvest.

Quite early, around the end of September, Ivan had cattle in the byre to feed for Christmas. This was the beginning of his winter's work. Then he began to grumble. He did not care for cattle; he loved his horses. On the whole, however, I am sure he was much happier than at Royston. On the other hand, I now led an utterly different life. The house was not nearly as attractive as the one at Braeside. It had an ugly corrugated iron roof, which I hated. We had a fair-sized living room, a front room and two back bedrooms. An attic was reached by a ladder and trap door. Later, I made the attic into a playroom for the children. A porch around the front door held a sink and running water. I cooked on an open peat fire. The biggest difference lay in my surroundings and my contact with neighbours.

Littleton farm house and steading, although it was not as isolated as Royston, was still out of sight. Only a small part of the steading roof was showing, along with the tops of the trees surrounding the farm house. At the end of the dip, but quite clearly visible, was the church of Millbrex. To the left, running the length of the howe, was the burn of Littleton. On an incline to the west of the burn, stood three croft dwellings. To the north-east at least another seven farm houses were visible. One farm was perhaps about 60 to 70 acres and could hardly be classified as a croft, but the others were in the region of twelve to twenty acres. All were happy homes with industrious people winning a livelihood from the soil. But where are they now? They have vanished, leaving only the rubble of their homes and sometimes not even that.

I had relinquished my little oasis surrounded by green fields. Around the corner stood another dwelling, Burnside Croft, the home of Mr and Mrs Ironside. While I had little contact with the farm and its day to day affairs, I saw the Ironsides daily. They were about ten years older than Ivan and me. They had two children, a boy and girl, both newly started at school. A friendship began with them which lasted over 50 years. During that year, I came to understand and appreciate the crofting way of minding and managing a small place, the crofters' cheerfulness, their friendship, all part I think of the art of neighbourliness. Their first love was their land; the good Lord came second.

Burnside farm was about twenty acres. James Ironside had taken over from his father. He kept one horse and two cows along with perhaps nine or ten yearlings and a similar number of calves. They also kept pigs - a few breeding sows. James had one particular favourite which answered to her name. I liked animals, but pigs were not my favourites. I thought they were ugly, dirty and perhaps a little bit smelly. Once I really came to know them, however, I had to change my opinion for if pigs are given the right conditions, they are as clean as any other animal and they are intelligent and loveable creatures.

Pigs were quite a paying trade, but the main source of income on the Ironsides' croft was their hens. I am sure Mrs Ironside was a pioneer in this branch of poultry industry. For a long time hens were the Cinderellas of the farm trade, living in a scruffy corner of the steading, picking up any odd scraps they could find. When she had need of an egg, the farmer's wife went out and searched the farm yard until she found a few. In the 1930s a few began to house their birds and feed and care for them, which paid a dividend in eggs for sale.

Mrs Ironside took this up in a big way, housing 500 birds. She was the first I met to have an oil heated incubator for hatching out chicks. It took 100 eggs at a time. There were bigger incubators, but this one suited her best. Newly hatched chicks were transferred to a brooder, again oil heated, and reared in special houses scrubbed spotlessly clean, draught-proofed and fitted with glass windows for plenty of light. The houses were moved on skids or runners to fresh ground for the chicks to forage. Mrs Ironside reared about 400 to 500 chicks each year to replace her stock. Each day she collected her eggs and washed and packed them in boxes which held 30 dozen. I think on an average she sold ten of these each week. At first the grocer handled the eggs but later a cooperative was formed and a lorry called each week to lift them. At that time eggs were making from one to two shillings or two shillings and sixpence per dozen. Not a great deal of money one may think, but overhead costs were low as little extra food was bought in. The hens' principal food was oats - home grown. A big boiler kept in an outhouse was filled most days with potatoes, again grown on the croft. The potatoes were mashed up with sids and other mixtures brought home from the meal mill. This mix was used both for pigs and poultry. Feed for the young chickens had to be bought in and later, when eggs made more money, the hens' oats were supplemented with layers pellets, consisting I believe of the same elements as in the crofters' own traditional mixtures. There was a lot of hard work in keeping hens but for many years they guaranteed a comfortable livelihood for hundreds of crofters all over the countryside - that is, until the big boys came in and spoiled it.

The Ironsides were a hard-working couple, grand neighbours, and they always had time for a chat and a bit of fun. I remember Jamie telling me a story: the threshing mill had gone to a farm but, instead of the farmer, it was his wife who appeared on the scene to give the men their instructions on how and where to set the mill. She did this with every confidence and great expertise. When she went back to the house, the mill men said to the farmer, "I doot min the wife wears the breeks."

"Oh maybe", replied the farmer, "but I hidna sic a gweed pair or I got her."

The freedom of my small flock of birds was somewhat curtailed. A fence had to be put up along the side of a field of oats belonging to the Ironsides for, if the hens and chicks had got in, they would soon have destroyed quite a lot of it. Yet in a way I was lucky for, of the two other fields which adjoined the house, one was in grass and the other in turnips. A few weeks after we arrived I had an extra bonus. A brown hen with eight chicks appeared suddenly from nowhere. I knew by her colour she was out of Mrs Ironside's flock, and suspected she had gone broody and set herself - an annoying habit hens have. Mrs Ironside had no time for one small, recalcitrant hen and I was allowed to keep her.

At Christmas my sister-in-law gave me a duck for the pot. I had never cleaned or cooked a duck before and I was stupid enough to try and pluck it like a chicken. The duck was full of down and tears fell before I got it even half ready for the oven. After my tale of woe, I was given two live ducks to compensate, and to supply Ivan with one of his favourite meals - a duck egg. Ivan made them a small lean-to duck house - they had to be shut up each night or else there would be no eggs. All ducks like to wander and these two were no exception. Usually, in the morning they made for the burn and were not to be seen again until evening. They got one feed per day in the evening. They were very exact in this routine. If eight o' clock was feeding time, they were there on the dot and you could hear them squawking at the door. It was the two ducks which led to my fall-out with Mrs Thompson, the grieve's wife.

I seldom met any of the other farm workers. I might have had a welcoming shout and word from some of them when they were working in the fields near the house. There were two, though, who liked to play pranks on us. Often, I opened the door in the morning to find peats stacked on the doorstep. One of their very annoying practical jokes was to let the ducks out. Anyway, I eventually decided I would pay them back.

Down among the tobacco plants at the foot of the hedge, thistle-like plants grew in abundance - burdock. They had rough leaves and large burry heads which would stick like glue to any sort of clothing.

I collected quite a few of them and, one night when I knew the men were all away from home, I went down to the farm with Ivan when he went to collect the milk. The farm house stood well away from the steading and the chaumer where the men slept was at the back, so while Ivan went to the kitchen door it was quite easy for me to slip into the chaumer unseen. Very thoroughly I set these plants into the men's beds, between the sheets. Oh, how I would have loved to have seen and heard those lads when they came home that night and crawled into bed.

I did not hear from them but Ivan did next day and I am afraid he got the blame, for it was only around our house those dandy burdocks grew.

Mrs Thompson went wild with rage as they were very difficult to get off the sheets. One night soon after, I decided I should go down with Ivan to the farmhouse and explain and apologise. But, I hardly got my mouth open before she flew into a rage, called me a bitch and several other Bs. Ivan tried to calm her down but to no avail, so we just quietly walked away. After we rounded the corner, I sat down on the bank of the dam and went into hysterical fits of giggles. Ivan thought me quite daft and I think he was glad to get me home. The men still played pranks on us, but the ducks were left alone.

In my new life at Littleton, I did miss one person from the old: George Watson the grocer and Jack-of-all-trades. If I had been in need of anything he was sure to supply it. My new grocer was alright but just not a Mr Watson. He came from Lethenty and owned a small country 'shoppie' but was 'neen the waur o' that'. These shops stocked goods to satisfy all the needs and wants of country folk: food, coal, paraffin and petrol, often the newspapers and sometimes they doubled as the local Post Office. Not all these country stores had vans, but at Lethenty the Chapmans, father and sons, had a van out and about daily. They also owned a garage with a petrol pump and ran a car hire business. All these motor vans with their various goods were, like the poultry industry at that time, just coming into their own in a big way.

A baker's van came from Fyvie but I cannot remember a butcher. Ivan just went down in the evening to New Deer or to Fyvie for meat. At that time all shops stayed open until around nine o'clock, for country folk did not have a day in the week off work or even a half day for that matter, and seldom finished work before six o'clock. Some Sundays they had free, but all shops were shut then.

That year of 1936 must have been a memorable one, for the old king had died and a new one had reluctantly taken his place, a king destined never to be crowned. All the scandal and tumult that followed was but a ripple on the surface of our lives. We had no television, no wireless and few newspapers to bring the news to our home. Christmas came hard on the heels of the abdication. The Christmas I spent at Littleton bears little resemblance to today's festivities. In England the big celebration was Christmas but in Scotland Hogmanay was the highlight of our year. Perhaps Scotland was still bound to an ancient, pagan tradition. In those early days, we did in our hearts rejoice in the birth of Jesus, but I think few now remember whose birthday they are celebrating; it is all an orgy of present buying, eating and drinking. That Christmas of 1936 I do not think I even had a Christmas card. I do remember my mother baked me a fine cake and gave the children small gifts and we exchanged presents. I tried to get the children some toys. Ena got a tricycle, which had taken months of saving. She flew around on it, bumping into the fire and upsetting a kettle of water - this time with no ill effects.

A sweet recollection comes vividly to mind. It was New Year's Eve. My mother was staying and the three of us were sitting quietly by the fireside waiting to welcome in the New Year. The bairns were fast asleep, my mother was reading, Ivan was asleep in his chair and I was knitting. Beside us, on a small table, stood a bottle of ginger wine with three glasses all ready for a toast. Just a few minutes before midnight, Ivan awoke and got to his feet. We both went to the door and looked out. It was a clear, frosty night and a brooding stillness lay over all, as if the whole world was asleep. Then, from out of that stillness, loud and clear, came the sweet sound of bells at the Church of Millbrex, barely a mile away. That lovely sound came floating up through the howe, reverberating all around. Not a word was spoken between us, but we drew close together, standing thus for a few minutes, two people in complete harmony. It was one of those moments when one knew that God was near, giving a sense of peace and eternity. That night, when the bells rang out their New Year message, was a turning point in my life. The things that I had once held dear to my heart slowly began again to take on a new meaning.

We turned back into the house, drank our toast and went off to bed. There were no 'first footers'. In the background, unknown to us, dark clouds were gathering. They receded somewhat when Neville Chamberlain returned to Britain with his scrap of paper guaranteeing "peace in our time" but not altogether. About this time preparations for war began. Everyone seemed to be knitting but I joined an evening class for First Aid run by the Red Cross and St John's Ambulance Society. Mina Spence, a daughter of one of our neighbours, was keen on the First Aid course but she had no one for company. So Mrs Ironside persuaded me to go, offering to look after the children if Ivan was not available. The classes were held in the evenings twice weekly at Fyvie and we had over seven miles to cycle.

It was a nice break and I enjoyed the outing, meeting and mixing with other people. We were honoured in a way by having as a member of the class the wife of the Laird of Fyvie Castle, Lady Anne Forbes Leith. She was a plain woman with no airs or graces. Often she would arrive very late dressed in a pair of old shoes and a raincoat that certainly had seen better days. We sat together and talked on all sorts of subjects. I had no great difficulty in picking up the various techniques we were being taught. Once she asked me if I was a teacher. I told her I wasn't but I did not elaborate, never letting on I was just a cotter wife.

We had completed a written paper and on our last evening we had to do a practical and oral examination to win our First Aid certificate. Lady Anne, as usual, arrived late, but apologised profusely and asked if she could go first, explaining that, for the past two nights, she had been held up and she had spoiled the dinner at the Castle by putting in a late appearance. She dared not do it a third time for fear that the cook would hand in her notice - and good cooks were very hard to come by. We just smiled and said she could go on ahead. I was quite thrilled to have my certificate and an A grade. I longed for someone to practise on, but no-one obliged except Jamie Ironside's dog, Bobsie, who got one of his legs torn on a wire fence. I very carefully bathed and dressed it and expertly bandaged it up. Alas, the ungrateful pup that he was, next morning the bandage was lying in tatters. I wonder if Lady Forbes Leith was ever able put her certificate to practical use when, during the war years, Fyvie Castle was used as a military hospital.

Both our children were growing up healthy and happy bairns. There was no recurrence of David's tummy trouble but oh, he was a lazy lad and he was eighteen months old before he walked. An uncle of mine was a shoemaker in Fyvie and on a visit to us he remarked that he had a pair of small brown buttoned boots which, though unfashionable, might help David to walk. He brought them up and, once they were fitted on David, he almost immediately set off. They provided just that little extra support his ankles needed.

The children were full of pranks and escapades. The hens which the previous tenants had kept were unhealthy, many had contracted some disease and died. To rout this disease out, Ivan bought a bag of quick lime and, after cleaning the hen house, he white-washed the inside and sprinkled lime on the ground round about. Ena must have been watching her Dad.

One morning a few days later, I put David outside in his pram with Ena playing around, while I got on with the washing. From outside came sounds of laughter and joy and I did wonder what they were up to. Suddenly the laughter changed to howls of pain, which I knew came from David. To my horror I discovered that Ena had found an old pan, filled it with lime and was broadcasting it all around. Quite a lot fell into the pram and her last handful landed full in David's face filling his eyes. I quickly picked him up and held his head and face below the water tap. The cold water washed out most of the lime, though he had very sore, red inflamed eyes for several days.

Another day they were put up in the loft to play. I only did this when it rained or it was too cold to play outside. They had all their toys up with them. They usually enjoyed themselves, coming to no harm, and it gave me a little break. Although I could not see them, I could hear them and I thought it was impossible for them to get into real mischief. How wrong I was. There was a prolonged hush in the attic and I decided to investigate. I could hardly believe my eyes when I saw the shambles. Someone had once tried to make the loft into a bedroom and had practically papered it all over. One part was only newspaper, but the other had a pretty flower-pattern wallpaper. The paper was almost completely stripped off and lay in ribbons all over the floor.

Then there was the day they both disappeared. It must have been in the spring time, I had been busy in the house and it was some time before I realised I had not seen or heard of them for quite some time. Looking out and not finding them did not alarm me at first. Although they were forbidden to go on their own to the Ironsides', they did occasionally disobey. I would find them either with Jamie or Mrs Ironside. But to my dismay the Ironsides had not set eyes on them. Mrs Ironside and I searched all the out-buildings before parting company - she went up the road, while I hurried down the burn side, up to the farm steading and round past the dam. This was the one place I feared for their safety. The ducks were on the dam and all was peaceful, without a child in sight. I hurried back to the house hoping some miracle had happened and I would find them returned, but no, they had just completely vanished. I knew I must go to the farm and contact Ivan. Mrs Ironside said Jamie had gone to the mill and she thought he would be back soon. Even as we were standing talking, the horse and cart appeared round the corner of the steading at Littleton and trundled up the road towards us. To my utter joy the two prodigals were seated beside Jamie in the cart. As he was riding up the road on the other side of the farm, he had found them both sitting by the roadside. I was so pleased to have them back safe, I do not think I even scolded them.

It was a washing day and Mrs Ironside had gone out to the back to peg up the clothes. David wandered up and, finding the living room door open, he went in. Whether he discovered the cupboard door was open too, or opened it on his own, we will never know but, when Mrs Ironside returned, she found him very busy. When she scolded him, all he did was point to a shelf where she kept a tin of biscuits - his way of telling her he wanted one.

At that time, most grocers sold cereals and sugar in one or two-pound brown bags though they bought their supplies in bulk hundredweights. Once I was badly let down with this practise. I had a pan of milk on the boil for a flaked rice pudding and sprinkled the rice on the milk. It immediately went up in a cloud of foam. Looking at the bag, flaked rice was clearly marked on it, but my taste buds soon told me that it was flaked soap.

In February of that year Ena celebrated her fourth birthday. She had arrived in a snow storm and her birthdays were often snowbound. It was so that year. I had planned a small party. Jack and Doris Ironside would come for their tea. Although we had a good supply of water on tap, the cleanliness and quality were in doubt and we were in the habit of going each day to fetch water from Mrs Ironside's well. With the snow piled high, the children were sure I would never be able to make the daily round trip to the well and there would be no tea. But there was tea and there was also a cake with the message emblazoned in pink icing, 'Happy 4th Birthday Ena'. The bairns thought it marvellous.

One Sunday I decided to take Ena to church with me. Most of the neighbours attended and it was easy for me to join them. Though it was quite a walk for a little girl, it was not beyond her. We found a seat about the middle of the main body of the church which faced the choir and pulpit. The trouble began during the first hymn. She could not see over the seat in front and demanded to be lifted up.

Standing on her seat she joined the singing and when the hymn ended, continued in her treble of la, la, la. The girls in the choir began to take notice and smiled at her. The little monkey knew fine and played up. I have often heard of churches with bats in the belfry, but this one had 'doos'. You could hear them cooing and one flew across the aisle. This of course fascinated Ena and, in the midst of the sermon, she began asking all sorts of questions, not always in whispers.

I was getting more and more embarrassed and then came the final folly. The collection was taken up with a long handled ladle. When the man came around I gave her a coin to put in the ladle. Somehow she missed and the penny went rolling down the aisle. As quick as lightning, she was down on all fours chasing the penny down to the choir. She retrieved it and straight away took off to the other side of the church chasing the man with the ladle and shouting, "Hey min, hey min". I was glad to get her out of that church, but some people, the minister's wife amongst them, gathered round and said what a sweet and dear little girl she was. Dear little my foot. I never took her back.

I met the minister but never really got acquainted with him. He was a character, well liked, and his pride and joy was his Morris car, in which he travelled across the countryside giving lifts to all and sundry. He was an atrocious driver - in those days no test had to be passed. The parishioners were quite scared to get in the car with him and would often refuse a lift which must have hurt his feelings. Once he offered a lift to Mrs Ironside whose pride and joy was a flock of Brown Leghorn hens she kept for breeding. One day, she was setting out to fetch home a cockerel from Gight, about three miles away. The minister arrived on the scene and insisted he took her across. Rather reluctantly, she agreed. They arrived at the place with her considerably shaken and collected the bird but on the return journey the cockerel somehow escaped from his basket. His flapping about the car upset the minister's concentration and they all landed in the ditch. They were not hurt but his nibs managed to make an escape. The minister and Mrs Ironside took half an hour to round him up. She then set out for home with her pedigree cockerel and the poor minister had to get someone with a horse to pull his beloved car out of the ditch.

That year seemed to slip past so quickly. In early March, Ivan's hopes were again raised that he might get the tenancy of a croft. It was in the Ellon district. Ivan got off work early one evening, hired the Lethenty car and Jamie and I went with him to view the croft. It was just on the big side for Ivan's bank balance. When you took over a tenancy, all the crops, granary corn and the first, second and third years' grass had to be valued and paid for to the outgoing tenant. Fencing and dung were valued too and any new buildings had to be paid for.

However, Ivan thought he might just scrape through and an offer was made. It took some weeks for a reply to come back. This, in itself, prepared us for the answer. If he had any chance, he would have been called into the estate office for an interview. When the letter came, it just said that the farm of Mosstown of Ellon had been let and thanked him for his offer.

About this time Mr Thompson let it be known he was giving up the grieve's job. He and Mrs Thompson were retiring to a cottage at

Gight. When the grieve left a farm, all the other workers did the same. This meant that Ivan would again be without a job and we would be on the move once more. Moving from place to place really got me down. I knew most of the people around me; I liked them and they, in turn, I think liked me.

During this period Ivan made no effort to find himself another situation but kept on saying he was for no more cottar jobs. When I tried to talk the matter over, he retreated into a silent world which I could not enter; those moods troubled me. Meanwhile in the outside world the fears of war were temporarily forgotten as all rejoiced at the thought of the imminent coronation of the King and Queen, on the 12th of May.

One night, a week or so before the coronation, Ivan went out, not saying where he was going. He returned two hours later with the news that he had fixed us up with a house quite near belonging to a Mr Petrie, the farmer of Asleid. He offered little more information; I never knew how he had come to know of it. I was somewhat dismayed. We would have to pay rent. If there was no work, how would we manage? There was no dole or anything of that sort in those days.

However one of our problems was solved; we would have a roof over our heads. On the 12th of May the weather was beautiful and for me it was a happy day. Nearly everyone had a holiday and Ivan had at least part of the day off. We took our bikes and our children, I packed a picnic box and we set off for the Old Mill House, Cairnbanno, which was to be our next home. Ivan had his spade slung across his back and, on the carrier of the bicycle, a bag of potatoes, for we were planning to plant the garden. Ivan was in a happy, teasing mood and for the meantime my misgivings were laid to rest. The garden was across the road from the house and as it was occupied we did not go near. We did see the family, six or seven of them, carrying small flags, set out in the afternoon, presumably to celebrate the Coronation. They gave us a wave and we waved back.

It's strange that I remember so many of the details of that coronation day but none of our actual move to Cairnbanno which took place only three weeks later. Still we made it. But oh where was our dream croft? It was nearer than we thought.

CHAPTER FIVE

THE OLD MILL HOUSE

MY NEW home pleased me well, but it was a real mess when we moved in.

Before we arrived, two families had lived together in the house. They caused Mr Petrie a great deal of trouble. The week before we were due to move in, he had to resort to the law to have them evicted for non-payment of rent and, as a result, it was stipulated by Mr Petrie that we must pay our rent six months in advance.

It was a sturdy granite house with a combined kitchen/living room, a large room to the front of

The Mill House, Cairnbanno, today

the house, a hallway and a staircase leading to two bedrooms, both with dormer windows. A smaller room was built off the kitchen along with a lobby, a larder and a porch leading to the back door. It took me weeks to clean the house.

The house was in good condition, except for the havoc that those previous tenants had wrought. We did nothing to the front room except clean it and use it for a store and a playroom for the bairns.

Once I got the hall and staircase clean, I was charmed by the paint work which was dark blue, almost navy, with gold scrolls - very unusual and really quite elegant. The living room resembled a pig-sty more than anything else, but with hard work, a tin of paint and a few rolls of wallpaper it took on a more pleasant aspect.

I was glad Ivan was at home to help, but still I was relieved to hear Mr Petrie offer him work. We were saddled with a house and rent to pay, and there were none of the customary 'perks'. We were lucky that Jamie Ironside had gifted us a load of peats and we had meal and potatoes from Waughtonhill. Soon, we would be able to dig our own from the garden. I was able to arrange a supply of milk from our nearest neighbour, Mrs Gordon of Cairnbanno House, and there were many occasions when I had enough eggs to sell to cover our grocery bill. We were once again on Mr Watson's customer list and I was delighted. For some time his was the only van that called. Later on through the summer I had more vans than I needed. Crighton of Methlick was my baker and my old butcher, Mr Hadden from New Deer also appeared. Once a fortnight, an ice cream van called late in the evening to give Ivan and the bairns a chance to indulge them-selves. I thought it was a downright extravagance - I had the money to look after.

When Ivan was in work we were, strangely, slightly better off than before. By the day he got five shillings, by the week it was twenty-five shillings but if he put in six single days, he came home with thirty-five shillings. Riches indeed. The other day an old friend and I got talking, comparing prices of today with those of the 1930s. At the time a loaf of bread cost four pennies, though I can remember further back when it had been tuppence. Our discussion ended with the staggering fact that buying one loaf per week for 52 weeks, a year's supply, would have cost a little more than £2. Today that money would only buy three loaves.

I liked my new abode but there was one disadvantage - there was no water in the house as there had been at Braeside and Littleton. Here I was back to a well almost identical to the one at the bottom of the garden at Fridayhill but much farther. This well was situated at the side of the road nearly 500 yards away below the steading . It was a very weary haul up the steep incline to the house. I have always been very economical with water and hate to see any wasted, even up to the present day. After the breakfast dishes were washed, the water was used to clean the potatoes or other vegetables. Then it was added to the pot of peelings and scraps for the poultry, even with all those detergents and washing liquids I had used.

We often got an extra supply by collecting rain water off the roof. A few weeks after we arrived at Old Mill, Ivan fitted a wooden barrel below a spout at the back of the house. This eased the burden considerably as it usually supplied all the water for washing and cleaning purposes.

Our house had once been a meal mill and croft. Below the house, in good repair, there was a small compact steading but there was no trace of the old mill; it was weeks before I found the ruins. Daily, at about one o'clock, the bairns and I walked across to Cairnbanno House for our milk. The correct route was by the main road but we crossed the bridge and turned right to the steading, then we walked the back path along a short avenue of trees to the big house. It was a lovely manor house and I found Mrs Gordon, a widow, very friendly. One day I decided to explore and took a short cut and that was how I found the old mill.

On the opposite side of the road from our house was a big dip and at the bottom ran the Cairnbanno burn. A field, which I am sure once had been part of the mill croft, stretched out from the top of the small valley. The gate was opposite our entrance and it seemed a much closer approach to Cairnbanno House. I took this route one day and found the ruins of the old mill lying quite near the bank of the burn. It had been a long time out of use but the outline of the main buildings was still clearly visible. It was a pleasant alternative route to Cairnbanno House but only passable by stepping stone when the burn was running low. This was quite fun for the bairns and the burn was my biggest problem where they were concerned - they were fascinated with it. It was quite deep in places and I forbade them to go there alone. But a two and a four year old are seldom very reliable. Ena would take her shoes off and throw them into the water, jumping with glee as she watched them float away into the distance. This happened twice and she lost her shoes. I was forced to give her a good spanking. Had her father known he would not have sanctioned it, but I think it did her good, for the prank was not repeated.

Another day, I heard David screaming and I can tell you he could make good use of his lungs. It may have saved his life, for I found him in the burn up to his neck in water. Ena too was very wet. It was mid-summer, a very warm, sunny day, but I took them both straight home, stripped them, put on their night-clothes and sent them upstairs to bed, where they remained for the rest of the day. It worked and they never, that I know of, went back on their own. They were also forbidden to go out on to the main road, as cars were beginning to be a hazard. They did obey this order. I impressed on Ena that she had David to look after, and I was amused to see her, when she saw a car approaching, pull him into the side of the road and sit on top of him until the car had passed.

For the first few weeks Ivan had work at Asleid but once the hoeing of the turnips was over and the hay crop secured, he often had days with no work. On one of those inactive days, he went up to Burnside to help Jamie Ironside. Late on, after supper, he returned and I knew immediately something was up. It was no good my asking what the problem was; he would get round to it in his own good time. It was only when I said I would go and get our bedtime drink that he asked did I mind on Jamie's old blue cow? Of course I did.

"She had a big bull calf the day."

"Jamie'll be pleased" I replied.

"Pleased enough. But her daughter is due any day and he'll hae tae sell the auld een tae mak room. He was gaun tae sell her afore she calved, but she cam on early."

"That's surely a pity," I responded, but I was beginning to wonder what all this was leading up to.

"Aye," Ivan continued, "she'd a lot o' good years in her yet an he wunna get muckle noo she's calved and forby he means tae keep the calf."

"Well that'll be up to him but I think I'll awa tae bed noo."

Then came the question: "Fit aboot us buyin the coo? I'd get her at a bargain price."

"A bargain? Dinna be daft. Fit wid we dae wi a coo? "

"Weel, I was in past Asleid on ma way hame the nicht an Mr Petrie says we can hae the byre for her. We can keep her a while then sell her for a profit."

"Oh," says I, "so Jamie and you have already been discussing it; we've nae grass, nae food or bedding of any sort. The hale idea is completely daft."

But Ivan had all the answers. Seeing I was friendly with Mrs Gordon would I not ask if she could graze her during the summer?

Very unwillingly, I agreed for I still could think of it only as a most impractical idea and I went off to bed in a huff.

When I approached Mrs Gordon next day, she quite readily agreed to rent us, for a small weekly sum, the grazing of the field across the road. I tried hard to dissuade Ivan from the idea, but next day he went back to Millbrex and bought Belinda. How she came to have that name I have no idea but she became my beautiful, blue cow Belinda. She was at least ten years old, maybe more and would have cost around £6 to £8. Ivan's idea, when he bought her, was to let her go dry, fatten her up and then sell her at a slight profit. But things did not work out that way. Chiefly it was my fault. Ivan had milked cows since he was a youngster, but I had to learn afresh. Watching Ivan, it looked so simple, but there was a knack to it. Once I acquired this knack, the milk flowed freely. There was a ntion around then that blue cows were poor milkers, but Belinda produced very good milk, filling a two-gallon pail three times a day. I could not bear to see all this milk go to waste, but I would not buy eqipment for butter or cheese making. The hens had pans full of the milk but they were never great milk drinkers. I used to get great amusement though just watching them make an attempt. They would

Our first cow Belinda

all crowd round the dish, dipping their beaks and heads into the milk. Then up high went their heads and they shook a spray of milk all over themselves. Only a few drops went down their gullets.

What were we to do with the milk? I suggested we buy a calf. There were three or four stalls in the byre and Belinda occupied only one. In fact, we bought two calves and into our lives came Douglas Panton, a cattle dealer from Maud. He was friendly with one of Ivan's older brothers and throughout our farming years, three generations of the Pantons have supplied us with calves.

During that summer, another animal came into our lives - a little pup called Lassie, just the image of the Lassie in the films. One Sunday Ivan went to visit his brother. I had to stay at home - it was too long a journey and the children were getting too big to carry on our bikes. When he returned home they were in bed but not, as I thought, asleep. He was in the habit of leaving his bike at the back door and I had heard him arrive and so had the children. He took some time to appear and I was beginning to wonder what was keeping him. When he came in carrying a big box both scallywags came bounding down the stair. Of course, being Ivan, he had to tease and he would not open the box. The strange high-pitched noise coming from the box had me puzzled, but from the first moment I saw the little pup I liked her. She was shivering and whimpering, a very bewildered puppy, only about six or seven weeks old. I gathered her up in my arms soothing and cuddling her and I was rewarded with a wet nose and tongue caressing my cheek. Ivan suggested we warm some milk and give her a drink. It was good to see her lapping it up and she soon recovered and began to explore the room.

Ena was determined to take the pup to bed with her but Ivan said she would have to stay in the byre with the cow and calves. But for this first night some soft rags were put in a box and we decided to put her into the small room in the lobby next to the back door where we kept odds and ends such as potatoes and poultry food. I got the others off to bed but stayed behind for a while trying to comfort the pup and get her calmed but I am afraid I was not very successful. For such a small dog she made a dreadful noise and, though she seemed to settle the next day, the second night was a repeat of the first. When I could bear it no longer, I crept downstairs and took her through to the living room. I made her a bed and stayed a while talking to her before slipping quietly away. That was the end of our trouble. Her box was set down behind the armchair and like a good dog she crawled into her box when she needed a daytime nap. But I know fine she never slept in it during the night. Mind, we never caught her in the armchair, but the warm cushion with its tell-tale dent betrayed her.

I could hardly believe that this adorable bundle of fun could be so destructive. The children's shoes were chewed to ribbons, cleaning cloths and brushes all disappeared and she even dared to tear some of my books to tatters. The chickens were chased and feathers flew. Yet, when she sat and looked at you with those beguiling brown eyes, all was forgiven and you just hoped that one day she would become an ordinary, biddable dog.

One day she did get into serious trouble. The shepherd from Asleid often passed the house with his two dogs en route to his sheep pens. Somehow his young dog, Laddie, and Lassie clubbed together and began to chase my chickens, catching and killing one of them. The shepherd was angry at his dog and he gave it a good thrashing and I did the same to Lassie. Afterwards we got talking and he warned me I would need to take Lassie in hand and give her some proper training. She proved a willing pupil and soon learned the basic commands. I found that a good training chore for her was to fetch the ducks home of an evening from the burn. It took a wee while till she learned that she must not hurry them and nip out a few feathers at the same time. Once this message got through, she was very good indeed. I began to take her with me to fetch the cow from the field and again she was a help, though she had one bad habit I was never able to eradicate: snapping and nipping at the cow's heels.

In the mornings Lassie was always the first to greet you. But one day there was no welcome. She was in her box looking very miserable; she would not touch her food, nor would she even take a drink. When our friend Mr Craighead the postman called, he missed her and I took him in to see her. He thought she might have eaten something bad, perhaps poisoned food and he made up a mixture for her - mostly salt. He forced this over her throat and it made her very sick. Telling us to keep her warm and give her nothing to eat - just a drink of warm water if she would take it - he left. Next day she did not seem much better but at least was no worse and Mr Craighead was pleased to find her still alive. He had brought her some powders; he mixed one up and put it over her throat, the other he left for me to mix and give her later. That day she was able to get out of her box and go outside for a 'walk' and by the next morning there was a big improvement. The children had been so upset about their playmate and it was strange to see them creeping about so quietly, fearing to make a noise and disturb her. I have always believed a pet is good for children and that children are good for animals. They learn to take care of their pets and this nurture forms and broadens their characters. And I am sure animals, especially dogs, benefit from the company of children.

Mr Craighead continued to visit Lassie each day. After the powder, he brought her pills and in about a week she was almost her old self. Traditional tales of dogs biting postmen never applied to Lassie and our postman. She had always made him welcome, but now her welcome was threefold. She would set off down the brae when he was due, trot along the road and wait for him on the bridge. He began to give her the newspaper at the bridge to carry home. One day Ena pondered why Lassie never went out to meet the postman on a Sunday, at which point David chipped in that Lassie knew the postie never came on a Sunday.

That summer of 1937 seemed to pass so quickly. Ivan was seldom without work, just the odd day. Breakfast was the only meal he had at home so there was little cooking to be done - the children and I preferred picnic snacks. Our social life was nil. I had been back for evening visits to Mrs Ironside but I was unable to keep my promise to other Millbrex friends. Ivan made an occasional Sunday visit to Jamie Ironside and he returned the visits usually in an evening. We never saw the Asleid farm folk. Below Asleid on our left was Silverlea, a smaller place farmed by a James Bruce. But it was only during the harvest that I got acquainted with him and his mother, who kept house. Cairnbanno House came next and the owner, Mrs Gordon, I came to know very well. Her husband had died very suddenly the year before and she had two children at school - John and Alice. She too liked to read and we often exchanged books. The road up past our house led to another two steadings, both called Grainhill where the Gordon and Soutar families farmed. Jenny, the youngest of the Soutar family, came past daily on her way to school. I think the children attracted her and she began to call, along with Alice from Cairnbanno House. Another person with whom we became acquainted was Dickie Dempster, Mrs Gordon's grieve, whom she later married. He was quite a character and he stayed in our lives for many years. I met him first when he showed me where to put Belinda, but I did not altogether like or trust him and I always made a point not to be left alone with him. One day he brought another animal into our lives: a small piglet. The deal was if I would take care of it, I could have it. Otherwise it would just die; it was the runt of the family and what a poor little runt it was, all covered in bites and scratches inflicted by its brothers and sisters.

A wooden box was found and stuffed with straw and a hot water bottle was filled to keep the piglet warm. The steading was quite a distance from the house and, as the piglet had to be fed often, I kept it with me. At first I tried to spoon feed the animal, but I ended up using a baby's bottle and teat. Soon, our piglet was on its way to the byre and then to a new home in a small sty which Ivan had fixed up. Being so small, it was very difficult to keep in and often escaped. We had great times giving chase, but Lassie usually came to our aid and cornered it. In no time 'piggie' was eating out of a trough and got so big that it could not get through the bars of its pen. Then came the day, alas, that piggie went where all good porkers go.

One day Ena came into the house shouting, "Mam, mam, Belinda's oot o' the park - she's up at the quarry playing wi a big black coo". I could hardly believe her, but my heart almost stopped beating when I saw the two animals - Belinda and the Aberdeen Angus bull from the farm - careering along the edge of a disused, water-filled quarry. I took Ena, David and Lassie and dumped them in the front garden, enclosed by a hawthorn hedge. Shutting the gate, I bade them stay there until I got back. Fortunately, it was the midday break and the farm hands were around the steading. They soon had the bull back in its field and Belinda was brought home to imprisonment in the byre. It had been Ivan's intention to have Belinda sold for slaughter but when she was found to be in calf, the idea was rejected. No one could have been happier than I was at this turn of events. I think she must have been over seventeen years of age when she died. In later years, she gave us four or five more calves and she was such a good milker she helped to raise many more.

It was a good summer and when the corn and oats - it was oats they grew then, not barley - were beginning to yellow, Ivan knew he would need to think of getting harvest work. A harvest engagement lasted between a month and six weeks, sometimes running into eight weeks if the weather held up the work. The working wage was about £2 a week, but this was based on 'productivity'. Someone who could build rucks or stacks always commanded a better wage. The custom at that time was for anyone seeking work in the harvest field to go to Aikey Fair wearing a buttonhole of green corn heads. Mr Petrie had tentatively suggested that Ivan might come to Asleid at harvest, but no formal approach had been made and one day Ivan set off to Turriff and Cheyne's market, which operated as a kind of 'employment bureau' for farm workers. He did get an engagement, but a distance away, with a Mr Farquhar Dorley of Auchterless. Just after this, Mr Petrie did come and offer work. Ivan was disappointed and Mr Petrie was none too pleased, but a bargain was a bargain. Today I expect it would have been broken with little compunction. I think Ivan was away for over two months because they were very short of workers and he was kept on till the thatching of the ricks was completed.

Then I myself got a chance of some harvest work. The offer was made by Mr Bruce of Silverlea, though I do not think he was much taken with me - I did not exactly look the part. I assured him I could fork and handle a horse and cart, but I think it was against his better judgement that we struck a bargain. Whenever it was a suitable day I would go in the afternoons and do a bit of pitch and toss with the sheaves of corn. I had to be ready for work at Silverlea prompt at 1pm and it was usually around 7pm when we finished. Before I could have afternoons free, however, I had the children and animals to feed and organise. The cow was brought in early for midday milking, the poultry were given their afternoon feed and the broody hens, with their flocks of small chicks, were also fed and shut up in their runs.

It was something of a novelty for the children and they adjusted well. They played hide and seek amongst the stooks. The hired hand, a young lad of seventeen, was so good with them - he had so much patience and they got rides in the cart. His name was Roger and his folk had a croft in Blackhills of Tyrie. Much to our surprise, we found we were related - my aunt's husband was his uncle. At the end of the day, while the men stabled and fed the horses, the children and I had our supper in the farm house - Mrs Bruce was somewhat mean with food. Each person's allowance was set down on the table and I had to watch the bairns like hawks in case they took some of the men's portions. Then it was off home. Before we reached the door, Lassie's excited bark greeted us and there was always a scramble to get the door key, which was hidden below a stone. Washed, fed and then upstairs to bed, they were soon asleep but I had another hour's work ere I could follow. Belinda had to be milked, the calves and pig fed, eggs collected and the poultry shut up. The ducks had come home but had gone back to the burn and being tired I often left them. Tired and weary, I crept upstairs to bed. My earnest desire was often that it might rain next day and I would have a day at home. The pay was not all that attractive and I sometimes wonder what the workers of today would think of my paltry earnings. The rate was two shillings or two shillings and sixpence for an afternoon's work - a seven hour stint. Altogether, I would have earned £2 for the time I was employed.

Young Roger kept up the friendship and he often came down to the Mill House. He left Silverlea at the November Term and, when he failed to find another suitable job, he joined the Army. War broke out a year or two later. He always kept in touch and I remember him paying us a visit on one of his leaves. I had one postcard from France but like so many more young lads, he did not come back.

Soon after Ivan finished the harvest, he went as horseman to Jack Fowlie, who had the farm of Mid Culsh at New Deer. Ivan kept that job until the end of November. The children seldom saw him, for they were usually in bed before he got home and still fast asleep when he left in the early morning.

Belinda had to stay indoors now. Jamie had sold us a load of turnips and we got straw from Cairnbanno. The two calves had gone down to Waughtonhill - they were not ready for sale and would fetch a better price in the Spring. The cow still had a good supply of milk and Douglas Panton was again in touch - he brought us a blue heifer calf which we called Dimples.

One night in November I went up to Asleid to pay the rent and fell in love with an Aberdeen Angus bull. Since Ivan had refused the work there, there was no more communication with the Petries and when November came round I was sent to pay the rent. When I was shown through to their sitting room, I met Mr Petrie for the first time. He seemed a frail old man and he needed a stick to get around. Yet he made me welcome and was quite pleasant. Once our business was completed, we got talking. The subject nearest to his heart was cattle, especially black ones. I knew so little about breeds - a cow was just a cow to me - but I was surprised to learn that the Asleid herd of Aberdeen Angus cattle was famous. Mr Petrie showed me newspaper clippings and a picture of a bull which he had bred at Asleid. It had taken the championship at a Perth sale in 1935 and was sold for £1,050, an unheard of price - compare that with the average sale price of £30. I must have listened and asked intelligent questions for he suddenly asked if I would like to see his herd. This I felt was an honour and I immediately said yes. He shouted through to the kitchen for someone to light a lantern and we proceeded outside. In the first building were a few cows and some younger stock. He mentioned their names and the prizes they had won. Inside another building were three cows - all different colours - and two black calves, a bewildering mixture. One cow was an Aberdeen Angus, the next was a red Shorthorn and the third, a Freisian. Mr Petrie soon explained - the Aberdeen Angus cows were poor milkers and those were special calves, so the Freisian cow, which gives a plentiful supply of rich milk, was fostering one and the other calf had both his mother and the Shorthorn cow to suck. When we entered, a calf stopped suckling and came towards us. Even in the poor light it was a magnificent sight. Its mouth and eyelashes were smeared with frothy milk, which gave it a slightly comical look. But, oh that beautiful head with ears like butterfly wings and the black velvet coat. At that moment my love affair with Aberdeen Angus cattle began and I vowed that one day I would have a herd of them.

When Ivan's work finished at Mid Culsh, he got a six month engagement at a farm with the quaint name of Peel't Egg; only a few miles down the New Deer road. He was the only worker and got treated like one of themselves. Unless there was extra work, he came home on a Saturday for his supper and did not go back until Monday morning. With his wages he was given a stack of hay, not first class as it was the gatherings of the field, but good enough quality for Belinda's and Dimples' winter fodder. With a few loads of turnips, we were able to feed both animals throughout the winter very cheaply.

My memories of that Christmas of 1937 are scarce. I do remember that it was Ena's first encounter with Santa Claus. At the end of summer I took the children across to Cairnbanno School to have injections - for diphtheria or smallpox. They did not enjoy this visit and when it was getting near to Christmas, the school master called to invite us up to the school's party. He said it might give them a happier image of the school - Ena was due to start the following Easter. I took them to the party and they met Santa Clause complete with white beard, red cloak and a sack full of presents. Both were overjoyed with their small gift from him and, once we got home, I was bombarded with questions, especially from Ena. I just told them the customary story and she demanded to know why Santa had never brought her a gift. "Oh", I said, "it must just be that children have to go to school before Santa knows about them." She seemed to accept this, but I later found her looking up our chimney. She turned and said, "You know, Mummy, Santa will never get down our chimney with his sack. He's far too big". I was able to satisfy her by saying he just dropped them down and Mummy and Daddy picked them up and put them in their stockings. Later I heard her later telling David all about it. She added that when she went to school, she would tell the teacher to tell Santa about David and then he too would have a present next year. David just sat and listened, believing every word she said.

At New Year, my mother came for her usual visit. I remember the event because I did one of the daftest things ever. She was arriving by bus from Aberdeen at the Greens cross-road - only a short distance away - and Ivan had gone to meet her. During the day, I put a hot water bottle in her bed and for a little more comfort I had lit a fire in the bedroom. After Ivan left I refilled the bottle and, taking a shovel of coal, climbed the stairs. To get to the fireplace, I had first to pass the bed which was on my right. I threw the shovel and coal on to the bed and was in the act of bending down to place the hot water bottle in the fire when I came to my senses. I cannot describe the awful feeling of dismay when I saw my lovely white bedspread.

The dark clouds of war were drawing ever nearer. Hitler was on the march, but here in our small corner, we went about our daily jobs undisturbed. I even got myself involved in a salmon-poaching prank and I caught a fish of fishermen's dreams - squarely if not fairly hooked. When Ivan left for work, I too usually got going and I had the milking done before the children awoke. The cow was fed, mucked out and milked and to finish she was given a pail of water fetched from the burn. This morning, the daylight was just filtering in and, as I crossed the slope down to the burn, I could feel the grass crisp below my feet. When I bent down to fill my pail, my eye caught a silver flash and I saw the biggest fish I had ever laid eyes on in the water resting completely still amongst the tangled weeds. I stood absolutely still until I heard a noise behind me. It was Alex Grant the shepherd with Laddie. I put my fingers to my lips and he crept up beside me. He whispered, "It's a salmon, what a beauty, is it deid"?

Indeed, it was lying very still, but then there was a slight ripple in the water followed by a flick of its tail. "We will have it out", he said and slipped away, returning with the byre graip. He made an effort to get the prongs of the grape below its body, but the fish awoke and had other ideas. Heaving up with a mighty swish of its tail, it sent Alex off balance and he went straight into the water. In my efforts to help, I too went in. The salmon twisted and turned, lashing out with its tail with almost unbelievable power. It was determined to get away and we were equally adamant we would catch it. After a short but mighty struggle it lay spent on the grass bank and two very wet and bedraggled specimens of humanity looked down on it, grinning all over.

When we tried to lift it, it kept slithering through our fingers. Thinking I might find a piece of rope, I went back to the byre but all I could find was an old sack. The fish wouldn't fit into it so we just wrapped it round the middle of the fish which allowed Alec to lift it and carry it up to the house. Putting the empty pail and the graip in the byre (this was one morning Belinda had no drink), I picked up Alec's coat - the only article of his clothing that was not wet - and followed him to the house.

With a sharp knife we cut the throat of the fish, tied a piece of string around it and weighed it with a spring balance. It turned the scales at 18lbs. We did not measure it but it must have been nearly five feet long, for when we hung it on the back of the kitchen door, the tail touched the floor.

Our wet clothing was now making us very miserable and Alec had to go to tend his sheep. Fortunately both he and Ivan wore much the same size in trousers and underclothing. Giving him a dry towel I sent him through to the front room to change. My own things were soon discarded for dry garments and while Alec drank a cup of tea, his boots dried before the fire. I just hoped that no one had seen him leave the house or eyebrows would have been raised. The children never woke till much later and I doubt if they even noticed a strange man's clothing hanging on the line. They were excited about the fish, saying how clever I was to catch so big a one.

I had Alec's clothes dry and ironed for him when he called back in the evening and a good portion of the fish cut up for him to take home. I had always liked tinned salmon but had never tasted the real thing. This was the real thing and far, far better. The Ironsides got a cut, Ivan took a portion with him down to Waughton and even Dickie Dempster enjoyed some. It would have been so handy for us to have had a deep freeze but at that time they were unknown in a household. I wrapped the fish up which helped to keep it longer and I do not think any was wasted but we must have consumed an awful lot of fish.

In that spring of 1938, Ena was five years old and come Easter would have to attend school and the question of how was causing us some concern. Cairnbanno was her nearest school but it was over two miles away, too far for a small girl to walk on her own. Alice and Jenny went to New Deer Secondary School with their cycles and except for the two Petrie children (whose mother took them by car), there were no other children in the area. The school teacher had suggested asking Mrs Petrie to give Ena a lift, but she was not at all approachable. If there had been someone I could have left David with, I would have taken her on my bicycle, but there was no one. Nevertheless, I got her school outfit ready. My mother had knitted two pairs of long black stockings - in those days little girls wore long knitted stockings in winter and shorter ones in summer. I had been able to buy navy-blue material through Mr Watson, which I hoped to make up into tunics. One afternoon I cut out a pattern, intending to sew it up, but my mother's old Singer kept breaking needles. In disgust, I gave it up and as it was time to feed the hens, I put away my sewing and went downstairs.

Unbeknown to me, a man had been knocking at the door and as I barged out, I was almost on top of him. After we had both apologised, he said, "Excuse me madam, but is your sewing machine sewing all right". It was such a coincidence that I burst out laughing and explained what had happened. He offered to come upstairs and see it but hummed and hawed, "Yes it might repair, but it would be expensive". I would be far better to buy a new one, he said. He was there from the Singer Sewing Machine Company to sell me one and, when he left, I had committed myself to buying a brand new machine. Until that moment, I had never heard of hire purchase but it was beginning to come in. He was to buy my old machine for about ten shillings and, if I put down another £1 and ten shillings, followed by ten monthly instalments of £1, the machine would be mine - £12, for me, quite a sum.

The minute he left I regretted it. I was sure Ivan would murder me over the hire purchase but, surprisingly, he was quite complacent and told me not to worry. But that was the one and only time I ever got anything for the house on hire purchase and my machine was paid up on the first instalment. It was a good buy in the end and gave years of service.

Soon after the machine incident, Jamie Ironside unexpectedly appeared one evening and I could tell at a glance that he was excited about something. It was not long before he turned to Ivan and said: "I think I've found you a croft". It appeared that one of the crofts beside him would be up for rent. It was occupied by a John Webster, a relative of Mrs Ironside. For some years he had been running both his own croft and his mother's farm. Now, his mother was retiring to a cottage in Fyvie and he would be giving up the small croft to work the farm. Jamie knew the owner quite well - a Mr Ewing from Millbrex. He was sure if Ivan went with him to see Mr Ewing, a bargain could be struck and that is exactly what happened. In a few weeks it was all settled. After such a long time and so many disappointments, we found it hard to believe that it had now really happened. It also solved the school problem. Ena would not go to school until June when Mrs Ironside's daughter would be able to take her along to Millbrex. The last few weeks passed in a flash. Once again our goods and chattels had to be gathered together and packed. I had spent happy days at the Mill House and I did have some regrets at leaving. In a way, though, it was not too hard to say goodbye. The thought of having our own place overshadowed everything else. The happy thought was that Ivan and I would be going home and there would be no more packing. We left the old Mill House on the 26th of May, 1938.

CHAPTER SIX

CROFTERS
AT LITTLE MILLBREX

AT LAST our dream had become reality and Ivan and I stood on land given into our keeping, a little kingdom all our own. It consisted of only about twenty acres but in past years it had been well farmed and was in good heart - "weel vrocht grun".

There was no despondency and there were no doubts when Ivan and I took on our croft. I have little memory of the actual removal

Ivan and I, Ena and David at Little Millbrex

from the Mill House to Little Millbrex. Shortly after the settlement of the lease, Ivan went down and spent a night at his family home in Waughton, talking over business details with his brothers. Gordon attended various farm auctions and sales and collected essential machinery for Ivan - a cart, a plough and harrow. Near the time we moved in, a load of machinery arrived at Millbrex, along with the two calves I had reared and three or four others, a young red Hereford cow and an old mare called Gyp. Our household goods were moved by lorry by the same Mr Chapman who did our moonlight flitting.

We were only hours at the croft when, as the lorry was being unloaded in the close, Lassie gave a yelp of joy and bounded off along the croft road to greet a figure on a bicycle, clad in postman's garb. Postie Mowat wasn't to know that this huge brown and white collie dog only wished to show affection and give his face a friendly lick. His leg came off the bike and his boot shot out giving Lassie a hard blow in the ribs. Poor Lassie wailed in anguish and disappeared to hide in some dark corner and lick her wounds. Mr Mowat turned out to be a neighbour - he combined his croft and the postman's job. Once we told him about Lassie's fondness for the other postman, he did try to make friends but Lassie would have none of it. He was the one and only person I ever knew her to take a firm dislike to. When he called she got behind me, softly growling. Often I felt uneasy as to what she was contemplating.

We were separated from the farm of Littleton by a moss and our old home lay only two fields away. We were mostly surrounded by crofts, the Taylors below on our left, the Mutches above on our right, and a little further down was Burnside, the Ironsides' home. The house and steading had nothing to recommend them. The steading, typical of other crofts around, was built in a semi-circle with the house in the middle. As you entered the close, on your right lay a cart shed and on your left, an open, lean-to built up against the stable wall. Two hooks or slugs hung from the main beam of the roof where the cart shafts rested. Last year, we returned to the croft on a nostalgic visit. Where the dwelling house had stood, there is now a very modern bungalow. What amused me was that, after fifty years, the cart shed was as it had been, complete with hooks. But now it was used as a shelter for the owner's car.

The stable had stalls for a pair of horse with a space for storing hay. Mr Webster had built a wooden tool shed on to the stable wall, and we had to pay for that too at valuation. On open ground near the stable, which may have been at one time a garden, stood an object which I disliked. I should have appreciated it, for now there would be no more heavy pails of water to carry uphill from the well. It was our only water supply but to me it was just a cantankerous, frustrating lump of metal. Next to the house, wire netting enclosed the hen run and hen house. A gap between the hen house and the barn gave access to the peat stock and ash pit.

The door of the barn was only a few yards away from the front door. The barn sheltered a small, compact thrashing mill, which also had to be taken over at valuation along with its petrol-driven engine. I came to know that engine intimately, for it was the bane of Ivan's existence. The little demon was lodged by itself in an outhouse alongside the barn where, through a hole in the wall, it was coupled to the threshing mill by belt and pulley. An hour before operations began, a plug was extracted from the engine and warmed by the fire. Then, the engine was filled with petrol and, with a lot of coaxing and hard cranking, it might, or it might not, be persuaded to start. And, just when you were congratulating yourself, imagining the barn filling with fresh smelling straw, that engine would begin to cough and splutter and peter out - where there had been the sweet hum of the mill's music there was silence. Often in utter desperation, I would go over the hill to fetch its previous owner. He would bend down and, with a few gentle taps and some soothing words, it would start, purring sweetly, like a contented cat lapping cream.

The byre stood next to the barn. It had one long double stall for the milk cows and three or four smaller stalls, along with two pens for calves. A turnip shed, with a pig house at its back, was built on to the end of the byre. At the back of the stalls, was a railway carriage which the Websters had converted into a poultry house.

We built the corn and hay ruck as near to the barn as possible. All the foundations of the stacks were marked out with stone circles and, to ease thrashing, made in straight rows. In the slack period before harvest, the circles were cleared and a pole put in the middle to guide the building. A farm's prosperity was judged by its corn yard.

Finishing the corn stack was the crown of the farmer's year, filling him with the satisfaction of knowing that man and beast would have ample food and fodder for the winter.

To many of my generation, the corn yard holds nostalgic memories - memories of moonlight escapades, moments of joy and fun, mystery and enchantment. As boys and girls we played tag and hide-and-seek around the rucks. One such incident almost ended in tragedy. Robert was about ten or eleven, the youngest of a pack of five or six, all enjoying a moonlit game of hide and seek. He found an old cement trough lying partially on its side and crept below it to hide. In doing so he upset the trough's balance and it came down on top of him. At first this did not dismay him - 'They will never find me here', thought he with glee. We kept shouting for him, but either he stayed quiet or we could not hear him. It was getting late and, as he only lived a short distance away, we thought he had gone home. Much later his mother awoke the farm folk and then there was panic. But all was well when someone thought of lifting the trough and found Robert fast asleep. Luckily, the trough had been resting on a piece of wood which had allowed plenty of air to circulate.

The corn yard was also a meeting place for many courting couples, the lads and lassies of the farm toon. There must be many romantic memories of times spent there. I know, because I too was there before I met Ivan.

We were lucky to have that mill in our barn. Jamie Ironside also had a mill, but we were the only two in the locality- the other crofters had to depend on a travelling threshing mill, pulled by a monster, grinding and hissing steam. As a child, I was terrified at the sight of those steam engines. They were so big and clumsy and I had a horror of being crushed below one of the big iron wheels. The engine lumbered up to the farm late at night. You heard it long before you saw it and when it appeared out of the darkness, it looked like a huge apparition with two glowing red eyes.

The day when the mill arrived was all business and bustle. It took fourteen to sixteen men to keep the mill in operation, but all in the community rallied to each other's needs. Ivan and Jamie too were needed and were paid back with a load of straw or help in completing another farm job. It was also a busy day's work for the crofters' women folk. All those men had to be fed and the women seldom had much help. With the men folk away, the other wives had farm duties to attend to. Preparations began early; a big baking of oatcakes, scones and bannocks was done the day before, a pot of potatoes was peeled and the vegetables for the soup were prepared. Sometimes the mill arrived the night before and the driver and his companion often required bed and breakfast. About ten o'clock, a 'piece' - tea and scones - was carried out to the workers. This was followed at midday by a meal in the house. I can tell you it took some arranging in the cramped surroundings to get all seated around the table. Usually the menu was broth, followed by beef and oatmeal dumplings, or it might just have been tattie soup with the beef cut up through it. But I think the favourite was mince and tatties. A pudding came next - a currant dumpling, or custard and stewed fruit. A piece was brought out again to the workers about three o'clock. By late afternoon the threshing was over and all went home, as most had cattle to feed.

Having a mill of our own was much easier. It was extra work but we could do it in our own time and avoid all the extra hassle. One end of the barn was reserved for the corn sheaves, the other for the straw. I fed the sheaves to the mill and Ivan looked after the corn and chaff and took the straw away. We usually had to thresh twice a week but a fill of the barn lasted two weeks.

In those years, most farms and crofts were part of a large estate. Ours belonged to a local farmer who, instead of working the land, had decided to rent it out. He may have thought that it would be suitable for his retirement.

As the incoming tenants, we were required to take over at valuation certain things which belonged to the outgoing tenant. This should have been done before we moved in, but there was a misunderstanding and it had still to be arranged. This put us at a disadvantage because we were unable to get our cattle out on the grass. The fencing, dung, and the mill, along with the first, second and third year's grass had all to be taken over. Except for a small supply of hay for Gyp, we had no animal feed. We were known in the area and most of the neighbours, when they heard of our trouble, came to our aid. Some gave straw, others a load of turnips. Both parties had to arrange for a separate valuation to agree on the price and it was here that John

Webster, an auctioneer from Maud, came into our lives. He was the father of Jack Webster, author of 'A Grain of Truth'. John was also the son of the old lady at Allathan who called me out in the middle of the night. Later on, he proved a good friend, giving Ivan valuable advice on buying and selling stock. Belinda, or 'Beldie' as she was now known, knew I am sure that she was back on her native heath. The first time she was put out to grass, she made for the top of the field. Then the tail went up, nostrils sniffing the air and she danced around the field; I am sure she was celebrating. The other cow, a young Hereford carrying her second calf, never acquired a name. Ivan just called her the red cow. The breed was just beginning to find favour among the standards - Aberdeen Angus, Shorthorn and Freisian.

Our Hereford had come as a calf from England, probably a Panton calf. Ivan favoured the breed, or rather a cross between the Hereford and Freisian, which gave you a black animal with a white face, still our favourite breeding cow crossed with an Aberdeen Angus bull. To me, no animal could ever compare with the Angus, but I did get fond of another breed, the Murray Grey. They were a cross between the Aberdeen Angus and the Shorthorn. But so many breeds - mostly from the Continent (Charolais, Limousin, Holstein, Blond d'Acquitaine) - have now come in that it is utter confusion. When we took possession of the croft, both our cows were dry. Beldie did not calve until the end of June and the other still later. So, again we had to depend on neighbours and we got a supply of milk from the Ironsides. Better neighbours we could not have had, for they helped in so many ways. Soon after we arrived, Mrs. Ironside gave me a whole batch of chicks - over 80 - which she had hatched in her own incubator. Ivan gave me a brand new hen house and we acquired a second-hand brooder. Before I left the Mill, I had hatched a few broods of chicks.

When Gyp arrived at the croft, she was almost ready for retirement. A brown mare with a white face, she had a very docile and lovely nature. I could handle horses and ride bareback, but I had little knowledge of harnessing them up and over this task I found myself in trouble. It was no good asking Ivan anything for he had little patience in showing you how. Anyway that day he was not around and I found I had to put Gyp into the cart and fetch something home. I had not taken much notice, but had seen Ivan many times just offering her the collar and through went her head with no bother. I did not realise I had to offer the collar upside down and once the head was through, turn it around. At the first attempt, she did what was expected of her but to her annoyance her head just got stuck. On the second attempt, with the collar still in the wrong position, she would not even try and away up in the air went her head - on her high horse. I could achieve little standing on the floor so I climbed the fore sty.

Then I realised what I had been doing wrong and offered her the collar the right way round, but still with no success. I slipped from my perch and fell among her feet. However, I was not one to give up easily, so again I climbed up. But it took several attempts and a lot of coaxing before that collar lay snug on her neck. The rest followed easily and I led her proudly out and back to the cart and even fetched her favourite titbit, an oatcake. She loved an apple and was awfully fond of the fine carrots we grew in a small field lying next to the moss. Her fondness for oatcake often landed her and me in trouble. When the barn was filled for threshing, the sheaves had to be left outside the door. These were brought from the corn yard and the cart was tilted on its axle to let the load of sheaves slide off. While Ivan forked them into the barn, Gyp had just to stand quietly. But if by any chance she got a glimpse of me at the door, she was across trailing the cart, scraping the end on the rough surface of the close and scattering the sheaves.

First on the agenda after taking over the tenancy of the croft was getting Ena off to school. I had had her clothes ready for some time but I cycled down to Fyvie to my shoemaker uncle and bought a fine pair of stout shoes for her. I had always gone to school in boots and boys still wore them, but for girls boots were now a thing of the past. Very much to Ena's delight, my uncle also gave me a small leather school-bag. To Ena, this was a treasure indeed. I had taught her the prayer that I had said as a child and to my mind so clearly comes the vision of that little girl by her bedside saying, "Gentle Jesus, meek and mild, bless this little child tonight". And ending with the words, "Keep my bag safe". Before climbing into bed, she hung her precious bag on the back of a chair where it was the last thing she saw before she fell asleep and the first when she awoke.

I had been using a small book to teach her numbers and 'A B C' and on the night before she was due to start school, the book along with her school slate and a box of slate pencils were all carefully packed into her bag. Next morning I added a "piece" for the midday snack and a note for her teacher, giving her name and date of birth. Thus, the first morning a very proud and excited little girl went off quite happily with her friend, Doris, for her first day at school. You might think that for the first day I would have gone with her to school, but it would have taken up most of my forenoon, time I could ill afford to lose. Doris, Mrs Ironside's daughter, who was about 2 years older than Ena, had come across for her and I did accompany them through the track that led across the moss to join the Littleton road.

Doris's brother Jack and quite a few others all came down the road. With a cheery good-bye and a wave of her hand, off she went, not even giving me a backward glance. I turned away, and retraced my steps across the moss with a lump in my throat and a tear in my eye, realising that my little girl was quickly growing up and going out into the big world all on her own.

When the hands of the clock crept round to four o'clock, David and I went eagerly to meet Ena. Where the moss bordered with the Littleton fields, there was a steep rise in the ground, which kept the road hidden, and we waited there. She was pleased we had come to meet her, but oh what a lot she had to tell us. It had been a first day at school for a few others as well. We were told all their names and how nice the teacher was. She had called her Georgina and could she now be called by that name. And the book I had given her - I only put it in to her bag to please her - was no use. She had another new lovely one. Such and such a one had this and that for dinner and could she have some of this for next day? On and on she went, with David getting bewildered by all the chatter and wanting her to come and play. But she was so full of all she had seen and done that she had no time for her baby brother. When her dad came in, he too had to listen to all her tales, but she did get tired that night and went to bed early. She was asleep before David and, when I tucked him in, he said, "Oh mam, can I gang to school tomorrow?"

For the first week or so, I took time to walk with her across to where she met the others but she loved the school and there was never any trouble getting her away. David missed her very much and, whenever the clock came round to 4pm, he was off on his own through the heather to meet her. One day, she came in alone and, as I knew he had gone off early, I got some-what alarmed. But we soon found him - he was fast asleep lying in a hollow on a heath-ery bank. Ena had walked past without seeing him. Another morning, she had only been gone minutes, when she rushed back, very scared and excited shouting, "Mam, mam, a big black bird flew fair at me. 'Go back, go back,' it said. It did mam, it did."

Ena rigged out for school

I had to keep from smiling for, being brought up beside Mormond, I knew well the call of the grouse. It took a little explaining and, although I did promise to come back through the moss with her, she was very unwilling and wanted the dog for protection. Eventually, we were able to persuade her to join the others, but there is little doubt she had quite an exciting story to tell them and her other school mates too. For a few days after that, I too had to take the morning walk. She soon forgot all about it.

To Lassie, her new home was a place of delight. No more was she my dog, for she had transferred her allegiance to Ivan almost over-night. She now slept in the barn on a cosy bed of straw and had her food outside the door. Lassie was large and our living room small, so she was not encouraged to visit the house. Later on, during the winter evenings, she was allowed in and stretched herself out on the floor beside Ivan's chair. He took her out with him when he went to supper the horse and she was allowed a dander around before being shut up in the barn. Suppering the horse was a bedtime task. Gyp was taken out for a drink, given some hay and bedded down with straw for the night. If Ivan was away, I loved doing this. She responded to affection and I can still recall the lovely feeling of her soft velvet nostrils nuzzling my hand and neck in search of a piece of oatcake.

As a lad at the Hill of Dens, where there were a lot of trees and funn dykes, Ivan and his brothers had enjoyed poaching rabbits. It was their staple diet and also brought in a little pocket money. Old habits die hard and Ivan again succumbed to the temptation of poaching. Lassie was an apt pupil and the pair of them enjoyed many a happy hour together. Rabbit was on our menu twice a week, once for dinner and once for supper. The legs were tied together, it was stuffed with oatmeal and onions, and roasted in an iron pot hung on a peat fire - a dish fit to set before a King. It also earned Ivan some pocket money. He sold the rabbits to the butcher for I think about sixpence a rabbit. I always liked those little furry animals and I have had hours of enjoyment just watching them playing and nibbling around. I hated the idea of killing them but they had to be kept under control, for they did quite a lot of damage to the grass which we could ill afford, and destroyed large patches of corn and turnips. The other little beastie, the ferret, I never did like. On one poaching expedition Ivan found one and brought it home. It was kept in a hutch and I had to feed it with bread and milk. It had a wicked look and once it bit my finger. He had the ferret for some time, but eventually lost it and I was not one bit sorry. Poachers regularly used ferrets to catch rabbits. They were sent down into the rabbit holes to chase the rabbits into a net where they were entangled and dispatched by hand. Rabbits killed in this way were much more in demand than those killed by gun - it was a cleaner carcass without lead or pellets. Lassie, of course, could not go down a rabbit hole but she was very good at digging them out with her claws. When Ivan was not around, she often went and stayed away for hours, poaching on her own, but whether she caught any I never knew, for she never brought one home though she may have eaten or buried them.

Something that used to puzzle me was that Lassie not only knew the postman did not come on Sunday but she also knew that our baker came on a Thursday. Those country men always liked to keep to a strict timetable. It would have been about one o'clock one Thursday, when the van man slowed his vehicle down to turn off the main road. He saw Lassie seated on the top of the bank, which flanked our side road and spoke to her from the open window of his cabin, which would have been just about level with the top of the dyke where she sat. Effortlessly, she leapt and landed on the seat beside him. When they arrived at the house she was rewarded with a biscuit. Next Thursday, to his surprise, Lassie was again seated on the same spot and, after that, few Thursdays passed without her being ready and waiting. The question I have often asked myself is how she knew when Thursday came round? Often I watched and I never knew her to disappear any other day. Just for amusement, Ivan did once try to shut her up in the barn, but she evaded him, slipped through the gap, made off across the field and disappeared over the dyke, quite in the opposite direction to where she was going. She was not a disobedient dog, but that day paid no heed to her master's call or whistles. But she returned with the baker as usual.

It would have been into August when one day I found that a box of my precious books had been left behind at the Mill house. How could I have done such a thing for, to this day, I mourn their loss. With faint hope of their recovery, I went that evening to the Mill house, but the lady who answered my knock on the door knew nothing of them. She had only just moved in from another district and knew nothing of the previous occupiers. Hoping Mrs Gordon might know something, I paid her a visit, but again she had no knowledge of the people who had moved in after us. She said they had only stayed weeks and left after an argument with the Petries. Nothing, I thought, could come of giving Asleid a visit, so I went back home very disappointed, for the books had meant so much to me. They had encompassed both shattered dreams and days of happiness - another person, another me that I had put away in a secret place.

Remembering it today brings it all back. Those books, my school text books and my favourite fiction reading had been bought second-hand but a few had been given to me by one who had become very special. Jim Kellas was our Minister's son and when he first came into my life I was in the last year of my Techmuiry school and he in his first year at college. During his holidays he came as an assistant to the minister of the old parish church at Fraserburgh. Techmuiry was a part of this parish and his duties included teaching the Sunday school of which I was a pupil. The following year I had gone to Strichen school but I still remained at the Sunday school. As he too had been a pupil at Strichen, he took an interest and offered me some of his text books which were a big help. All school books had to be paid for and those of the secondary were expensive.

That year, I had taken over the teaching of the infants on the Sunday and also become a member of the bible class and thus a friendship began to build up between us. I had an enquiring mind, had been very well versed under my grandfather and I could converse on bible subjects quite well. He had a very happy-go-lucky nature. We had fun and laughed a lot. There were also arguments and discussions on many topics. One of these was politics. The labour movement was in its infancy and was at the time called socialism. Changing the name to labour was a stroke of genius. Working class people knew or cared little for politics but the word labour symbolised to them that it was their government. Jim was an idealist and a world where all were equal appealed to him. The school teacher at Techmuiry, a Mrs Morrison, was a die-hard Tory and it was often with some amusement that I used to listen to the arguments between them. At that time there were just two parties Liberals and Tories. At home I had often heard my grandfather say that working class people were always better off under a Tory government. To me that wise old man could never be wrong and my allegiance followed his; I have never changed.

Our friendship continued through to his fourth and final year of the University. He was working hard for his BD degree and I seldom saw him though I did have the occasional postcard, letter or magazine. Each month he passed on to me his favourite magazine, edited by Arthur Mee. One of these was in the box with the lost books. When the University pass list was published it was with joy and pride that I saw Jim's name at the top of the list with an Honours Degree. He was back at Techmuiry that summer and to me the sun seemed to shine all the time. That summer was one of the happiest. I saw him each Sunday and often he would pay me an afternoon or evening visit and sometimes I would go down to the manse at Rathen. In the nearby hall, he taught me to play badminton and then we went back to the manse for tea and up to the attic rooms which were crammed full of books. There were books of all kinds which I was allowed to borrow. It was there I found Charles Dickens, Walter Scott and the lovely book Lorna Doone.

There was a complete set of Dickens' works that I came to love and I read the lot. Two spare copies - one of The Old Curiosity Shop (Little Nell) and the other A Tale of Two Cities - were given to me to keep. I also had a copy of The Cricket on the Hearth, Vanity Fair, a small print of Milton's poems and one of Robert Browning's were all added to my collection and were among the lost books.

Sure by Tummel and Loch Rannoch and Lochaber I will go...
If it's thinking in your inner heart that braggart's in my step
You've never smelt the tangle of the Isles.

The lilt and sound of these words, how sweet they were to me and always when I hear them I am transported back to a hilltop on Mormond, surrounded by the fragrance of purple heather in bloom and the hum of insects wafting around the breeze. It must have been in September, Jim and I had tramped to the top, rested a while, then in bantering mood had set off down the hill hand-in-hand. In the exuberance of youth, we began to run and burst into song. As our young voices rose in cadence, through the air came floating back - "Hey ho come to the fair", followed by the words of the Hebridean song. At the bottom we collapsed and for a few minutes lay in exhaustion. Looking at his watch, he suddenly pulled me to my feet, saying it was time he was going as he had a meeting. Standing close together our eyes met and he softly murmured my name and I whispered his. It was a magic moment that I have, all unknown through the years, held within my heart. We pressed to the end of the road where his bicycle lay and I watched him go with a feeling of contentment.

We met again on Sunday and shortly afterwards I was at the manse on a Saturday afternoon for I was now back at school, in my final year. Jim and his sister with whom I was ages, had our tea alone. His father's health was beginning to give some concern; he was in bed that day and Mrs Kellas had joined him in the bedroom for tea. I gave Kate a help to clear the table and wash the tea dishes then went up to find Jim in the attic. Soon afterwards, Mrs Kellas appeared. She had never done this before and we were somewhat surprised. If she had expected to find us in some compromising situation, she must have been disappointed. Jim was seated on a table in the far corner deep in a tome of a book and I was on the floor next to the door, taking notes for a school subject. She was, like her son, a very lively and happy person and never short of words but tonight she looked ill at ease and was finding difficulty in making conversation. Eventually it came out. Were we aware that our friendship was attracting some gossip? Jim was ten years older than I was, we were not of the same class, and our behaviour might hinder his future career. I must indeed have been very naive for it was a long time afterwards before I really understood what she was getting at. I looked across at Jim, but he kept his head down and said nothing. Neither did I, but picking up my notebook I got out of the room and quickly went downstairs, found my bike and soon I was on my way home.

When we met on Sunday I evaded any personal contact but he did manoeuvre me into a few minutes' private conversation. He thought his mother was very wrong in saying what she did and apologised for her behaviour and hoped it would make no difference to the short time we would now have together. He was due to leavethree weeks later for America where he was taking up a scholarship at a theological college in New York. I felt so very embarrassed. Her words had been such a shock and I felt as though he was a stranger and no longer my friend and companion. He was Mr Kellas, the minister. He did call one evening at my home but I was down at the neighbouring farm. He left a note and a book on bible knowledge which had been his own and as it had been a help in his studies he hoped it might aid me in mine. That book too was lost.

The Techmuiry folk were all very sad at losing their minister and bade him farewell at a small social gathering in the school. It was with others, and I would not have wished it otherwise, that I said my good-bye. He wished me success in my studies and said he would be looking forward to my letters.

I continued with the Sunday school but my main effort was with my school work. My prospects were fair but there would have to be much hard work and burning of the midnight candle ere I could gain my Higher Leaving Certificate. This would qualify me to sit my pre-liminary exams for entrance to the University, thence fulfilling my dreams of offering my services to a Missionary Society and following in the footsteps of David Livingstone and Mary Slessor.

When his letter came there was no mention or hint of the upset. He found the city of New York fascinating and gave me an amusing description of his life there. Sometimes he was just a wee bit homesick for he missed Rathen but the studies he was pursuing fulfilled him. He was looking forward to the day when he would be his own master with all the work it entailed. Often he discussed my problems and gave me all encouragement to pursue my ambitions; I think he was the only one who knew of them. I usually had a letter once a month and answered accordingly. I kept some of those letters and they had been in the box with the books. I now had to forego the pleasure of visiting the attic at the manse, for I had returned all the borrowed books. Jim's father, Mr Kellas, was a quiet and scholarly gentleman. I think he liked me and would have made me welcome, but I was not sure of his mother.

Winter passed and spring came which brought the school year to a close. I got my highers but was able to savour the sweetness of that success for only for a few short weeks. A tragedy came to the family which changed my life.

A young girl, my cousin, unwilling to face the disgrace of an illegitimate child, took her own life. The father had emigrated to Canada, likely knowing nothing of the child and in those days Canada was far, far away and there had been no correspondence between them. It was a strange coincidence that her father, my uncle had also emigrated - to Australia - and Marjory was born nine month later. I didnt know her mother but our grandmother had brought her up. The night they brought her home I went to see her and standing by the bier, something happened to me and a great doubt filled my mind. How could God, whom I had loved all my life and cherished as a caring father, let this happen? That night I could not sleep. Early in the morning I left my bed and fled to Mormond and when I returned hours later, all my world had come crashing down and I was left in a land of desolation. That simple faith that had been my grandfather's and had been mine was gone; the mainspring of my life was shattered and the one who might have helped was far away . More was to follow; my grandmother, getting on in years and not as active as she

96

had been, needed more care and the family tried to persuade her to leave the cottage to make her home with some of them. She would hear none of it. "Na, na - the quinie can bide wi me and I'll manage fine." The quinie was me. All my hopes of a university career vanished. Rebel I did, but not too determinedly; the vision for going had vanished too. Actually, at that time, although I carried on as usual, life had no meaning for me. All my dreams were locked away in my inner heart and the key was thrown away. It was only when Ivan came on the scene that I began to live again and only gradually over the years the spiritual conflict adjusted.

James Kellas in New York knew little of the distress and tumult I went through. I wrote less often and the usual spontaneity of my writing must have been missing but if he sensed the change it would have been put down to the disappointment of my being unable to go to College. His letters were full of concern, trying to give me hope that if God had meant me to carry on his work, a way would open up. His father became gravely ill and a few months later he was home, only completing eighteen months of his two-year course. We met almost as strangers and soon afterwards, with the death of his father, he had to take up the burden of the parish and finish his father's term of work, enabling Mrs Kellas to qualify for a minister's widow's pension. He gave of his best but somehow he did not please the Rathen people. I went to church and also attended his Bible Class, but I am afraid I only gave lip service. A prophet hath no honour in his own country and thus it proved with Jim. The situation was not helped by his mother and his sister Kate, for they had been quick to condemn our friendship.

When his term of office ended I think he was glad to leave his native Rathen and go to Fortevoit in Perthshire where he had been appointed parish minister. Our involvement with each other now almost ceased. He stayed only a short time in Perthshire and then came to Aberdeen looking after the larger and more affluent parish of Mannofield. He got married and had twin sons but only twice was I able to take the opportunity to attend a service. On the second occasion, after the service, I went round to the vestry and made myself known. He was delighted and insisted that I stay on for lunch and meet Mrs Kellas and his family. I accepted but I think on my part it was a mistake. She was gracious, as befitted the lady of the manse, but distant. I did get the feeling, though I may have been wrong, that she felt I was not of their class but only a country yokel who knew little of town life or the refinements of upper society (she was a wealthy ship owner's daughter). As I left he said good-bye, shaking my hand and kissing me on the cheek, the first and only time he did so. We did not meet again. He faithfully served the congregation of Mannofield for over 30 years and when he began to find himself less fit, he again moved back to Perthshire taking over a small country parish. Shortly afterwards it was with much sadness I read in the papers of his death. Always, in corner of my heart, I keep those cherished memories both happy and sad and sometimes I wonder if those lost dreams had been fulfilled and my Lochinvar had come out of the West, what my life might have been?

No more romancing, for I have digressed too long. Let me get back to 1938. I have little memory of the harvest that year. The crop belonged to Mr Webster, the previous tenant, and was not ours until valued and paid for. This was done when it was ready for harvesting and I can recall that payment reduced our bank balance almost to nil. Our only income was from the sale of eggs, which in winter was erratic and often barely enough to cover our food bill. Always something new was needed, simple things like boots for the bairns or a replacement fork or spade. The rent had to be paid half-yearly, the second instalment due at Martinmas in November. Very much against his will, Ivan had to think of looking for work. This, of course, would mean a much bigger share of the workload falling on my shoulders, turning a lot of the tasks that had been a pleasure into a sort of drudgery. Ivan did find work and we got by.

Money, money. Why should it play such a part in our life? It was the serpent that entered our little Eden. It never seriously upset the harmony of our lives, but the want of it did tend to make us more ambitious and we wanted better things for our children. In my sights, even then, was a field with black cattle, a sale ring in Perth, a lovely Aberdeen Angus bull and me holding aloft a silver cup.

CHAPTER SEVEN

ANOTHER WAR
ANOTHER SON

THE YEAR 1939 came in with despondency and gloom; everyone knew war was imminent. The euphoria that followed Neville Chamberlain's return to Britain from Munich brandishing the scrap of paper that guaranteed 'Peace in Our Time' had vanished.

It was a particularly mild winter, for only once were the roads blocked with snow and Ena was prevented from going to school. Unlike most children, she was not a bit pleased about this. She loved school and the fact that, more often than not, she was nearer the foot of the class than the top did not worry her. She just looked to learn things and did not mind how long it took her.

Spring came early and with the lighter and brighter days and the awakening of the earth came a feeling and an urge to get going. At that time most womenfolk indulged in a frenzy of house-cleaning but although I too had this urge, I was more concerned about getting on with raising broods of chickens. No more clocking hens for me for we had now acquired a second-hand incubator. I intended to have three fills this year rearing, I hoped, over 100 young hens, for the earlier I had pullets, the earlier I would be able to fill the egg basket. Around August the older flock went into moult and the laying season came to a halt. Pullets come into production at about six months old so if they were hatched in March or April they were ready by September, letting us have eggs to sell and money for our basic needs. The price usually rose during the winter months. For hatching eggs I had two pens of breeding stock: one of Bass Rock hens, crossed with a Black Leghorn cockerel and one of pure Brown Leghorns. Both pens were kept well away from our dwelling, the Brown Leghorns down in the bottom corner of the grass field next to the moss, the other pen on the opposite side next to the road beside a high dyke, the same dyke where Lassie lay in wait for the baker's van. The Leghorns were known as the lighter breeds. They were prolific layers but too light to make good table birds. They originally came from the Mediteranean, Italy I think, and were bred in the US in the 19th century, coming to Britain later. Rhode Island Reds, Light Sussex, Whyndottes and my favourite the blue Bass Rocks were but a few of the heavier breeds. Today few country folk under 50 would know these names, but in the thirties and up to the fifties they were as familiar as those of Aberdeen Angus, Shorthorn and Ayrshire today. How many boiled and roasted chickens I have enjoyed, yet I never killed one. That was always a task for Ivan, not one he liked either, but economy demanded it.

There were few crofts that did not have one or two pigs and no scraps were ever wasted. Anything the dogs or cats could not consume, potato peelings and even dish water were all added to the pigs' pail. Like Jamie Ironside, quite a few crofters went in for breeding, but our one and only attempt ended in disaster. We had one house which held three pigs and our usual consignment was three pigs, three times a year. I fed and looked after them and when they were sold the proceeds were added to my housekeeping money but out of this I had to pay for the replacements. One of these seemed a promising young sow and it was decided that she would fulfil her destiny and become a mother. She had been kept in a makeshift house and pen Ivan had put together, but now that the cattle were all out to grass the byre was empty and a stall was converted into a maternity ward. When she was due she was moved in. During that time the children caused us some amusement. Their father had put them out of the byre which they both resented but Ena was always very resourceful and had made her way into the barn and climbed up on to the top of the wall dividing barn from byre. David had, of course, followed and both were able to watch the proceedings unseen. She was quick and soon had eight piglets. No other animals are so quick on their feet after birth as piglets. They just come out, get on to their feet, and run. Both children knew how chickens came out of eggs but although they knew that our cows had calves, they had never given the matter a thought. Puzzlement and excitement made David give the show away first. He could not make out where they were coming from and suddenly burst out, giving voice to his thoughts, asking in rather uncouth words as to which end they were coming from. Looking up, it was so funny seeing their little faces peering down at us that we both laughed and told them to get out of there. But their query went unanswered. Although we successfully weaned the litter, it was our first and our last.

Ivan went to feed her one morning shortly before her second litter was due. Usually he was met with delighted grunts and squeals but this morning when called on she did not even appear. Immediately Ivan knew something was wrong and when she was on her feet he saw that a terrible carnage had taken place. All around were bits of skin and small bones. She had given birth to dear knows how many, but had eaten the lot. She had to go for we could not trust her not to do it again. Over the years I weaned and fattened many a bacon and pork pig but that experience upset us so much that we just could not bring ourselves to have any more breeding sows.

Spring had been early and an early harvest followed. This year, Ivan had arranged for one of his neighbours to come with his tractor (a Fordson) and binder to cut the crop. The year before he had borrowed a binder and Gyp, and another horse had done the cutting, but it did need a pair of fit horses and Gyp, though able to do light work, was now past her best and needed a rest from heavy duties. Before they cut the crop, the field had to be opened up to make a path for the binder to operate. This was a job for a man with a well sharpened scythe and I can recall Ivan, with a scythe stone in his hand, caressing one side of the blade and then the other until he was satisfied that it was sharp. Then the swish and rhythm was beautiful to watch. My task which followed was not easy. I could fork and build loads but this was something I had to learn - how to gather up and bind the sheaves. The scythe laid the straw in neat rows. These 'bouts' were gathered into sheaves and from them a few straws were taken, divided into two, then twisted together and used to bind the sheaf. All very simple but

101

often, when you lifted them, they would fall apart and it was only by practise that you achieved satisfactory results. It was for me a back-breaking job. I did it for years, not only in opening up the fields but also in bad years when the crops were heavy and got badly twisted and flat, but I never became an expert.

Today I often wonder how our various tasks got fitted in. Ivan usually arose about 6.30 or a little later. In the dark mornings, lamps that had been cleaned and filled the night before were lit and taken out to the stable where the animals' needs were attended to. In the summer, it was a walk over the fields to see if all was well and bring in the two cows for milking. By that time I would have surfaced and before going out to the byre had cleaned up the hearth, laid and kindled the fire and taken out the ashes. I would have filled a big black kettle and hung it over the fire in the hope that it would boil before I returned. I milked both cows only keeping enough for our own needs; the rest of the milk was fed to a few calves. I did occasionally make cheese but not butter as Ivan considered it much more impor-tant to rear our own stock. Then back to the house for a quick breakfast. What could be more simple? Ivan had his bowl of brose, which he made himself; no man would ever have allowed a woman to make his brose. We then shared a pot of tea and had a slice of bread, Ivan's spread with syrup, mine with marmalade. We reserved the luxury of a piece of toast for Sunday mornings. How good it used to taste, toasted before an open fire, far, far better than the toast made today in an electric toaster.

Then Ivan went forth to his usual jobs while I fed the pigs. All hens and chickens, including those housed across the fields had to be let out and given breakfast, all before the children were got up, given their breakfast and put off to school. Then there were dishes to wash, water and peats to fetch in, beds to make and dinner to cook. The postman came around ten o'clock. Then I always tried to have a break: no tea or coffee, just a look through the mail and a read of the newspaper. Twelve was our dinner hour. The meal over, Ivan liked a nap and there was just Lassie left to feed. She had only one meal a day, sometimes left-over scraps from the dinner, but usually brose, and when at home Ivan always fed her himself. For me it was back to the byre for more milk to feed the hungry calves again. In season

I had to visit the brooder hous to fill up the chicken trough and see the lamp was O.K.. Back to the house to clear the table and wash dishes and then, if I was lucky, I might get a half-hour to myself for a wash and general tidy-up and perhaps put on a clean overall. Later on, the poultry rounds had to be done again and the eggs collected and washed. About this time I would have had an average of ten to twelve dozen eggs to pack per day. Around four o'clock, Ena came home from school so I had to spare a little time to listen to all her news while she changed her clothes. For about four months of the winter they were provided with hot meals at school but for the rest of the year we kept something from our midday meal which she had when she came home. The pigs had to be fed their second meal then and supper for ourselves was prepared for six o'clock. Then there were supper dishes to clear and wash up and sometimes, if time had been short and it often was, I still had eggs to clean and pack. A supply of water and peats with sticks for the morning fire had to be provided, but when the children were old enough this was one of their jobs. Then the children had to be got to bed followed by a quick milking routine and all the poultry had to be shut up in case of foxes.

This was the daily routine but also there was washing day, when all the water was carried in pails and heated in a pot hung over the fire, baking day, with batches of oatcakes, scones and bannocks, ironing day and house-cleaning chores. Then there was mending and darning all to be fitted in with the seasonal jobs: chick rearing, peat cutting, helping with hay and harvest, potato planting and gathering and, in the winter, thrashing.

And yet we still had time to socialise with our neighbours, have a chat and gossip, play and have fun and games with the children and Lassie.

I remember that harvest of 1939 well. The year before, our cash problems had been acute but Ivan had been able to have his own crop secure and to fit in a few weeks of harvest work at neighbouring farms. The grieve at Littleton had hurt his back and his misfortune was Ivan's gain, as he had fully a fortnight's work building stacks.

This year he was going full-time to a Mr Dalgarno at Cairnbanno, but had arranged for our crop to be cut by tractor and binder and this was done just before he started at Cairnbanno. The day was Monday

4th of September. It would have been the first time a tractor was on the croft and also one of the first models in the Fordson range. I did not like it; to me it was an ugly, smelly, green monster.

How am I so sure of that date or has it now rung a bell? At dawn on the 1st September 1939 the Germans invaded Poland. Britain had given her pledge that if this happened we would go to her aid and an ultimatum was given that unless the Germans withdrew, war would follow. At four o'clock on Sunday 3rd September, the ultimatum expired and Chamberlain told the country we were at war.

On that Monday morning James Cardno, farmer of North Millbrex, arrived with his tractor and was in the harvest field at the back of the house. I can still see the edition of the Press and Journal. A black border surrounded the first page and at the top, also in black, was the word WAR in very large letters. It was time to take the men folk their piece and I took the newspaper with me. Clear and fresh as on the day it happened, that moment comes back. The sound and sight of the rustling golden corn, two or three rows of neat sheaves left lying in the tracks of tractor and binder, James Cardno, a stout cheery figure leaning slightly on the green monster, which was now quiet. Ivan had slipped down from his perch and seated on the binder platform. Both men were drinking their tea and munching away with a sense of enjoyment, a scone which I had liberally spread with rhubarb jam. Standing between them, holding up the paper, I read the awful news of a country at war, the basket and tea kettle at my feet. "It won't last long; we will soon sort that mannie Hitler and it will be all over by Christmas," said Mr Cardno. I answered that I was not sure. All Ivan said was that it was a terrible business when you had braced yourself for a supreme test of courage and endurance and when nothing happens you feel relieved, but also sort of let down. Such, I think, was the mood of Britain at the end of 1939. Poland had been obliterated, which was very sad, but it was a long way away and not many people even knew where it was.

The advent of war changed our lives but little. Restrictions on lighting did as much as anything to remind us, for even in our remote corner you dared not show a light. "Put out that light," or worse, was a common cry. We were all issued with gas masks and had to carry them everywhere.

The government had decided that in case of bombing raids, thousands of children and mothers of children under five from all the main cities would be evacuated to the country. We had all been sent forms to fill in as to what accommodation we had and if it was possible to take in children. I had only the three small rooms and so was exempt but several other families in the district did have them - our nearest neighbour took in a mother and two children. They came, I think, from the slums of Glasgow. Mrs Mutch was appalled by the fact that they had lice, wet the bed, and both mother and children used terrible language. The mother did no work but sat around smoking. The children chased the chickens and when they caught them pulled their feathers out. Both the dog and the cats ran for their lives. The final insult - Mrs Mutch was in the byre milking when the two children appeared and pelted her with earth clods which went all over her and into the milk.

Others were not so bad, but none in our district really settled and all were gone by Christmas. About this time a little lad, not an evacuee but one of Ena's classmates, whom an elderly lady had been fostering, had been sent back to Glasgow as she had been taken ill and was unable to look after him. Ena had missed him at school; she had picked up some information but was still puzzled about his absence. When telling me her story, she added to my amusement, "I think they must have taken Percy away to the knackery".

At first it really was a 'phoney war' with both sides taking up imaginary lines. Nothing seemed to happen. "Hang out the washing on the Seigfried line" became a popular ditty all over the country.

Actually, the first action and tragedy of the war was in mid-October when a German submarine crept into Scapa Flow where our fleet were sheltering during the hours of darkness. It was supposed to be safe waters but one of our finest ships, the Royal Oak, was sent to the bottom. Only 396 were saved and 1200 lost their lives. The teacher at the school must have been telling the children about the tragedy and when Ena told us the story she added: "And all the little ships lying around were shivering."

Ration books were issued, as were clothing and sweet coupons but although some commodities got scarce the rations were ample and there was no hardship. We were buying very few new clothes anyway and actually lots of people began to buy more sweets than they were in the habit of doing, just to make use of their coupons. The price of eggs, and a few other goods being sold from the croft, began to rise in price so overall - though there was still plenty of hard work - our life on the croft was slightly easier.

The winter passed and with the coming of April 1940, David started school. Up to that time, he was in the habit of sleeping till about mid-day and, always having work a-plenty, I let him sleep. I thought the task of getting him off to school would be a big one but it was much easier than I feared, though he never liked school the way Ena did. He had grown into a big sturdy boy, as dark as his sister was fair. She was a chatter-box; he spoke few words. I did not go with him to school that first day; he just went off with Ena and found the others at the moss end. A task he had enjoyed had been taking the newspaper up the road to our neighbour and I still remember feeling so lonely that first day without him. I recall making my way up to Mrs Mutch. "You have no newspaper boy today for my little lad has gone off to school."

"Aye," she said "gone today and it will be like tomorrow when he leaves." She had just finished a baking, the kettle was put on for tea and we enjoyed a new-baked scone as we sat and talked awhile. I came home feeling a lot more cheerful. The following May they gave up their croft and returned to a cottage at Millbrex. Their croft was taken over by another farmer and like so many others since, the house and outbuildings were later left to go to ruin. One can but mourn their passing for it was a good and simple life untrammelled by the stress and strife of the present day.

At first the bigger boys teased David and gave him a rough ride, but he did enjoy the day of the school picnic at Peterhead. The sea and sands fascinated him. He joined in all their games and took part, whatever the others' ages, in all the races. He got a lot of attention and lots of sweets and pennies too. Some years later my old school at Techmuiry arranged a picnic to Fyvie. Mrs Morrison, who had been my teacher, was still the Head and I wrote her asking if we could join them. The picnic was held in the field adjoining the main road outside Fyvie and during the afternoon some of us thought we would walk up to the castle. We were told it was quite near but on that warm summer's afternoon, both adults and children found it long and tiring. Coming to a shady nook with a seat, we decided to rest awhile, then returned to the picnic park. If we had but known, the castle was just round the corner. It was well over forty years later that I had my first view of the magnificent Fyvie Castle. On leaving the bus at Millbrex on the way home, David said: "Are we going to the picnic now Mummy?" I did not cotton on till we arrived home and his Dad said to him, "Well, did you have a good time at the Picnic?" and David answered "No. We never went to the picnic just for a long walk". I then realised that a picnic to David was Peterhead, sea and sand.

Another incident upset him very much. It was at the Christmas party and happened the year before he went to school. The children had all had a lovely time with games, good things to eat and Santa Claus giving presents. Mrs Ironside had been in the kitchen and before I went home, I went through to help her to wash up the dishes. By that time Santa had got rid of his outfit, which consisted of a complete cloak with wig and mask, and had hung it up on the back of the kitchen door. David had followed me through and suddenly let out an agonising cry and ran to me, hiding his face in my skirt, sobbing for all his worth, "Suntie's dead, Suntie's dead". I had dealt with the Cairnbanno Santa to everyone's satisfaction, but this one took some explaining I can tell you.

The phoney war continued, but it was only the lull before the storm. In June, all hell broke loose. The impregnable Maginot Line proved useless and the German army drove our armies and those of France (our other allies had

David on his way to school carrying his gas mask

107

deserted) back to the sea. Then there was the miracle of Dunkirk. Although thousands of our troops died, all shipping was commandeered; big and small ships, including herring boats, brought the bulk of our army and those of General de Gaulle safely back to British soil, to fight another day.

The fact that they did rally was due to Winston Churchill and those words of his: "We shall fight on the beaches, we shall fight on the landing ground, we shall fight in the fields and in the streets. We shall fight in the hills, we shall never surrender." One couple near us lost a grandson and another a son-in-law, and it was indeed sad news for me when I learned that my friend from the Blackhills of Tyrie would not be returning.

We seemed far from the conflicts of war and life continued on the croft in a contented way. That spring I acquired my first Tilley lamp. It was a handsome one; Ivan had bought it at a sale. It was all brass with a double burner and a white shade but it gave a poor light.

My first chickens were due out in April and once they had hatched I would be tied up. I was in need of a new coat and had saved two pounds. I made up my mind I'd have a shopping spree. It was a cold but bright afternoon when I set out on my bike to New Deer where my old grocer Mr Watson had his shop. Ivan was busy with horse and cart, taking off the last of the turnip crop prior to ploughing and getting the field re-seeded. Both children were with him and I gave them a wave as I went up the road.

When I arrived at the shop, several customers were there and I had to wait for attention. He had a well-stocked shop for not only was he a grocer but he had a drapery and ironmongery department, so a dander round was quite a pleasure. As I made my way towards the coats, my attention was drawn to a stand where an object I had dreamt of was displayed: an Aladdin lamp and all for the price of two pounds. They had not been long on the market but my neighbour Mrs Ironside had one. I thought of the times I had sat below our lamp struggling to thread a needle, an almost impossible task if you were using dark thread. How marvellous it would be to have one of those. I went and looked at the coats. One or two were quite nice and would have suited me well with prices quite within my range. The quality was far superior to today's materials. The coats checked, back I went to the lamp weighing all the pros and cons. Then yet another prowl around the shop and back again to the lamp. When a voice said "Can I help you?" I said, "Yes, I will have the lamp."

The journey home proved a nightmare. From a bright cold day it became, towards evening, a night of howling gales, snow and blocked roads. I had a cousin who was the miller at Auchreddie on the outskirts of New Deer and once I had finished my shopping, a visit there was on the agenda. The snow had come on quite early, beginning as light flakes drifting down like small white feathers, but by the time I was ready to visit it was snowing heavily, covering everything in a

Ivan clearing a path through the snow

white mantle. Before I left home I had mentioned that I might visit and stay for supper, but on seeing the snow I only took a quick cup of tea and decided to set off for home. The wind had now begun and once I left the shelter of the village and came to the open road, I found it difficult to make headway. The full force of the wind and snow was in my face making it impossible to stay on my bicycle. It was hard even to keep walking, but I struggled on through a white wilderness. Once or twice I was tempted to seek shelter but the thought of Ivan and the children at home kept me going.

As I moved, so slowly, up the road to Greens then on to our own part known as the Waggle Hill, the snow and wind seemed to increase their ferocity and often I was in despair. Leaning on the cycle helped as the wheels slipped through the snow more easily than did my feet. At last I turned off thankfully into our own road end, finding that the high dykes gave me much needed shelter. Going downhill with the wind now at my back and the thought of home being so near, I soon made it. I had no idea what time it was, but I had left New Deer between five and six o'clock. When I entered our own close a faint light was showing from the stable. I made for this, finding Ivan quite unconcernedly bedding down Gyp and giving her some feed. I thought he would have been distracted with worry but all he said was "Oh, you've got back have you?". In reality Ivan had had no idea it was such a bad night. The croft buildings were low down and very sheltered from the north wind. It had been snowing when he had come into the house but having his own and the children's supper to make, then getting them off to bed, he had not been outside and had no idea of the storm. He had not worried about me as he thought I had tarried with my relatives. Next day we read in the paper the full story of the unexpected April storm. Several roads were blocked and a young girl was found dead in a drift of snow on the road leading out of New Deer over the Red Hill, quite near to the one I had been on.

Ivan was not at all taken with my lamp and thought me a bit silly not buying the coat I was badly needing. However, I was very happy with my Tilley, and today if the electricity gets cut off, the same lamp can still give us a reasonably good light and I did get my new coat for a birthday present.

During that summer, Ivan got a few weeks work as a local postman. Mr Mowat our neighbour and postman was off work for several weeks and Ivan covered for him. Never had I thought he would like a job of that sort but he revelled in it, cycling around the district, delivering his neighbours' mail, having a chat here and there and getting to know people. He found it somewhat difficult sorting out the mail but that was overcome quite easily. He adjusted his route so that he had only three or four calls before he came to his own abode. Then, while he was having a cup of tea, I sorted them out in neat bundles in order of delivery. In later years, he used to like to say "when I was the postman". The other day I was speaking to an old acquaintance still on his farm where Ivan delivered. Ivan's name came up and he remembered him coming round as postman.

Ever since Dunkirk, invasion by the German Army had hovered near like a dark shadow. Little news was allowed to filter through the newspapers, but we did know that bombs were being dropped quite near us. From friends, we knew that Fraserburgh had been badly hit and lives lost and that even Aberdeen had been visited by the German Luftwaffe, but it was only after 1945 when the war ended that we realised the full horror. At the time it touched our lives but little. That May, Ivan's brothers moved up from Waughtonhill to the farm of Little Byth which brought us nearer to each other.

I got the feeling about this time that, for Ivan, the croft was losing some of its enchantment. His brothers moving up to a larger farm may have been one factor, but in his conversation the word "if" came up often. "If only I had more ground... If I was able to keep a pair of horse... If I was not depending on others for work..." were some of his comments. The affairs of the croft were reasonably healthy: the crops were good, I was building up a profitable poultry flock and we were well stocked in cattle. On my last birthday in May I had reached the ripe old age of thirty and an insurance policy had become due. We decided to put the money - the vast sum of £50 - into the bank, so now even the bank manager met us with a smile. I'd maybe had visions of an Aberdeen Angus bull. We also had some savings which Ivan kept in a tin on the shelf in the box-bed. Like the older generations, our few valuables were also kept on the shelf but as yet I had no big family Bible. Although I often pondered on these spiritual things, I still had a long away to go before I really and truly believed that the faith of my childhood would never return. I did know, however, that Ivan's vision was now to have a larger farm.

That summer we added another cow to our herd, a black yearling Highland heifer we called Blackie. Ivan had bought her in high hopes, but she would never have become a butcher's dream. She developed huge horns. Later on these would have been cut off but at that time de-horning was not popular and was regarded as cruelty. We decided she might serve us better as a cow, but she had a difficult calving and we lost her calf. Whether all the pain she suffered caused her to feel resentment, one can never tell, but she turned on Ivan like a demon, lashing out with both head and feet. Strange creature she was, she treated me very differently when I approached and she was most affectionate. She licked me all over and then allowed me to milk her. No-one but myself was ever allowed to do this, which often proved awkward. A few weeks later, Ivan and I both went down with flu. One of our neighbours, James Tyler, who had assisted Ivan at the calving,

111

said he would manage but I am afraid he spoke too soon for he too had to give up. For one whole day she was not milked but on the second morning I struggled out to the byre. I have never forgotten the rapturous welcome I got. For all her drawbacks she was a grand little cow, rewarding us with pails of rich creamy milk. In later years she had no more calving problems but I was the only one ever allowed to milk her.

Still on the croft was Dimples, the late calf I had reared at Cairnbanno. She had not developed selling potential either and we had the idea that like Blackie, she too might become a cow. In the next year she had still not come into season and I knew Ivan was contemplating sending her to the sale ring. I shed a tear when I saw her departing for Maud but much to my joy, Ivan was offered such a poor price he decided to bring her back home. Somehow, she got mixed in with another herd and it was more than a week later when a much knocked about and battered Dimples returned. I was so pleased and happy to have her back and I am sure she too was happy to be home to her own pastures green. Almost next day she rewarded us by coming into season and became for many years our number one cow.

For those living in the towns, life must have been a nightmare that winter with thoughts of invasion as Hitler intensified his bombing campaign. In the summer, the blitz dwindled as Hitler, making his biggest mistake, invaded Russia. In the spring of that year, somewhat to my dismay, I realised I was pregnant. After David's birth I had been sent to Aberdeen for an examination and told that quite probably I would not have any more children and that it would take at least seven years for me to heal. David would be six in June. I decided that for as long as I could I would keep it a secret. Eventually, when Ivan did learn, he was upset and to please him we paid the doctor a visit. He was an old friend, Dr Crombie, and all he could do was promise to keep an eye on me. If anything seemed to be wrong it would be arranged that I go into hospital.

It was a slow harvest. There had been little sunshine and the corn was unwilling to ripen. There were days of wind and rain which flattened the crops and made it difficult to harvest. Ivan had again taken a harvest at Cairnbanno, but I had to adjust myself to being only an onlooker. That was ill to bear, for being outside was a joy in itself.

The stooking, the forking and the building of the loads of golden sheaves, with all the happy banter that went on, fills me with nostalgia still.

One morning Mr Dalgarno arrived with two horses and carts and the whole crop was harvested that day. Conditions could not have been altogether good for later several of the rucks heated and had to be turned, which meant rebuilding the sheaves. Mrs Ironside came and assisted Ivan at this. I was around, of course, and I went and stood on one of the foundations. The heat coming off the sheaves was so great I could feel it coming up through the soles of my shoes.

Bad harvest though it was, it did not prevent Ivan taking steps towards a bigger farm. He looked at several but offered for only one. Our banker, a Mr Redford, came up one day and took both of us down to see one on the Fyvie Castle estate: Camaloun. I liked the name and we both liked the farm. With high hopes an offer for the lease was sent in but a son of an employee of the laird was the lucky person.

Soon afterwards, Redbriggs came up. It lay in the Greeness district only a few miles away over the hill from Cuminestown. Bill Skene, an acquaintance who had a croft near Redbriggs, brought the 72-acre farm to Ivan's notice. It had been on the market for some time: a poor place, badly farmed and no-one was prepared to offer for it. The then tenant, a Mr Moir, was sitting rent-free. I can recall my first sight of it very well. Mrs Ironside had come to stay with the children so that we could both go. We took our bikes, meeting Mr Skene at the roundabout at the entrance to the Teuchar Howe. Another farm, also called Redbriggs (this in fact was South and ours was North) stood on the corner where the road divided. We went past it, left our bikes at the side of the road and went into a field. Quite naturally I thought the farm we had passed was the one we were visiting. I quite liked the look of it, thinking it would be alright. We crossed one field, then going up a rise in the ground another farm house and buildings came into view. I realised that this was IT, not the one we had passed. I was a bit disappointed, for the house did not attract me at all and I had the same feeling when we went inside. The people had been sitting quite happy and rent-free for some time and prospective tenants were not made very welcome. The kitchen and living room were combined. There had been a box bed but this had been taken out which certainly caused me no regrets. There was a big hole in the cement floor in front of where the bed had been and the wall at the back was plain, unadorned stone like the wall of a byre or stable. I also noticed all the inside doors were fitted with latches. Snecks we called them, and for some reason I disliked "lift the sneck Mrs and come awa in" as a friendly greeting. Snecks were alright for outside doors but for inside doors you turned a handle.

We were not shown over the rest of the house and it was only when we were leaving I saw, on the wall beside the back of the door, a sink and a tap with running water and then all feelings of disappointment vanished. Thinking and remembering the old iron pump which stood in majesty in our close, I had visions of a new life.

The farm was part of Hatton Castle estate and they were eager for a suitable tenant, knew the farm was very run-down and were willing to let for a low rent. Ivan thought he had nothing to lose and an agreement was drawn up. For the sum of £15 in two half-yearly payments of £7.10s paid at Whitsun and Martinmas, the lease of the tenancy of North Redbriggs in the parish of Monquhitter was ours. Entry was to be from the 28th May, 1942, to run for twenty-one years but having a clause at seven and fourteen, each party giving the other one year's notice. The deed was done and we would be leaving our dream croft. I was not entirely happy, for though it was small it was paying its way and I really had all I wanted. To me, the animals and working with them seemed enough, but the pull of land and more land had taken over the dream that Ivan had.

It was now November and my time was very near. Today no one is allowed to have their baby at home but then it was regarded as a natural process and very few babies were born in hospital. Dr Crombie never once asked me to come to his surgery, but regularly came on visits and towards the end, the district nurse called once a week. I considered myself well looked after.

November was ten days gone when, on a cold, very wet and windy night, Robert James came ashore. It was a right long ordeal but there were no complications. The only problem arose the next day when the nurse had difficulty in getting her car through. The Deershall road was awash with piled up sheaves of corn blown from a nearby field blocking her path. It was a sad and sorry sight to see all those sheaves, part of someone's livelihood, but the weather never cleared up and that year many fields had to be abandoned.

Mary Reid, the blacksmith's daughter from Gight, came and looked after my household. She earned her livelihood in this way, giving a week here and a fortnight there, attending to mothers and babies. We were much the same age. Shw was a grand lass and we became friends, keeping up the acquaintance for many years. At that time, knowing I would be a bit harassed, I booked her again for the 28th May to come and help with the flitting.

Ena was charmed with her small brother but David was not so sure. It happened that at that time I was due to give a chicken for school dinners. Mary had prepared it, and giving it to the children to take to school, she asked David which would he rather give away, the chicken or the baby. He promptly said "the baby". He was so much more attached to his mother than Ena and I think somewhat resented all the attention a little baby needed; this resentment remained with him for a long time. His father had given his second son the name of Robert James, but he has been known to all as Robin. I was the culprit there. I had been discovering Rabbie Burns and like all his other lasses, I had fallen in love with him, so naturally around the 25th of January all our thoughts centred around him:

This wally boy will be na couth
I think we'll ca him Robin

"Aye," I said, "We'll ca him Robin." And Robin he became.

That January of forty-two brought one of the biggest snowstorms I have ever experienced. It happened towards the end of the month and the side roads around the croft were still filled with snow in April.

It came on a Saturday night and all day on the Sunday it never stopped, accompanied by howling winds that lifted you off your feet and filled your eyes, nostrils and lungs with powdery snow. Ivan had difficulty in crossing the close to attend to his animals and though I had been able to milk in the morning, by evening it was nigh impossible to cross the close although it was only a few yards. I was utterly exhausted and choking with the snow. Coming back we clung together, holding hard and guarding the pail of milk. We had to leave

115

the poultry alone, for if we had tried to open a door it would have been torn from our hands.

We awoke on the Monday morning to a dark, eerie and silent world. Then we realised that the living room window was covered with snow with only a faint glimmer of light showing through and when the outside door was opened, a complete wall of snow met our eyes. We had to tunnel our way out using the fireside shovel. Thank goodness it was a strong one, the one we had bought from Cocky Hunter in Aberdeen.

Once outside, I stood in sheer amazement at the beauty of the scene that met my eyes. A

The snow piled high against our house

white wilderness in all its purity and peace, covering all in hoary frost, glittering crystal dew drops. Only once have I been moved in the same way. It was at Mount Scopus where from my bedroom window I gazed down on the golden city of Old Jerusalem shining in the sun. Like the snow scene, I have never forgotten it.

In many places the snow lay four to five feet deep. A severe frost had developed during the night, even our water pails inside the porch had quite a thickness of ice covering them. Outside, the snow was up to the eaves and the only clearance was where the wind had blown through a gap between the house and the barn. To both byre and stables a pathway had to be dug. I still have some snaps showing Ivan pushing a barrow load of turnips through a tunnel of snow more than three feet high. Most of the poultry were housed in the railway carriage and we found them reasonably comfortable but I can still remember the plight of the Bass Rock hens. Never have I seen such poor bedraggled birds, all huddled together on the roosts with tangles of ice hanging from their wings and tail feathers. They were packed

116

around with snow which had filtered through a broken window but in a way it had protected them and they all survived. It took not weeks but months to get back to anything like our usual routine.

All roads were blocked with not even the mail getting through. The railway line between Aberdeen and Fraserburgh was blocked at Brucklay, and I remember reading in a newspaper how on the Sunday evening, a minister from a Gardenstown Church had got lost between manse and church and found himself at a farm two miles away.

Week after week, Jamie Ironside and Ivan trudged miles across fields to bring our bread and groceries. The poultry must have made a quick recovery for the men also rigged up a sledge and pulled this across to the shops at Lethenty to deliver boxes of eggs. Even when the main roads were opened it took weeks before our side roads were clear of snow and for weeks on end vans had to be met. Times were arranged and a few of us met each week at the farm of North Millbrex which was situated on the main Fyvie/Millbrex road east of the church, home of the Cardnos.

This became quite a sociable occasion for while we were waiting for the van, Mrs Cardno made cups of tea and we all had a real natter about our own affairs, passing on hints as to how we managed or bemoaning our mistakes. One lady used to boast of her prowess as a baker and the marvellous scones she made out of just flour and water. I had doubts about this and was always sure that if I attempted to do the same, my family would not have eaten them. Even the pigs might not have regarded them as a treat.

The war still seemed far away and touched our lives but little. The Pearl Harbour incident bringing America into the war gave us, I think, a false sense of complacency. We were now sure the war would soon be over. Our preparations for moving had to be made but this gave me no pleasure. I liked the life in the croft and had no desire to move. The tenant had the farm buildings to keep in repair so the woodwork was expected to be painted every two years but the landlord provided anything new. Ivan had complained continually about the barn door which was falling to pieces but all his pleas had fallen on deaf ears. Now with a new tenant taking over, a new door was provided.

Our landlord was a Mr Ewan, who along with his son had a farm near the church of Millbrex. He also had a builder's business and though now retired, did all his own repair work. He brought up his materials and made the new door on the croft, and very much to my amusement, he did something that, thrifty and canny though he was, I had never seen Ivan do: he drew out the nails from the old door and hammered them into the new wood.

Prior to our move he did a lot of work around the buildings. Although it was no benefit to us I was still expected to feed him. I never grudged the odd cup of tea but I did object to him thinking he was entitled to his midday meal and offering me nothing in way of payment. Remembering this brings a funny incident to mind. For our next day's dinner, I had cleaned a chicken and put it in the cupboard in the porch. A large black and white tom cat who had come to us as a stray, a devious brute and an accomplished thief, had been prowling around and found the cupboard open; it was not beyond his capabilities to have opened the door himself. Mr Ewan was mixing cement in the close and suddenly I heard a howl of rage followed by heavy oaths that rent the air. I got outside just in time to see the cat and chicken disappearing round the corner of the cow shed and Mr Ewan in hot pursuit. In a few minutes he returned carrying the chicken and handed it to me saying, "here's ma dinner". After a good clean it was cooked next day so that at least that was one meal he earned.

The Germans were using an Anglo-Irishman, William Joyce, to broadcast propaganda to Britain. People thought it a huge joke and he was christened Lord Haw-Haw. We did not have a wireless but I had been at a neighbour the evening before and heard Lord Haw-Haw say that Hitler was coming in the Autumn to Balmoral to take up his residence and all we common mortals were to be transported to darkest Africa. Next day as he mixed away among his cement, I could not resist teasing Mr Ewan.

Did he know, I said, that Hitler fancied coming to Scotland that summer for some grouse shooting and deerstalking. And that he would be taking up residency at Balmoral. All the inhabitants were to be transported to Africa or some lone island and he might soon find himself restoring mud huts in the jungle. Did he think it might be a better life? I only got a grunt in reply.

Sometime in March of that year we had to say goodbye to Gyp. She must have been well over twenty years of age. The long spell of snow and frost had taken its toll. She had been unable to get much exercise, and several times she had needed assitance to rise. This time she was not to get up. Gyp was our first horse and I loved her like no other. Before they came to take her away, I sat in the stable with her head in my lap giving her a drink of water out of a basin which she enjoyed, then a piece of her favourite oatcake. When I heard the knackery cart coming down the road I gently laid her head back in the straw murmuring, "Goodbye, Gyp old girl" and fled to the house. I am not ashamed to say I shed a lot of tears that day. A dog may be a man's best friend, but a horse is not far behind.

Into her place came a young grey mare. We had her such a short time I cannot recall her name. She came from a farm near Byth for about £30. With moving to a bigger place, money was again a cause for concern. Redbriggs would need three horses to carry the work load but we might just manage at the beginning with a fine pair. A mare in foal had to be spared heavy work, so I was surprised to learn she was in foal and felt that Ivan had been unwise. But although it could be an added risk, it could also be an added bonus.

After the work of putting in the spring crop at the croft was completed, Ivan went across to Redbriggs and with his mare and one of Alan Moir's horses cultivated a piece of ground ready for planting the potatoes. When he returned in the evening, the mare was sweating a lot and, although she drank plenty of water, refused her food. This got Ivan worried and when next morning she still refused to eat and seemed distressed, he sent for the vet. A blockage in the bowel was diagnosed and she was given some medicine but when the vet returned next day she was no better. They took her out and walked her up and down the yard and after further examinations it was found to be a twist of the bowels for which nothing could be done. Again, in a matter of weeks, the knackery cart came and called. He'd had high hopes for his bonny grey mare and the disappointment for Ivan was bitter. In a matter of weeks we would be moving to the other farm with no horse. It was a daunting thought.

May term was the usual time for farms to change hands, bringing about lots of farm roups and Ivan attended most of them. He picked up one or two things he needed but still no horse. All went far beyond the price he could afford. It was getting dangerously near the 28th,

119

when the farm sale at Littleton took place. It bordered with our croft with only the moss lying between us. It was a three pair and single horse place but they were all young and able horses and would command a good price, so Ivan's hope of securing one of these was not very high. After an early dinner, Ivan left for the roup but by six o'clock he had not returned. Being a little on edge I went out to look for him and got quite excited when I viewed him coming through the moss leading a large grey horse. Both bairns and I ran through the small field, leaping the ditch and met him on the path. I expected Ivan to be beaming all over but he met us with a rather subdued and sheepish grin. Later I learned why. Reaching up I gave the animal a clap. He tossed his head in the air and gave a snort as much as to say, "I haven't seen one like this before." We learned little from Ivan as he led him to the stable except that his name was Clyde. He found our stable door rather low and needed a lot of coaxing to go inside but when he did he fairly filled Gyp's stall. We all helped to give him a feed and bed him down, but it was not till after supper and the children were in bed that I got more details. We were just in the middle of those when an old acquaintance, Dickie Dempster from Cairnbanno and a horse dealer by the name of McKenzie, came to call. They had come, they said, to do him a favour as they were sure by now he regretted buying the horse and they were prepared to give him a good offer for his bad bargain. Bad bargain indeed. The cheek of them, I thought, for Ivan had already told me it was a marvellous piece of luck. Clyde was a shire horse, a slightly heavier breed of horse than the Clydesdale but unfortunately one that was inclined to have greasy feet which, if neglected, developed into a chronic disease.

Clyde was only six years old but the workers at Littleton had neglected him and he had one leg badly affected. This in no way impaired his strength and he was a big powerful brute, able and fit to tackle any workload. In winter it gave him no trouble but during the summer, especially in a hot spell, it gave off a fluid with a nasty smell which attracted flies and the feet had to be regularly bathed in disinfectant. Our two worthies kept on about his feet, he would foul our grass and cattle would not thrive. Ivan said little but I stormed into the attack and was thankful to see them depart without Clyde. Clyde was like a miracle. Ivan had bid up all the other horses to a high figure, more than he could afford but had got none of them. Clyde came last but no one seemed interested. Few were prepared to be bothered with him and he was too big for a crofter's home. The auctioneer was Alex Bell. He knew Ivan and his bidding on the other horses had been noted. When no bids came he hesitated for a second then knocked him down to Ivan for £7. The horse's owner Frank Beaton, not knowing the circumstances, had expected to get £100 for him.

Next day, a Sunday, our pair of so-called friends again made an appearance but Ivan was not at home and I soon sent them packing. Ivan also purchased one of the Redbriggs horses but the sale must have been near moving time for the horse never left his home. Clyde proved his worth and without him we would have been badly off. A trailer was borrowed from the postman and all our implements, hen-houses, furniture, goods and chattels were taken safely across to our new abode by Clyde. Mary Reid had promised to help with the flitting. In the evening before we were moving, the cows were milked early and Jamie Ironside, his son Jack, Ivan and I set off with the whole stock, accompanied by the two dogs. (We had another collie, a black and white dog called Sammy. David had brought him home about six months earlier from the grieve at Littleton.)

We had the three cows, Beldie, Red Cow and Blackie, Dimples who was due to calve that summer and about another fifteen animals. It took us three hours to get them across. Lassie kept them moving from behind and Jack and Jamie went in front guiding them past entrances to side roads or any openings. I can still see that small dog streaking on in front and whenever he came to a gate or opening of any sort sitting down and not one dared pass him. He was only a young dog but he did so well only to disgrace himself in the end. When we came to the farm, the byre door where the animals had to enter was open. He made for this and planked himself squarely in the middle. No words of command did he hear, or if he heard he did not obey and it was only a boot on his behind that moved him. Poor lad, he had a short life for he took ill that summer and died. We had only one mishap, a calf not more than a week old got so tired that it collapsed at Redbriggs. The farm people took it in and gave it shelter and next day it was none the worse.

On the last day Clyde had to make two more journeys. We had to be up early but it was one of those dewy mornings that only come in May, like the morning we set out for Fridayhill. It had been a late Spring but with the snow lying around so long it had done the land a power of good and the promise of all good things was there. I knew I did not want to leave this place but there was no time to think, no time to indulge my feelings, just get up and go.

Mary had set off on her bicycle when the first load left. She would milk the cows, attend to the chickens and the other animals and perhaps cook something for Ivan and herself. David had gone with his dad on the lorry. It would take some hours for them to return for the last load.

Stray hens were collected from the railway carriage and put into a box beside the two ducks, awaiting transportation. A basin of bread and milk was taken to the byre for the cats we were leaving behind, in the hopes it might tide them over till the new arrivals came; the cat we were taking wailed from the box where she was confined, Ena talking to reassure her. The clock stood alone on the mantlepiece. I went to the pump and filled a trough with fresh water for Clyde when he returned. We had a meal of sorts, let the fire go out and cleaned and made the hearth tidy.

Soon, the load was on its way and just as it turned out of the close I caught sight of my bicycle still standing in the cart shed. Clyde was halted and a few minutes later he was on his way, disappearing for the last time up and over the brae and out of sight.

Nothing more to do now but tidy up and go. I was walking to Redbriggs. Beside Robin in the pram we packed the clock, some valuables, a setting of brown Leghorn hatching eggs and our cat. Ivan had expected Ena to go with him on the lorry but she was, like her mother, not keen on leaving and had decided at the last minute she too would walk. Doris had come over to help and she decided to keep us company as well. I have never measured the distance between the croft and Greeness but it must have been over four miles and took us more than an hour. We had kept the brush to sweep everything clean before we left and Doris carried this as she and Ena walked beside me. We had some milk and biscuits on the way and Robin slept the whole time. Over the hill Redbriggs came in sight; we had arrived, but it was yet to become home.

122

CHAPTER EIGHT

FARMERS IN THE TEUCHAR HOWE

THE HAMLET of Greeness lay at the heart of the Teuchar Howe and Redbriggs was in the North-West corner. It had been a 'Howe of Sorrows' at least twice, death and desolation having swept through the glen. Situated in the Parish of Monquhitter it would, in those far distant days, have been off the beaten track. Those small communities were not so much troubled with warring factions seeking power, as were their coast-wise brothers. Except in the case of Robert Bruce who, before he could keep a crown upon his head, had to eliminate John Comyn, the Earl of Buchan. Bruce defeated him at Barra near Oldmeldrum, then at Brucehill only a mile or so from here and then continued destroying every building that his soldiers set eyes on, burning, looting and laying all to waste. Greeness did not escape. This was in December 1307, but if possible, a worse disaster came 300 years nearer our time: 'the seven ill years'. Ill years indeed, for the whole population of the Howe except one or two families were wiped out, dying of starvation. For seven whole years, one after the other, every summer had abnormal rainfall and the weather was cold without any sunshine and there was a constant shrouding mist. An early frost stopped the ripening of the crops which became a mess of rotting vegetation. The surrounding districts in Monquhitter shared the same fate and I read that many who died in the later stages had no cemetery burials. Some were laid in a handy hollow and simply covered up. The human suffering must have been appalling, the hunger and despair terrible beyond all comprehension. What is certain is that the time came when the glen was empty as the remaining people and stock died or were forced to leave. The landlords re-populated the area with sheep. Eventually, the people came back and with new ideas of farming, better husbandry, seeds and fertiliser, the Howe became alive once more.

When we arrived in 1942, Greeness was a fairly prosperous community of several crofts and farms, a shop and Post Office and a two teacher school. Our farm lay on the poorest land in the North; it was dour and cold. At that time I knew nothing of the tumult and despair this land had witnessed, but at moments I could feel an atmosphere of struggle, a clinging force, as of those souls who had suffered and died. I felt that I did not belong here and I never came to love it. We arrived at Redbriggs as tenants and bought it later but, even though it was the first land to belong to us, it made no difference.

I entered quite a different way of life. Over at the croft the house and steading lay in a hollow and, although surrounded by other dwellings, we were isolated and had our privacy. Not so here, for the dwelling was only yards from the main Cuminestown to Fyvie road which cut right through our farmland. We had 36 acres on each side of the road. A side road led across to Birkenhills and the Turriff and Aberdeen turnpike. On our other side, on the main road, were the school and schoolhouse and across from these, separated by one small field, the croft of Netherton. Only a few yards further on lay the shop and Post Office with yet another two farms.

All the farmers were self-sufficient; they did not depend on their neighbours for a horse or plough or anything. I had come to be first a cottar wife, then a crofter's wife and now I had graduated to being a farmer's wife. One could hardly believe that people would be so different in character. The Wilsons had arrived at the same time as us but, unlike us, they were not newcomers to the district; they moved to Netherton from a croft further up the hill. I got to know them within weeks and I got acquainted with the Grays through patronising the shop and visiting the schoolhouse with the children. Except for these, our nearest neighbours, it took me years to get on speaking terms with the others. Our farm was known as North Redbriggs. Out of sight, but only four fields away, was South Redbriggs. It was here the small calf had collapsed and been given shelter. I spoke to some of the family that night, but in all the eighteen years we lived beside them, I was inside their house only once or twice and I cannot recall a visit from them. It had been so different among the friendly people of Millbrex; I knew them all.

Redbriggs in 1943

The children settled easily into school and thought it great to have only a five minute walk and to be able to come home for their midday meals. Mary was able to spare me three weeks of her time, which I very much appreciated. The house had been neglected and the paint work needed extra washing and the woodwork had to be scrubbed. I had six rooms, three up and three down, a porch and milk house. The upstairs rooms were somewhat confined, with only skylights for windows, but the children now had a bedroom each. The middle room upstairs was small but with a fitted frame to hold his bed, David used this for a few years. Ourselves, we had quite a fair sized bedroom downstairs and I still used the front room as a spare bedroom for visitors. Jack Ironside sometimes occupied the other room upstairs. He had just left school and came that first summer to help Ivan so it was a full house.

I remember going with Mary to a neighbouring farm along the Birkenhills road after they had a day of the thrashing mill and we were able to fill two chaff beds. I used these for many years at Redbriggs for they were the warmest and most comfortable of beds.

With our coming to Redbriggs, my daily routine was somewhat easier. Ivan was now occupied full time at farm work. In fact, the size of the place warranted another worker, but we were on a tight budget and could not spare the wages. The Ironsides did not need Jack all the time and that first summer he spent many a week helping Ivan, getting perhaps ten shillings or a pound, as the work warranted. Next year, the Ironsides too left their croft and went to a larger farm beside Oldmeldrum. We never lost touch, but our meetings were infrequent. Much later, when we both had cars, we met more often. James died a few years ago but as I write, Mrs Ironside is still alive and it's grand to have talks about the old days sometimes.

Ivan may have had the satisfaction of more land and his pair of horse but it was a much harder struggle to make ends meet. The poultry were still our main source of income and I supplemented this with pigs and fattening Christmas poultry. I still milked the cows and reared calves. Beldie came to Redbriggs with us but only survived a short time. She had her last calf at Millbrex and, when she failed to produce another, the old faithful cow had to go, always a sore point with me. Dimples took her place and was around for many years. Ivan bought a small brown mare from Alan Moir, but she was a high stepper and rather an erratic worker. Although Clyde had his handicap, he was the best deal Ivan ever made in horse flesh and, for many years, kept the plough turning over the soil.

I was not the only one that encountered a change of lifestyle coming to Redbriggs: Lassie did too. There were no dykes, and there was no master to take her poaching. But there was some compensation on the main road with lots of cars and bikes to chase. To me, she was a big, soft, lovely brown and white sable collie dog, but to those on bikes she was a yellow peril and we were forced to chain her up. She did not like this and one day she broke loose and disappeared. About a week later, Jamie Ironside came across and said she had been seen in her old haunts but that he had been unable to catch her. Ivan went back with him, but no trace could be found. Our other old neighbour, Jamie Taylor, who lived at the far side of the moss said he had seen her several times and thought he would be able to get her to come to him.

Although not a lot of correspondence passed between us, we had found Jamie Taylor a very good neighbour. He lived alone - his wife was dead - and a daughter kept the house until she married. The daughter often returned, staying a week or so at a time helping to give him a redd-up. Every year, when he had the threshing mill, she would come to cook the food and once, when she was unable to make the visit, I went down to him and made the meals.

Another time Jamie had not been seen out or about at his usual duties and Ivan suggested I might go down and see if all was well, after the children were off to school. I slipped down the side of the moss and made towards the back door without seeing any trace of him. To my surprise, the door was standing wide open and when I made to enter, a flock of five or six partridges flew out. The fire was out but a pail of peats and kindlers stood on the hearth. On a stool before the fireplace lay his boots and beside them straw spread out to dry. This I knew he had taken out of his boots, as Ivan often did the same - using the straw for insoles. His boots must also have had some corn inside. This was strewn over the floor and had attracted the birds.

Later, he confessed that he always left the door open at night, summer or winter. He liked the birds and beasts to come in for shelter. I went through the house and found him still abed. He had had a bout of vomiting, but was now feeling a bit better and would get up. I told him to stay where he was. His animals were all in the fields and only the hens needed attention. I took out the ashes, put his boots to right and got the fire going. Heating some water, I took it through to him for a wash and then fed the hens. Then we both had a cup of tea by which time he was feeling much better and ready to get up.

We were very grateful for his help with Lassie but it took him some weeks to get her back. Jamie Ironside said she was staying with him and we knew he was sorry to part with her, for he tried us to sell her, but I would not part with our dog and once she was back home she settled down. That first summer at Redbriggs she had her first litter of pups and we gave one to Jamie Taylor. We were all sorry and David was very upset when soon after we moved Sammy, the black and white collie pup he had been given, died. But soon David was to get another dog.

Ivan had a friend - a distant cousin - Jamie Bruce, who lived in Byth. Ivan was always a soft touch where a dog was concerned and on a visit there, Jamie Bruce persuaded him to bring home someone's unwanted pup. The pup was a black and white mongrel, a cross between a spaniel and a collie but one of royal pedigree. A girl from Byth was a housemaid at The Coppins, the home of the Duke and Duchess of Kent. They bred spaniels, but one of the pups had not come up to standard and the housemaid was given the pup as a present. She took it home to Byth and that dog was the father of our Flossie. At a very early age she attached herself to David and seldom have I seen a dog so devoted. If you saw Flossie around you could be sure David was not far away. She even tried to go to school with him.

Some of the finest agricultural land in Britain lies in Aberdeenshire. The land around Greeness may not have been the best of it, but still quite a few prosperous farms were to be found. However, the piece of land Ivan had taken to cultivate and wrest a livelihood from was the poorest I have seen. It had been neglected for years, neither worked nor succoured and was rife with weeds. Even the weeds were poor specimens. It barely carried the stock we had brought from the croft. The field next to the school - our first year's grass, which would be our winter hay - was valued at two shillings and sixpence per acre. At Millbrex our four-acre field had been valued around £3 per acre. This will give you some idea of how poor the soil was. When it came to corn crop valuation, I am sure the ten to twelve acres at Millbrex were as productive as the 30 acres here at Redbriggs.

The corn crop was undersown with grass seed which Ivan had to supply. The field was full of weeds and much to Ivan's annoyance, after the grass seed was sown, Alan Moir gathered the weeds into piles and set fire to them, which could easily have damaged our seed. The ensuing corn crop, which we had to take over at valuation, was poor, so short in parts that the binder just went over the top. The crows had to go on their knees to pick the seed. Surprisingly, it was the only field where we had our quota of corn as valued.

Our valuations certainly did not cripple us; all the crops were poor, the dung was not a huge expenditure and the fencing cost little to take over. The thrashing mill was of much higher value. It had been purchased by Mr Moir at the Royal Highland Show in Dundee where it had taken a first prize for the Garvie collection. It was a larger replica of the little demon at the croft but not nearly so temperamental. It did occasionally cough and splutter and it took a fairly hefty arm to crank. It still took three to do the thrashing but an elevator took the corn up into the loft and it was grand to be able to go and fill up a bucket any time.

When we came to Redbriggs, a Mr Redford of the Clydesdale

Bank at Fyvie was not too enamoured of our prospects. Our debts were high and our assets low. Ivan had borrowed £100 from his brother Jim, a chemist in London, the only one of the brothers who had left agriculture. We had £50 in the bank and perhaps another £20 in hand and there were our other assets: a lease of a 72-acre farm, a pair of horse, a herd of 26 cattle comprising four cows, six calves and sixteen yearlings, two pigs, a laying stock of 400 hens with 150 chickens, six ducks and three turkeys (a cock and two hens) a dog and three cats, poultry houses and a few essential implements, none of any great value. Our biggest asset was our will to succeed.

Ivan neither cared nor knew about the business side; the burden of this lay on me. When we were first married, he had the idea that I might be able to save some of his pay but later accepted that this was impossible. At the croft I was left to manage the best way I could and at times I was able to put some small sums into the bank. Here it required a different budgeting. Almost all expenses had to be met out of the egg money. There were no overdrafts and no cheques - those came later - and although small sums were allowed on credit, they had to be paid by a certain date. The bank was a place to save your money and it was a disgrace if you were in the red. Any returns Ivan got off the sale of cattle had to be ploughed back into the farm in the way of seed and fertiliser or buying in extra feed for the animals.

Ivan had two good friends in John Webster, the manager of Maud Cattle Auction Mart and Douglas Panton, the calf dealer. At the end of the year, he was able to buy cattle from the mart and pay for them when they were re-sold, thus enabling him to fill the byre throughout the winter and, with buying more straw, getting more dung to put back on the land. Douglas Panton also supplied young calves which we often paid six months later. Quite a few of the merchants operated in this manner and were, in a way, the farmers' bankers. You gave your order for this year's grass seed and at the same time paid last year's. In past years each district had its meal mill and a blacksmith and these services had supplied most of the farmers' wants. Gradually, however, other firms were taking over. The poultry population now needed so much more feed and, with the appearance of tractors to replace horses, bigger and different machinery was needed. These new service firms employed travellers to scour the countryside for orders, supplying them with motors for the job. One such traveller had come to the croft, an Eddie Thomson, who, as I write, is one of the old brigade and still doing business. His firm was 'Silcocks', now long since swallowed up into a bigger amalgamation. When the war broke out Eddie, answering his country's call, disappeared from the scene. Once the war was over, however, the travellers became ever more numerous and though some in time became friends, they were often a hindrance - valuable time was lost in idle chat. Ivan brought most of them into the house for tea and many a time my blood pressure was mounting as they kept on chatting, usually discussing anything but the business in hand and I so badly wanted to get on with either baking or ironing.

Quite a lot of the travellers were selling animal feed. The days of feeding chickens on meal and potatoes were fast disappearing and I was now using 'Baby Chick' rearers' and layers' meal. We also got layers' pellets which were very handy to mix with the oats, still the laying hens' principal food. I still had a boiler but this was only used twice a week to boil up scraps and potatoes for the pigs. I fattened and sold about ten to twelve pigs once a year and a little meal was also bought for them. There were several feed firms - Gill and Sons and the North Eastern Co-op are but two - and some firms also sold fertiliser. Then there were the machinery salesmen, like Shearer Brothers of Turriff and Neil Ross of Ellon.

Ivan's brother, Alex, had been for some time a traveller for Sellars of Huntly. They, too, are still trading but are now at Oldmeldrum. He often put bargains Ivan's way. Well, I suppose the menfolk thought they were bargains, but I have my doubts and I was often annoyed after I had saved up for some household item to find I had to give it away for some hunk of metal Alex had persuaded Ivan he needed. Animal welfare was not forgotten though and there were firms like Osmonds, whose representatives called regularly at the farm, offering drugs to cure all animal ills. Thinking of those salesmen brings back memories of Ian Blench who, shortly after we came to Redbriggs, became our vet. Ivan had disagreed with the Turriff vets over the treatment of an animal and next time he called in the New Deer one. Mr Blench was young and energetic, fresh from college with new ideas and determined to succeed. With dedication and hard work, he built up a large practice and eventually he also took over the Methlick district. He scoured the countryside far and wide for customers and spared neither himself nor his old car. But with the animals he was never in a hurry.

As it was mostly my task to look after our sick beasts, I came more in contact with the vet than Ivan did. Once he called - I think it was to see a ewe - and as it was up in the far corner of the furthest away field, he made me get into his car and we drove along the main road then up through the field. That was one of the most terrifying experiences of my life. What used to amuse him very much was saying, once he had got us up early in the morning, "My isn't it grand to get up in the morning". One particular morning it was anything but. It was a dark winter's morning full of wind and rain and out of a dreamless sleep I was woken by a distant voice, "Mr. Michie, are you awake? Are you awake Mr Michie"? As I struggled out from below the blankets, I gave Ivan a push but got no response, not even a grunt. "I'm coming," I shouted, "What's wrong?" Grabbing an old coat - I had no dressing gown - and putting my feet into my slippers, I fumbled for a box of matches to get the light. I saw it was not yet five o'clock. Giving Ivan another shake, I got some movement and a few grunts and then I stumbled through to the kitchen. In the darkness I could just make out a figure. Still clutching the box of matches, I lit a small lamp we kept handy for dark mornings and entered the room. I could hardly believe my eyes when I recognised Mr. Blench.

"What on earth brings you here at this time of the morning?" I asked.

"Oh, nothing much," he replied, "but I had an early call not far from here and though I'd kill two birds with one stone and attend a cow Mr Michie had phoned about."

"Gosh," thought I, "Getting us up at this time of the morning for that." All that was wrong with the cow was that she had calved and not cleansed. Ivan appeared looking a bit bewildered, but I soon got rid of the pair of them for all they needed was a pail, a towel and some hot water, which I got from the big black kettle that always stood full on the bink.

As they disappeared out of the door, Mr Blench half turned and said that, when they came back, a cup of tea would be appreciated.

131

"Right," I said and shut the door. All the time it had been standing open with a howling gale of wind and rain outside and the kitchen was like an ice house. I got a good fire going and then went back to the bedroom to get dressed. It took them only a short time to attend to the cow and they soon re-appeared. But, by this time, the kettle had boiled, tea was made and a boiled egg with some toast was waiting. For all his bravado, Mr Blench was very tired and I can picture him to this day stretched out in Ivan's armchair. He had cast off his Wellington boots and his oilskin coat. He was dressed only in breeches and his legs, encased in long, grey woollen stockings, were stretched up to the blazing fire. Half an hour was all he allowed himself before he set off back to New Deer and I am quite sure that he began his day's work right away.

Another favourite greeting was, "Hello Missus, how's the ducks?" I had a flock of young ducks, who somehow developed a trouble we called 'the gobs' - they would open and shut their beaks uncontrollably. I enlisted Blench's aid and we gave them some pills, which he assured me would put matters right. They were young ducks, the pills were long and I had great difficulty in getting the ducks to swallow them. I only succeeded in doctoring two and next morning I found those two lying stiff and cold. The others recovered. It was some time or I saw him again, but he remembered and asked if the ducks had been cured. "Oh yes", I said with a laugh, "They never had another illness in their life". He never said anything but I have the feeling that I was given the wrong pills by mistake.

He was a good vet and a great character and it was with deep sadness that a few years after we came down here, I read in the papers that he had met his death through a car accident.

Another fraternity who gave me cause for concern were the vans that kept on calling. At the croft, I had one grocer and one baker; now there was seldom a day but a van of some sort called. The Chapmans from Lethenty had served me well and might have continued to do so, as the distance was not all that great, but they were short of staff. Two sons had been called up and, when we left Millbrex, a daughter was driving the grocery van with her younger brother, a lad of fourteen years of age.

For a grocer I now had Giles of Fyvie. He had expanded from a small shop into a big business. From groceries he branched out to poultry feed, converging then on the Christmas market to buy up all sorts of fat stock: ducks, geese and turkeys. He also ran several lorries to move cattle from and between farms. In addition, he had a lorry which called each week to collect the eggs. The following week, when the grocery van called, I was paid my egg money. At the peak season, my weekly income would have been about £20, wealth indeed.

At Millbrex I spent money only on necessities but here the temptation was great, for with us being so near the main road there were vans galore. Several butchers stopped but I chose one that came twice a week and the same applied to the baker. I just had the one grocer but there was a fish van and, in the summer months, an ice cream van. Other vans selling drapery, carpets, sheets and towels called periodically, so you could quite easily secure all your needs without ever going near a town. Nevertheless, the small shop run by the Grey family was quite an asset to that corner of Buchan. The Chapmans had supplied my newspapers but I now got these from the Greeness shop, which meant a weekly visit. Once in the shop, you always found a few more things to purchase. Then the bairns had to have their sweets, something I regarded as an extravagance. As a schoolgirl I had my two pennies a week pocket money and at first this was what I allowed my own children. But I found we had gone up in the world and I had to increase it to sixpence. Ena spent hers on sweets, but always shared with her baby brother. David did not have the same sweet tooth and kept his until he was able to buy something more lasting.

Alongside the general store, the Greys ran the Post Office and a public phone. I had always been in the habit of giving the postman our letters and money for postage, but now they were supposed to be stamped and put in the post box at the shop. Old habits die hard though, and I am afraid we kept up the old bad ways and still do. Over the years, the ways of the postmen too have changed greatly. The principle - the mail must go through - has certainly gone by the wayside. They had no holidays and delivered on Christmas and New Year's Day. Lately, I have known the postman deliver mail on a Friday and not be seen here till the following Tuesday and, forbye having three weeks holidays, they have umpteen days in between.

It is with affectionate thoughts that I remember John Rynd, our

133

Greeness postman, who served the community on his bike for many years. The district was notorious for being snowed up, yet I cannot remember a time when he did not appear, often arriving on foot hours late, but for him the mail had to go through. He was a great reader, wise in the ways of the countryside and he could converse on any subject. He also loved music and appeared regularly on concert platforms. When the Post Office decided to change their routine, John was ready for retirement. All mail had come from Aberdeen to Turriff for distribution by van to the various rural areas, where most of the postmen had cycles. The postmen were given vans but had much larger areas to cover, the result: fewer postmen. They kept changing the drivers around, so you never came to know your postman personally and you were lucky sometimes if you got a greeting of any sort. Often if you had no letter box - and few country houses had one - the letters were just thrown on the floor and if you had a letter to post, you had to be quick off the mark. Many an old person must have missed the postman badly for often they were the only contact with the outside world. I have known John to carry someone's old age pension to them on occasion.

I joined a mail order club, which Mrs Grey ran, paying a small amount each week on some household goods and items of clothing. One of the first things I got was a stair carpet - no Axminster or Wilton - just a plain cord. It covered the stair and had enough for a runner on the landing between the upstairs bedrooms. I thought myself braw. At that time you were well off if your floors were covered with lino and a few rugs and I'd had to economise before I got those. The kitchen, which served both as a living and dining room, had a cement floor that had to be washed each day and scrubbed once a week - the only comfort there was a fireside rug, usually home-made.

The War still dragged on. The coming of Churchill early in 1940 united the country as he won the support of every party in the House of Commons. After the evacuation of Dunkirk in June 1940, Britain was alone and before Germany could invade this island it had to conquer the air. Although Churchill offered the country nothing but blood, sweat and tears, he rallied the spirit and the will of the people with the now famous V sign for victory. The 'Battle of Britain', which followed in May 1941 was fought with gallantry and skill. Our lives depended on so few, but here at Greeness it all seemed so far away.

Further rationing came into force. We grumbled a little, but adapted to the war-time economy and the market price for our produce was always rising, so there was no real hardship. We had plenty of chicken and rabbit but little other meat and what we did get was mutton. Aberdeenshire has never been a mutton consumer and who could have questioned our taste when we bred and reared the Aberdeen Angus cattle, the best of British beef. Week after week along came the butcher with his van and fatty chunks of old ewe. It was roasted, boiled, served up hot and cold and made into broth and soups, but nothing could disguise the fact that it was mutton. I had never cared for it and now I came to loathe it; to this day it is seldom on my menu.

With the shop so near, the children saw to it that we used up our sweet coupons and I am sure more sweets were bought than ever before. We had potatoes and our own oats were still being taken to the meal mill to be ground into meal. With the advent of so many new suppliers of animal feed, several of the rural mills had to close down. But we were still able, at that time, to take supplies of corn to a mill at Greens and get meal for our own consumption and other products for the animals.

The other day, clearing out some rubbish, I came across petrol coupons that were in use in the 1940s. Petrol was in short supply and rationed long after the War was ended. We used petrol only for the engine in the barn and often had coupons to spare; those with cars were not so fortunate. The petrol for private use and agricultural use was coloured differently and anyone found with dyed petrol in their car was heavily fined - and plenty were caught. There were so many government restrictions and forms to fill in, even in those days and those in high places made some awful and amusing blunders. One farmer found his petrol allowance for his milking machine was insufficient and when filling up the application, he pointed out that he worked a seven day week. Back came the answer - they were not stupid and they knew perfectly well he did not work on Sundays.

Most farms were committed to plough up a certain acreage to provide food. One farmer in the district found that he was unable to fulfil his quota of ploughing, as it was time to start lambing. Back came the reply: "Postpone lambing and get on with the ploughing." Some task!

Cuminestown, our nearest village, had its Home Guard. Later, to most folk, they became 'Dad's Army' and their antics can still be relied on to raise a smile. Ivan went to a meeting once. A neighbour farmer, John McBoyle, who helped to run the local group, tried to get Ivan interested but he came back more amused than anything else, saying it wasn't for him. He would do his part helping to provide food for the nation, but it was little good, he thought, donning silly caps and armbands and going around looking for Germans if they arrived in force. When the meeting had been at its height, one of the speakers had been rallying the cause and paused a moment for effect. "We will . . ." In the pause, a voice from the back of the hall shouted, "Ay we will all run."

There were also first aid classes, but I already held a Red Cross certificate which I had gained at classes in Fyvie. Then there were what they called 'knitting bees', but I was not keen on them as I felt I had enough work keeping my own family in warm woollies. The women taking part gathered in each other's houses and begged or bought wool, from which they knitted socks, gloves, helmets and scarves to send to the troops.

That first year I socialised little, but I did become friendly with one person, in a way, Mrs Rankin the school master's wife. Something attracted us to each other, but it was a strange relationship. Except we both had babies in the pram - Mrs Rankin's daughter Beryl was two months younger than Robin - we had little else in common. We met first soon after our arrival. She called one afternoon, the baby all nicely dressed in her best frock and bib and smiling up from a very posh pram. I was a bit grubby, having just finished scrubbing out a chicken house. My Robin was in the garden sound asleep in his pram which, after having its third occupant, now showed considerable wear and tear. That was not an auspicious meeting and what she must have thought of me it is difficult to guess. I thought her snobbish and I am sure she considered herself very much my superior. However, in spite of all this, we did become friends.

The Rankins had only been a short time at Greeness before we arrived. Rankin taught in Aberdeen and, at the outbreak of war, had been called up. However he was discharged as unfit for wartime duties. William Rankin was a Buchan loon - his father was a joiner in Longside. The father had been married twice and Bill, as he was known in Greeness, had a half sister and brothers, but was the only child of his mother, the second Mrs Rankin and had, I think, been spoiled. He was a very happy-go-lucky sort of fellow and full of fun. I always enjoyed an evening in his company. He loved women and drink, which was his downfall and caused the break-up of his marriage.

Kate Rankin came from Fife. Her father was dead but her mother lived in Kirkcaldy. They had been working-class folk and Kate left school at an early age. But she had been able to get herself into the position of a traveller with McVitie's Biscuits. She was now the schoolmaster's wife and felt she had a position to keep up. I wish he had been of the same mind, for I often thought with his principles he should not be teaching children. The friendship between us had its ups and downs and I soon became aware that she was a very unhappy woman. I got far more involved in their affairs and quarrels than I would have wished. In the end, when they inherited some money and property in Aberdeen, she left and moved there. One of the pleasing and happy memories I have of Kate is her bringing me down a bowl of snowdrops that first Christmas. They were just beginning to peep through the earth and later in January they became a lovely bowl of white perfection. After the bulbs had finished flowering, I planted them in the garden hoping they would grow and multiply. Alas, I never saw them again. I am sure some field mice must have had a meal of them.

There was a small garden in front of the house but, like the surrounding fields, it was poor, very hard and stony ground. Pottering about in a garden, sowing seeds and gathering plants to grow was my delight. But I had little time to devote to it. I tried lots of different flowers - annuals and perennials - but my only success was with nasturtiums or 'Tom Thumbs'. They were a glorious riot of red and yellow.

The rest of the garden was in grass but later on when the boys grew older, they grew vegetables and strawberries and planted some goose-

137

berry bushes. The garden was partly surrounded by a wooden fence. On one side there was a beech hedge with a copper beech guarding the gate. At the other end we had an elder, in one corner an old rowan tree and beside it quite a young plane tree. In another corner, much to my delight, a lovely chestnut grew. It was one of the things I did like about Redbriggs. Chestnut trees were not very common in Buchan - this was the first time I had seen one growing. There was also a straggly white lilac which grew on the gable end of the house. A winter gale broke it and the part that was left I nursed, putting in fresh earth and dung at its roots. It grew and flourished and in the spring was covered with lovely garlands of white blooms. I cherished both it and the chestnut tree, but much to my sorrow and to the shame of those that followed us, relations though they were, they destroyed both trees.

To me at that time, Christmas was not all joy. I loved giving presents to those nearest and dearest to me on their birthdays and at Christmas, but this entailed a lot of hard work beginning away back in the summer when batches of early turkeys, chicks, goslings and chickens had to be reared. That in itself was a pleasant task but it was now, approaching Christmas, when the grisly work began. To pay for my presents they had to be sold, but first they had to be killed and plucked. This gave me no pleasure and in fact it was one job I loathed. It is hard to believe that over all the years I have lived on a farm and had chickens around, I have never once killed one. When one was needed Ivan, or later one of the boys, obliged, though I had to do the plucking. The young cockerels and geese I had fattened were lifted alive by Giles, but the chickens for private customers and others for presents had to be plucked along with all the turkeys. It took us days but Ivan and the children enjoyed the change and novelty. Once plucked, the turkeys were packed and sent by carrier and then by train to London. Uncle Jim had been able to get a much better price there than we could at the markets here. We did that for many years and the money bought us things we could not have afforded otherwise.

Our own Christmas and New Year's dinner was usually a chicken, or perhaps a piece of pork, but never turkey. That, we thought, was far too expensive. One year, I thought I had reared so many that surely I could afford one. The smallest of the turkey hens

138

was chosen and, although it was well cooked and tasted delicious, Ivan had to spoil it all by saying he thought the chicken had been just as good.

I think with coming to Redbriggs, Ivan and I drifted apart. No time now to stand still, no time to sit and speak. All our talking seemed to end in argument. Often my thoughts drifted back to the croft and the many happy moments when there had been time just to sit and talk or go for a ramble around our domain. The black moods to which he was subject seemed to come more often and caused me hurt and much unhappiness, with many a silent tear. What caused the moods was a mystery I was never able to solve and I never came to terms with them. But in later years, when they slackened, I did come to accept them. The fact that I could retreat into a world of my own, a world of books and other pursuits that Ivan never entered, kept me sane. I also had a thirst for knowledge, something that has never left me and through the years it has been my delight to probe and ponder many subjects. One winter, soon after we went to Redbriggs, I sent for a correspondence course on history run by the Postal Service. I had never cared for it at school, but reading stories - Jane Plaidy's historical novels - of the various Queens and Kings, I got deeply interested. Where I found the time to read I do not know, but usually it was when the others were asleep. I built the fire up a little, pulled the armchair close and the world and all its cares vanished. I would comeback to reality in the 'wee sma hours' to find the fire was out, I was stiff and cold and my books and papers lay scattered at my feet.

That first winter at Redbriggs my love was Rabbie Burns. How I revelled in him and marvelled at the feeling and simplicity of his poems. Wordsworth, Longfellow and Browning have all been favourites, but this man Robert Burns was the king of them all. If it's true that each time we see a shooting star, a baby is born, whoever saw the star that brought Robert Burns into the world must have been dazzled by its radiance and beauty. What can excel the feeling and simplicity of these words:

Had we never loved sae kindly,
Had we never loved sae blindly,
Never met or never pairted

We had ne'er been broken hairted.

I loved the humourous but terrible satire against cant and hypocrisy in 'Holy Willie's Prayer' and the tenderness of 'To a Mouse' and 'To A Mountain Daisy' but the poem I loved most was 'The Cottar's Saturday Night'; it was my beloved grandfather come to life.

I became quite well versed in Burns, joined the Turriff Burns Club and as Secretary of the Greeness Mutual Association I organised many a Burns Supper. Once, and only once, I answered the 'Toast to the Lasses'. The speech was easy to write but the delivery.. well I would rather forget it and no-one was ever able to persuade me to take on such a task again.

Just the other day Pearl Murray wrote in *The Press and Journal* of a Burns supper she had attended at Turriff. Although it took me a moment to realise it, I too attended that event; I think it must have been 1950. Mr Philip was in the Chair and Bob Boothby gave 'The Immortal Memory'. I remember well hearing him say in that great booming voice of his that Robert Burns had now taken his place amongst the great immortals on the summit of Parnassus. I knew what he meant but I would never have placed Burns there - it was so out of character - and, looking round the company, I wondered how many sitting there knew what he was talking about. The speech that pleased Miss Murray so much, disappointed me.

Other matters, matters more concerned with spiritual well being often occupied my mind. I could never discuss religion with Ivan. It is a subject most people find difficult to articulate yet I know he was deeply involved. Except for attending to his animals, he never believed in working on a Sunday, saying there was no need for it. In later years, even when pushed by a bad harvest, the boys had difficulty in persuading him to work in the harvest field on a Sunday. He had a great love for the church at Old Deer, where he had worshipped as a boy, and where he continued attending Communion twice a year. He would have no dealings with any other church elsewhere. Dr Kemp still served the community and, although I had only met him briefly, I greatly admired and respected the man. The few times I heard him preach I thought he was far too profound and learned, and he soared far above the common people. He had come to us at New

Deer, cycling up from Old Deer and baptised both Ena and David and, just before we left the croft, Robin was taken down to the Church at Millbrex for the ceremony. I had gone to that Church a few times - I have already described Ena's escapades there - but Ivan would never consider transferring his membership and the same applied to Monquhitter.

The minister at that time was the Reverend George Eddie Thomson. He conducted a Sunday School at Greeness with an afternoon service once a month. I sent Ena and David to the Sunday School and I usually attended the service. Although I never came to know him intimately, I found him one of the most saintly persons I have ever met. He spoke no evil, he saw no evil and did no evil. He never chided people for not attending. He had little interest, none really, in worldly gear. He had married late in life a lady said to be a life-long friend. She was only his wife for a few short years before he retired to Macduff but he did not live long to watch the sea in its gentle swell or in tempestuous moods. I remember him with great affection, for he was the means of the beginning of my return into the fold of a faith that has sustained me in sunshine and shadow.

It is strange that I cannot remember what started the train of thought that led me to a new understanding and conception. One night, Ivan and I had a bitter quarrel, the cause of which I have forgotten. Ivan went off to bed full of troubled thoughts; I could not rest and, donning my coat, I went outside. It was a dark night, but the sky was full of bright and shining stars and my eye soon got accustomed to the dark. I made my way up through the field to the wood and found a stump of tree for a comfortable seat. Very soon, the peace and tranquillity surrounding me soothed my troubled thoughts which began to wander and drift in other directions. Looking up at the sky I remembered a conversation Jim Kellas and I had once had. Doubts did sometimes arise in our Christian beliefs and once when he was troubled, he had been out on a dark night and, looking up at the beautiful sky above filled with a galaxy of shining stars, he also was filled with an assurance that God was out there somewhere.

Looking up at the stars that night and thinking of all Jim had said, there came a feeling to me that I was not alone, I felt a presence near me giving me back that faith that I had lost. Troubled no more and full of contentment I went home. Creeping into bed beside what I thought was a sleeping Ivan, he turned to me and said, "Far hiv ye been lass? I thocht I'd hae tae come and look for ye". Then, after a few moments came the words I had never expected Ivan to utter and I doubt that he ever did again. "I'm sorry lass for saying fit I did. I nivver meant it." I murmured, "Neither did I". And, for a time, there was a new comradeship between us. I felt it was a time of new beginnings and fresh hope.

And I said to the man who stood at the gate of the year, "Give me light that I may tread safely into the unknown." And he replied, "Go out into the darkness and put your hand into the hand of God. That shall be to you better than a light and safer than a known way."

CHAPTER NINE

REDBRIGGS AND THE LAND ARMY

YOU CAN'T build up a farm in weeks or months, nor yet in years; it takes a lifetime. Ivan and I both gave Redbriggs the best years of our lives, and at least set it on its way, for it is now one of the best farms in the Howe. When we left, another Michie took on the task.

Lassie and Gyp with Ena in the corn yard

Ivan set the plough deep, turning up red loam, which his critics condemned. But cultivation was what the ground needed and putting back just a little more than was taken from it in the way of dung and fertilizer. Clyde was his salvation, but he did not have a lot of luck with his other horses. To his aid, though, came a government scheme. The war dragged on, food was getting scarcer and it was rationed. "Grow more food," was the cry. Getting farm labour was difficult, as all the young men were conscripted to the war effort. The government set up this scheme to aid the farming community, providing tractors and other machinery at a cheap rate. Ivan employed machinery for the ploughing and then a tractor and binder to do the cutting at harvest time. Around this time the Women's Land Army came into force and we also availed ourselves of their help. We had three girls. One was a success but the other two were not.

The first to arrive was a very pretty blonde and, when first I set eyes on her, I said, "Oh dear!" She had a lovely figure, plenty of make-up with long tapered finger nails, and she tottered along on very high heels. She was living-in and, when roused in the morning, she appeared promptly looking much more with it', dressed in regulation uniform of blouse and skirt with flat shoes. She belonged to Glasgow, but she had difficulty in deciphering what we said, especially Ivan, as he took a delight in bewildering the poor lass and spoke at his broadest. At breakfast, I asked if she would have porridge, cornflakes or a boiled egg. She plumped for the egg. They were rationed in the town, but here on the farm, where we collected sometimes over 30 dozen a day, it would have been difficult to do so.

The fields were taking on a yellow hue, heralding the approaching harvest. The government outfit of tractor and binder was booked, but first the fields had to be opened up. A track had to be cut right round the field to give tractor and binder access to the crop and so as not to damage the ripened grain. That first morning, collecting the scythe, Ivan took her with him to the field to show her how to gather and bind corn stalks into sheaves. Remembering my own experience, I felt sorry for her as I watched the pair cross the close on their way to the field.

When they came in for their mid-day meal, little was said and again at supper time. She looked miserable and, as soon as she had a wash, she went off to bed. I asked Ivan how she had got on, but he just laughed and said not very good. Next day was a repeat. It was the habit at harvest time to have a tea break in the afternoon and I would take the tea and snack out to the field, but Ivan sent her home to get it. I had it just about ready when the door burst open and in she came in tears. "I'm not staying here no longer," she sobbed. "Mr Michie is a brute and I can do nothing right." That afternoon Ivan had to do without his tea. It took me some time to get her calmed down, but I thought it was little use trying to get her to go back to the field. However, we had our tea and we talked a little, and she became more reasonable. She really was a nice enough lass, just not suited to farm work. She came to the decision to give it up and I said I would contact the officer in charge of the land girls in our area. She lived in Turriff and this meant going to the shop and using a phone. Next day the lady called and, talking the matter over, decided to take the girl back with her.

That was the end of the first girl but the second arrived a few days later. Ann Grey was quite a different character, sturdy and with plenty to say for herself. Somehow I did not take to her. Yet, she seemed to get on much better with Ivan. But it only lasted a week. The officer in charge usually called once a week on a routine visit. None of those we housed had any agricultural training. Some stayed in camps and went out to the farms daily; others, like Ann, lived with the family. We paid the Land Army a sum of money and provided accommodation and food. The Army paid their wages and provided them with uniforms and working clothes but when off duty they were allowed, if they so desired, to wear their civilian clothes.

We had hoped and believed Ann was settling in, so it was a surprise when she announced she did not like farm work and was quitting. When her commanding officer called, she did little to persuade her to stay and, in a few days, she was gone.

Harvest was finished before the third arrived. This time we were in luck. Mary Parker settled in with no trouble and stayed for almost a year. She was about 19 years of age, came from Glasgow and our farm was the first she had set foot on. The first job she tackled was gathering potatoes and, almost from day one, she adapted. She was big and strong, with a good sense of humour, and she could laugh at her mistakes. She soon learned to milk and loved feeding the little calves. And, although I always did most of the poultry work, she often helped out and also fed the pigs. She got handy with the horses, fed the cattle and cleaned out both stable and byre. Ivan used to tease her a lot but she took it all in good part, and I marvelled at how she stuck in to the pulling of turnips, which in these days was all done by hand. It was a job I had seldom attempted and no joke on a cold winter's morning, with frost in the ground, having to pull a few cart loads. Her duties did not include housework, but she was not slow at giving a hand. At odd times I took advantage of this and slipped down to Turriff for an afternoon's shopping, leaving Mary to do the hens, look after the children and get the supper ready.

Once I came home to the smell of burning. Before I left, I had made a clootie dumpling for the supper, which needed three to four hours cooking. The dumpling was in a pot hung on the sway over the fire and occasionally the water had to be topped up. Mary had forgotten to do this. We quickly got the pot off the fire, added a little water and steam rose in clouds but, although a good part of the dumpling was inedible and the cloth would never hold another one, there was enough to go round. Poor Mary had the pot to clean and an awful lot of teasing.

Another time, Ivan had brought a batch of small pigs home from the mart at Turriff and Mary had the task of shutting them up, a difficult job. A short time afterwards a hullaballoo got up - the pigs were out. They were soon back in their pen except two which set off at a great pace, leaving the steading for an open field, with Mary in pursuit. There is something very amusing about small pigs. You'll always laugh rather than get angry and watching Mary chasing those pigs was hilarious. The pigs moved like lightning and Mary was big and clumsy. She was often close behind them and thought all she had to do was stretch out a hand and take hold of a leg or tail but, just at that precise moment when she thought she had one, it eluded her, leaving her lying flat on her back. Ivan and Lassie managed to capture one and in a final dive, Mary got hold of the other. There she was lying on her back piggie clasped to her bosom, squealing for all it could and Mary laughing fit to burst.

Like the rest of us, Mary had her faults and one she and I had in common was that we did not like getting up in the morning. The alarm clock was set for 6.30 am and Ivan promptly rose when it went off. I never heard it. When Ivan rose, he gave Mary a call and she was supposed to follow him out to the byre. I usually followed a little later on, got the milking done and came back into the house to prepare breakfast. Often Mary did not answer Ivan's call and I dared not go out without making sure she was up, or else when I returned, in all probability, she would still be in bed. Dare I confess that once or twice Ivan returned and found us both in bed. Did Ivan enjoy that? You bet he did, for nothing pleased him better than being able to pitch into someone. I was told if I went to my bed like other folk I would be able to get up. Yet, if we were going somewhere or something special was on and needed a very early morning call, it was always me who got up first.

Mary quickly made friends and enjoyed going out with the other young folk in the district. Sometimes, she borrowed my bike and cycled down to Birkenhills where she got a bus to Turriff and perhaps went to a dance or the pictures, meeting up with other land girls. Ivan and I once had a very enjoyable night out when we were invited to a social evening organised by the Land Army, meeting all the girls and the other farming families who employed them.

Mary had weekend breaks and holidays which were usually spent in Glasgow with her parents. Once, after she returned from one of these visits, she asked if she could have her parents up for a weekend visit. I gave permission gladly, and they travelled up a few weeks later and seemed quite decent folk. But I do not think they shared their daughter's enthusiasm for farm life. They were taken round by Mary and introduced to all the farm animals, which I think somewhat scared them. At her own request, I had taught Mary how to cook and, to show her parents how good she was, she insisted on cooking the Sunday dinner. I kept an eye on her and it all went well and we all sat together to enjoy the meal Mary had prepared. Mary came to us early in October, stayed throughout the winter and spring, and well into the summer. She was with us in June 1944, when the news came through of the Norway landing. We all rejoiced, for deep down in our hearts we had always been in fear of invasion. This, we were sure, would be a turning point and hoped the War would soon end.

In spite of all the war restrictions, there always seemed to be plenty of entertainment especially for the young folk - dances and concerts were taking place almost every other week. Mary took part and went out quite a lot and, although we were supposed always to enforce certain rules about coming in at night, I often heard her creep up the stairs long after the hour when she should have been in bed and fast asleep. Except perhaps for bringing it to her notice, we did not strictly adhere to the Army rules. Then, to my dismay one Monday morning, I found her bed had not been slept in. We made some discreet enquiries and learned where she might be. She had become involved with a son of a rather disreputable family. I went and saw Mary and persuaded her to return. Ivan and I were both fond of the lass and decided not to say anything to her commanding officer, in the hopes it would all blow over and she would see her mistake. For a few weeks all went well but I did have a feeling of disquiet. She was not her happy self and sometimes I could see she had been crying. We were told by friends that the boy she was going with was not much good, exempted from the army and out of work, and often involved in drunken brawls. Then, after a weekend leave, she again failed to return. We waited two days but when she still did to appear we had to report her missing.

They came and found her and took her away, and we did not even get to say goodbye. Her belongings were collected by the Land Army and we neither saw nor heard of her again. I was so sorry to part with her and the children missed her too. I hoped she might write but, when the weeks went past and with Christmas coming up, I wrote myself, forwarding the letter to her parents' address. It went unanswered. Another time, I came across the Land Army officer who had been in charge and I asked about Mary but all she could tell me was that Mary had gone back to Glasgow and was out of the Land Army. A rumour went around that she was pregnant, but I do not know the truth of that. Today, that would not have been a great sin but in those days it was looked upon in a different light. Today, young people's morals appal me.

In the next spring-clean, I lifted the stair carpet and underneath I found on the bottom step a shilling and a half crown. They belonged to Mary, for it had been a habit of hers when she had loose change, instead of going up to her bedroom, to slip it in beneath the stair carpet.

The harvest of 1944 was one of the worst we ever experienced. It had been a summer of little sunshine and the crops ripened late. In many farms September was well advanced before the sound of tractors and whirr of the binder were heard. Our crop - 30 acres of oats - was reasonably good and it was cut by the government outfit, the sheaves all lying neatly in rows ready to stook. Then, to complicate matters a little, right in the middle of this a new harvest hand, our youngest son, Alexander Douglas arrived. He did not exactly open the door and enter, carrying his suitcase, equipped for work. After three weeks in hospital in Turriff, it was mid-October before I returned to Redbriggs. When I left, the last thing I saw was those beautiful sheaves of grain all lying in neat rows spread around the fields. The sorrowful scene that met my eyes on my return was those sheaves still lying where the binder had dropped them, sodden, with the gold heads of grain slowly turning black. Between the day I left and the day I returned, there was almost continuous rain. Eventually, the bulk of the harvest was secured, but many sheaves were thrown away to rot by the dykeside. Others were fed to the mill, with only the head going through and the stalks discarded.

When Mary left, Ivan was able to get the services of a boy still at school, a neighbour crofter's son. He came on Saturdays and, during the harvest, he had an exemption from school. Help was also on hand from Ivan's brothers. I was now handicapped with another baby to look after and we began to think of getting a maid. Sandy was a happy, blue-eyed and golden-haired child, resembling Ena. They were all delighted with their

Ena with Ivan

149

brother and Ena, now nine years of age, proved to be a devoted nurse. David took to him much more than he had ever done to Robin and Robin just longed for the day when he would have a playmate. For some reason Ivan ignored the baby. Robin was now very much his favourite, but what a little chatter box he was, just the opposite of David. In character, all four children were so different but all I think favoured more the Michie side of the family than they did mine, in looks anyway.

In the summer we did have extra help. Ivan's niece Barbara, Uncle Jim's youngest daughter, came up from London. She wanted a life 'down on the farm' and she was going to an Agricultural College. It preferred the girls to have some knowledge of farming, so she came to us for a year to get experience. She got on fine, but by Christmas she was homesick and eventually returned to London.

Except for one boy we had no outside labour and, as spring approached, I found it almost impossible to cope. I could disregard some of the housework, but the rearing of calves and chickens could not be neglected. Somehow, domestic help would have to be got. The days when this had been easy were long past. Around the 'ferm touns' there are now no maids and even the farmer's wife has gone to find a job off the farm. Memories of those older times still linger. There may have been hard work, which never did anyone any harm, and there may have been drudgery, but it is the memories of all the happy hours of fun and laughter that remain. One farmer's wife who liked to climb the social ladder had a maid, a girl called Jessie who had been at school with me. Poor lass, she was not very bright. She was given all the mucky jobs about the farm; cleaning out the hen house, carrying pails of food to pigs and poultry, and washing out the kitchen floor and the cold cement lobbies. Seldom did she manage to get out of her heavy working clothes - a sack apron wrapped around her waist and big boots. She had little time to tidy and clean herself up.

However, one day her mistress decided to have an afternoon tea party and got the idea she would dress Jessie and train her to open the door and show the guests in. A black dress with a white apron and cap were acquired for Jessie and also a pair of stockings and elegant shoes.

150

The day came and you would hardly have recognised Jessie as she stood in the hall waiting for the front door bell to ring. In those days, in the larger farms, bells were in use and a board with lables reading 'door', 'dining room', 'parlour', 'bedroom no.1' and 'bedroom no.2' to show the maid where the summons had come from. Jessie's mistress sat waiting in the dining room and, when the first guest arrived, Jessie duly took her name and showed her in. Then, as she turned to leave the room, the mistress, to her horror, noticed that Jessie was still wearing her big heavy boots covered in muck and tied with binder twine. Below her dress her stockings could be seen lying in wrinkles around her ankles, exposing a large expanse of white leg.

My imminent problem was to get a girl to help in the house. The war had changed and widened women's horizons. Jobs in shops, offices and factories were now the thing and ordinary domestic work was unpopular.

Being close to the school, I had some idea who was nearing school leaving age and this helped in finding a young girl called Winnie who needed a few months to complete her schooling but a school exemption was easy got. She was a bright, clean and tidy girl and my problem was, I thought, solved. She was only with me for a few weeks when one morning she walked in and told me she was leaving at the end of the week and going to the schoolhouse. To say I was hurt was the least of it. Mrs Rankin and I were friends, and to persuade Winnie she would be better off at the schoolhouse was not the work of a friend. Mind you, she did not offer her more wages, but girls finding situations at a schoolhouse, manse or with a doctor were all considered much superior to those working on a farm.

My next girl came from Byth. Nell was untidy and had no idea of work, not even washing dishes. Each time she had to be told what to do and it was the same with most of her duties. One day, when our potatoes had run out, I sent her to the shed beside the back door for more. When there was no sign of her returning, I went to investigate. The potatoes were in a corner of the shed covered with tarpaulin. Nell had turned a portion down and seated herself on top, and she was peeling away at the potatoes and dropping them into a pail which had not a drop of water in it. She had a weekend off once a fortnight, cycling home to Byth on the Saturday afternoon and returning Sunday night. On her second weekend, she did not return. Except for making a discrete enquiry, we made no attempt to persuade her to come back.

My third girl was much better. Daisy was a local girl, a younger sister of the boy Mary Parker was involved with. Although her parents were of dubious character, I found her a pleasant, clean and tidy worker. She stayed with us for over a year and only left to find a job with more pay. She stayed in the district, married quite young to a local lad and often came to call, and even brought her first child to see me. Later on, when she did leave the district, she kept in touch for years with a Christmas card and, when she was back visiting her in-laws, I usually had a visit.

She always stayed in my mind and the very last horse we had was called Daisy after her. This Daisy was a yearling foal Ivan bought at a neighbour's roup and would have been about nine months older than Sandy. The children suggested calling her Daisy. It had been Ivan's ambition to rear a foal but he had never been successful. Gyp, our first horse, was too old and sadly our next horse, the grey mare, was almost due just before she died. Several mares had been served since, but the only one to hold also died, causing Ivan to give up the idea. In those days, men travelled a stallion around the farms during the breeding season and you paid quite a hefty sum for the service. It was beginning to die out in the 1940s and soon afterwards none of those horses or gentlemen were around. Tractors were replacing horses, besides there was a real scourge at that time, grass sickness, for which there was no cure. Many fine young horses died. We had one and I never wanted to see another animal go through such agony.

In June of that year, 1945, the war came to an end but we knew little difference in our lifestyle. There was no imminent end to rationing. In fact, I think more came in. We did learn more about the troubles and hardships the people in the towns had suffered with the bombing, which caused such a loss of life. All these things had been kept out of the papers. Aberdeen and the nearer towns of Fraserburgh and Peterhead had all been heavily attacked, and even the small village of Rosehearty had suffered, with many lives lost. Many rejoiced as loved ones returned, but many more held only a sorrowful thought for those who would not return, young lads who had gone so gallantly. Today, all those memorials in each town and country parish denote the thousands who made the supreme sacrifice.

Living out in the country we had escaped the worst of the effects. In fact we were getting better prices for our produce and our animals, which gave us some feeling of stability and an incentive to go forward. But the work was hard and it was often a struggle to make ends meet.

The winter of the following year was a desolate one, for Ena had to spend the whole of it in hospital. During late summer she developed a bad cold which seemed to linger on and on. She also had a cough which refused to go away, but her illness was brought to a head by a pain that only came during the night. It kept us both awake and, after three nights of it, I decided to get the doctor, Dr Forbes of Cuminestown. To call him one had either to contact him in perso or by phone. I remember the morning I decided to get the doctor vividly. I picked Sandy up, went upstairs and, to keep him out of mischief, shut him in the room with Ena while I went to phone from the shop. Some other duties called me urgently, so I told Ena that the doctor was coming and that I would return to tidy her room. I went downstairs and came face to face with the doctor. Ena was very quickly on her way to hospital in Aberdeen. Her cold had developed into pneumonia and this caused a spot on her lung - tuberculosis. She was back in the Sick Children's hospital where once before she had spent so many weeks. At that time, parents were not encouraged to visit, for their visits were believed to upset the children and this retarded their progress. My mother lived in Aberdeen and was able to visit regularly and report and, although we could not manage to go together, Ivan and I took turns once a fortnight on a Sunday. We cycled across to Birkenhills and got the bus from there. Ivan had Robin with him and I took David. The boys got a lift downhill on the carrier of the bike, but had to walk uphill. Robin would only have been five years of age but he can recall today how his father used to make him run behind the bicycle, something he very much resented. We were very grateful for the way our relations and friends gave up their coupons so that we could take sweets to Ena. I can also remember how surprised and touched we were when Mr Rankin brought a parcel of sweets which her class mates had contributed and, while Ena was in hospital, they contrived to do this once a month. Christmas was spent in the Sick Children's but all the nurses and staff really did give the children a lovely time.

Soon after the New Year, she was transferred to a sanatorium up at Newhills, just outside the boundaries of Aberdeen. It was while she was there that I bought her a grey dress with red spots. I had seen the frock in a shop window in Aberdeen. It was just made for her. It cost more than a man's wage for a week's work and it would have bought two calves. In fact, I did once buy a calf for ten shillings. If Ivan had known what it cost I think he would have murdered me.

She had so seldom had a new dress: most of her frocks were made out of old ones, some of mine, others given me, or from material bought as a remnant at a sale. The grey red spotted dress did not disappoint. It fitted and later I was able to lengthen the deep hem, which gave her longer wear. The last of it was stitched into a patchwork cushion. Ena was well cared for and happy at Newhills, and made friends with the other girls and, when she was well enough to be discharged, she felt just that little bit reluctant to leave. She came home in the beginning of May after more than six months.

The doctor paid her a visit, but said it would be some time before she was fit to return to school. The local children often came to play during their school breaks, but were envious of her not having to go to school. She herself began to express the wish to go back, so one day I went down to Cuminestown to see the doctor and suggest she return. But all I got was a good telling off and I was reminded about how serious her illness had been. She was not to go back to school till he had seen her.

I am afraid he never did and must, I think, have forgotten to pay that call. After the summer holidays I sent her back to school.

Dr Alexander T. Forbes or 'Tommy' as he was affectionately known to most folk, was an eccentric with a great devotion to his work. I first met Tommy when he came to the cottar house at Little-ton. He had followed in the footsteps of his father Dr Hugh McGregor Forbes and, between them, they served the community of Monquhit-ter from 1894 to 1960. Thankfully, we were a relatively healthy family and did not need him often, but the episode with Ena not going back to school was typical of him. He was the only doctor I ever knew who started his evening rounds about 10 or 11 o'clock, and paid his last visit after midnight. He said he liked to see his patients during these hours as people were usually at their lowest ebb then. Doors were left unlocked for him and it was said, whether true or false, that there were many occasions when he took the pulse of a sleeping patient and a close look to satisfy himself about something, and was back in the morning with a drug for treatment. On most days, he had a one-hour surgery in the morning and the evening. No appointments were made; if you had a complaint you just went along and hoped he would be able to see you. The waiting room was the Forbes' kitchen. Of the consulting room I have only a faint recollection - a desk, a chair and a couch, with the walls all lined with shelves full of bottles and boxes. There was no chemist in Cuminestown and there were no pre-scriptions; few pills were handed out. If no proprietary mix suited, he made up his own. In Tommy's view, medicine was not only a priority. It was everything.

Old Hughie, as his father had been known, went his rounds in a pony and trap, but after Tommy came in 1928 he bought himself a motor car. At first, he hired a man to drive and maintain it but when we arrived in the Teuchar Howe he was driving himself around. In the 1930s, when you purchased a car, you would be taken for a run in it, shown how to start it, how to steer and brake, how to get round a corner and how to stop. Thus equipped, you simply set off with no more in-struction, learning as you went along. It was much later that a driving test became obligatory.

I never saw Old Hughie, but was told that, although he was smaller in stature, Tommy was very like him physically and walked with the same rigid gait and short steps with his 'head in the howe o' his neck'. In Turriff Hospital when Sandy was born, the three doctors in attendance approached by an outside corridor and we used to know who was coming by the sound of the footsteps: Dr Ross was quick and sure; Dr Cameron thumped a heavy tread; but Dr Forbes sounded as though he was tip-toeing through the tulips.

I came to like and respect him and he served our family well. He retired in 1960, the year we left Redbriggs, but he and his wife lived in Cuminestown for many years in the house his father had built. It now serves as the Monquhitter Manse.

Both the Forbes and the community were, I think, disappointed that Sandy, their one son and only child, showed no interest in

155

following in his father's and grandfather's footsteps to become a doctor. Dressed always in a kilt of the blue and green tartan of the Forbes clan, he was well known. He was a talkative child and made himself agreeable to one and all, but showed little aptitude for school work. I once encountered him while waiting to see the doctor. He came through to the kitchen and started up a conversation with the patients. After asking my name, he seemed disappointed but returned in a few minutes with a small book. He was quite excited as he showed me that the name Michie was a sept of the Forbes clan and told me I should wear the same tartan as he did. Up to that time, I had little interest or knowledge of the clans or their tartans, but I had recently been deep in the fortunes of Bonnie Prince Charlie and had learned quite a lot about the fate of the clans on the battlefield of Culloden. That chance remark led me along many a delightful path exploring the Highland legends and stories. Old castles and their history began to fascinate me and one of the first to grab my attention was Dundarg here on the shores of Aberdour. The library was raided for material and I haunted the second-hand book shop in the New Market in Aberdeen whenever I could. Great was my joy every time I found an old book on the subject.

Ena made a complete recovery and had no recurrence of her illness. For a long time afterwards all her talk was of the nurses, the other girl patients, and what they all had done. Her great ambition now was to be a nurse. Unfortunately, she was a whole year behind with school work and was thirteen instead of twelve when she qualified. At this stage, the children had to leave Greeness School and go either to Turriff or Cuminestown. Turriff was a Secondary, with a higher curriculum which took them on to university. Cuminestown only taught to the school leaving age, which in the 1940s was fourteen. We were three miles from Cuminestown, but Turriff was eight. No bus was available for either but for Turriff you could cycle to Birkenhills and get a bus. If you were more than three miles from a school, grants through the School Board were available for transport. It was too bad that we were just under the three miles to Cuminestown so the children were expected to walk. Although I must have walked that distance to school, I did think it was too far. In winter, it would have been about 5.30 pm before they reached home. Ena went to Turriff. She had her own bike, for which she got an allowance, and free transport on the bus. David went to Cuminestown, but had no allowance for his bike and I can assure you it needed more repairs than Ena's ever did. We often threatened to make him walk.

None of my children had ever been any trouble to start at school, Sandy least of all. One day, when he was only four years of age, he was found wandering in the school playground. That afternoon, Mr Rankin had been showing the children some slides, something new which they greatly enjoyed. They took Sandy into the school and he too enjoyed them. Before I had missed him, one of the boys was sent down to tell me where he was. After that, he began to make regular visits and was only four

Robin & Sandy with Lassie

years of age when he joined the school roll. He was the only boy in a class of five girls, and they all spoiled him and made a fuss of him. One girl used to call on her way home and give Sandy sweets. Rosie now lives quite near here. I wonder if she remembers. I wonder too if a certain boy remembers that awful day when, after being involved in an accident with a motor van, he was brought to me mistaken for Sandy?

Both Robin and Sandy, had been home for their dinner and had just gone out to go back to school. Ivan was having a nap and I a little read before tackling the dinner dishes, when one of our neighbours, Mrs Wilson burst in saying that Sandy had had an accident with a motor. An awful sensation paralysed all my feelings and I said calmly, "Is he dead?"

"I don't know," she said, "but the doctor has been sent for and they're bringing him down." Mrs Wilson's husband Charlie and another man came in carrying the unconscious boy. I had known that

157

Sandy had just gone out and, at the time, would have been on the road - I never doubted that it was him. I bade them take him through to our bedroom and lay him on the bed. Then I went to him and again I will not forget the shock I got when, even though he was a terrible mess, I recognised that it was not Sandy but Patrick. Dr Tommy arrived about the same time and, after a quick look, he decided it would be best to take the boy home where he would be able to have a more thorough examination. It was only a short distance and, if I would come with him, he would take Patrick in his car. They wrapped Patrick, still unconscious, in the quilt he had been lying on. Where my own boy was I had no idea. When we arrived at Patrick's home, Tommy went in to explain. I sat in the car feeling terrible and I almost wished it had been Sandy. I had taken the shock and now this other mother had to take it too. It was no wonder that I was forgotten.

However, it did not turn out as bad as we had expected. After another thorough examination, the doctor decided to send Patrick into Aberdeen. This time his father took him in his own car direct to the Sick Children's where he spent many weeks, but came home fit and well. When I returned home, I automatically got my dishes washed and made things tidy, but had no feelings of either sorrow or relief. Then a policeman arrived seeking information and, when he left, the reaction set in and I just sat down and sobbed. The boys came home from school and found me. By the state of me they were sure Patrick must be dead.

While the children were growing up I had the dream that at least one of them might take up where I left off, but this was not to be. Ena was slow, but had a determined streak in her and would not give up. She was not clever, but she liked the school and she knew, if she was to fulfil her ambition and become a nurse, she had a certain standard to reach before she would be accepted for training.

She had the handicap of being a year behind, but stayed on at school till she was sixteen years of age, and she acquired the necessary grade. The only prize she ever took was for a book of pressed flowers. These were gathered mostly from our own farm where the terrain was varied. Right away on the furthest outpost was a bog where an abundance of flowers could be found. Then she had the burn side and the fields and, added to this, on our topmost border

158

was a wood and a piece of heath The flowers were all carefully pressed and mounted in a scrap book with the common and Latin name and the date and place where found added. I loved to help, for botany had been one of my favourite subjects at school and I could still find a thrill in finding a new specimen.

David took no prizes at school. It was an uphill task to pass his three 'Rs' and he was overjoyed the day he left school. David was such a quiet lad, like his father in so many ways, and often came up with quaint sayings. One day he had been cutting out photographs from the newspaper and they were mostly of brides. He carried them about with him or had them hidden around the house. I found one on the mantelpiece and put it away. Later I found him searching for it and, when I asked what he was looking for, I got the answer, "I've tint ma wummin."

After leaving Greeness school Ena, Robin and Sandy all went to Turriff but David did not qualify and went to Cuminestown.

I took an interest in their lessons and tried to help, but I could not do so now. Everything has so radically changed I could not even guide or help an infant. David seldom bothered me, but once I remember he did ask for assistance in writing an essay. I was not in a very good mood but he persisted as usual. "Right, tell me what you want to say - I'll write it for you to copy". The title was "What Would Improve the School From a Schoolboy's Point of View?" What could you expect from a 12 year old who had no great love for school? More comfortable seats with cushions, more playtime and not to go into school in the morning till 10 o'clock were but a few of David's ideas of making school a better place. I wrote it down, he copied it out and took it to the teacher. The teacher must have had a laugh. It was read out to the class and David was taken over the coals for his views and told that if it had not been good English he would have given him the strap but he did get full marks.

Robin, although he resembled David in looks, was quite different. He was quicker at learning but showed little desire for school lessons. An expert at asking awkward questions which often led into difficulties in explaining. He was a great favourite with his teacher Mr Rankin who used to tell the story of how one day he was showing the class slides of the Royal Family up at Balmoral. One slide showed the late

King George VI with a party tramping over the moors and through the heather, accompanied by dogs and carrying guns. When Mr Rankin asked the class if anyone could tell him what they were doing, up shot Robin's hand: "Poaching sir." Robin was a very clear speaker with a good carrying voice and at some function won a 1st prize for recitation. Mr. Rankin was often in demand as a speaker at Burns suppers and he took Robin along with him to recite 'Wullie's wife'.

Few if any of Mr. Rankin's pupils ever achieved academic fame but quite a few became budding gardeners. Surrounding the school house was a nice walled garden which was admirably kept by the senior boys. Mr Rankin had learned that they were much better with a spade than with a pen, but this did not exactly help in making the grade when they went to secondary school. Robin's school work did improve once he went to Turriff but, like David, when he reached the school-leaving age he was happy to leave.

CHAPTER TEN

BONNET LAIRDS

THE 1950s brought so many changes. All through my grandparents' lives and up till I was twenty, little change took place in the countryside. After the two world wars the speed of change was almost unbelievable. What would my grandfather think, I wonder, if he came back today and viewed the world around? I am sure he would take one look and quickly go back. Changes were needed and many were for the good, but others have had an evil influence and people have wandered so far from those simple things that were the very essence of our everyday lives. Barely two decades had passed since Ivan and I began our life together, yet those days at Fridayhill seemed almost a century ago, and the dream and fulfilment of our life on the croft remote and far away.

Cows were now milked by machines though I still did mine by hand and fed my 'cogget calves' with milk out of a pail. Even I had done away with incubators, however, and all my chickens were now bought as day old, sex-linked hybrids. It has been a wonder to me that hens which produce only female chicks have not been bred.

Daisy was now the only horse that grazed on the fields of Red-briggs. Old Clyde had passed on after a great many years of faithful service and Ivan had never had another so good. He had been unhappy to part with his horses, but one died and he had lots of mishaps and misadventures with others. Finally, much to Ivan's regret but to David's joy, we bought a new tractor - well I can't say it was a brand new one, for it was second-hand or maybe third or

Ena, David, Robin and Sandy

fourth. Ivan hated it and David later had a love-hate relationship with it. Temperamental was not the word for it. Often David had to leave it stuck in the field, come home and call an engineer from Scott's garage in Cuminestown. Sometimes a little twisting of nuts did the needful, but at other times only a crank made it start and, much to David's embarrassment, run sweetly. The most humiliating experience for David was when it got stuck in the corner of a shed and Daisy had to be brought in to pull it out. The tractor was regarded as a female which may have been the cause of its contrary temperament, or so suggested the mechanic when it was in for repair one day and they found it needed to be fitted with some sort of nuts called 'female olives'. The tractor was a big outlay, but it seemed the only way forward, even though Ivan and I had no love for this noisy, smelly hunk of machinery. The coming of the tractor may have eased the workload a little but it cost more to run, for the horses all fed off the farm whereas petrol had to be bought. And petrol was still rationed, for the restrictions on many goods stayed with us a long time after the war ended. Not only that but implements like the plough and cart had to be bought new. We both loved the horses so much and I remember their sweet smell and velvety touch, how you could bury your face in their soft necks and how they responded to your caresses. Time moves on and we must go with it, but what will replace the tractor I wonder?

Government restrictions seemed to multipy. Grants were given to aid farmers, something I never approved of as it is far better to give realistic prices for produce and have the public pay for the true price of production. Income tax applied to most farms and book-keeping became a necessity, which most farmers found difficult. Out all day in the fields working hard, they came in at night tired and having to sort out invoices and columns of figures to total was something they were loathe to tackle. If I had not been able to help Ivan, I am afraid he would have been in trouble. He was good with figures in his head, but committing them to paper was quite a different proposition. I was far from the world's best mathematician. It had been one of my weaknesses at school and, when it came to totalling figures, two and two never become four. Now I press a few buttons and the answer is there. At first, accounting was a simple exercise of balancing income and expenditure, but later it all became more complicated and I did at one time attend classes on book-keeping. Insurance stamps for the self-employed were now payable. Paying by cheque was also becoming common, but only for those with money in the bank. Our banking account was very small and it was often difficult not to be overdrawn. We owed no money except the £100 Ivan had borrowed from his brother. The poultry was still our main source of cash, and everything I got had to be saved and budgeted out of this income. Like most people, I liked to keep my house nice, but it was not a worry for me to do without. One thing I did fancy was a telephone and it took a while of careful saving ere I could afford one. Except for the shop and the school house, we were the first to have one installed.

Ivan never had any spare money in his pocket and he did not go out. Neither did he smoke or drink. In later years he often joked about the half crown he got for his dinner on mart days. He liked to go to Turriff on a Tuesday and seldom missed a sale. He was supposed to be home for his mid-day meal around one o'clock but often it was three o'clock and sometimes later before he put in an appearance, and by that time his meal was a dried-up useless plateful fit only for the cats. I got annoyed at the waste of good food and gave him the money to buy his dinner at Turriff. At that time, half a crown was ample for a meal: he could get a plate of soup, mince and tatties, followed by a cup of tea. He did occasionally buy something which he took a fancy to, like the wireless on one occasion. The wireless had begun between the two World Wars, but spread rapidly after the end of the Second War and few houses were without one. I had often expressed the wish for one, but Ivan thought it a needless expenditure and often said the bairns made enough noise in the house without adding to it. Again,

Ivan came up with one of his surprises. One day our plumber, who also carried on a wireless and television business in Turriff, had been called to repair a burst water pipe. Unknown to me, Ivan had been talking to him about a wireless set and, before going to inspect the damage, he called at the house, left a small blue set, a Bush, standing on the table, switched it on and told me he would call later to see what I thought of it. Of course, we got attached to the set and kept it. It gave us pleasure and served for many years. Ivan would seldom miss the early morning news, and to its sound I awoke most mornings.

Throughout her school days, Ena had held on to the dream that she would one day become a nurse and, shortly before her eighteenth birthday, after several interviews and disappointments, she was accepted at Morningfield Hospital. This meant more eggs had to be produced and more pigs needed to be fattened to provide her with a wardrobe for her new life in Aberdeen. And into the picture came Flossie, David's faithful old dog - her of the royal pedigree - and a pig called Susie. It just so happened that about six months earlier, Uncle Alex, Ivan's brother and an agricultural salesman, had been given a small pig whose mother, sisters and brothers had all rejected it - the runt of a large litter. The farmer gave it to Alex in the hope that he might find a home for it and in turn he gave it to Ena. We got a small bottle, a baby's teat - having reared quite a lot of orphaned lambs we had plenty of those - and a supply of milk, and the pig proved no problem to rear.

It just so happened that Flossie was nursing a pair of pups. She was not much good as a farm dog, but she had lots of those especially lovely pups and occasionally we were tempted to keep a few though we never had any difficulty in finding them homes. The night the pig arrived, we put it in a box filled with hay along with a hot water bottle and placed it in the shed where Flossie stayed. Next morning, to our surprise and dismay, we found the pig had escaped from its box and was lying snug, curled up beside Flossie and the two pups, which were then much the same size as the piglet. Kind and gentle, silly old Flossie did not seem to know she had a cuckoo in the nest and allowed it to suckle, washed and groomed it, the same as her own. Susie also had to have a bottle of milk but rapidly grew into a fine sturdy pig, leaving the pups far behind in size. For some time she kept sleeping

164

and romping with the pups, but dogs and pigs have different temperaments, and I think Susie sometimes had a wicked strain in her. She often bit the pups; one grew up with a hip out of joint caused by the pig's over-zealous attention.

Susie drew the attention of the newspapers and both she and Flossie had their photograph printed with their story in the local press. She was a character and very affectionate and, although she was a nuisance, we all loved her. She often managed to slip into the house and once, seeing her rub herself up against the lintel of the fireplace, I feared its demolition. She had a good life but a short one, for it took less than six months to make a pig ready for market. She fetched a good price - around £20 - which enabled us to fit

Ena's pig with Flossie

Ena out in style, with a complete wardrobe for her new start in life.

Nursing brought Ena no disappointments. She was happy, liking her work and making friends with her class-mates. Her pay was £2 per week, paid monthly. She had a day off once a week and liked to come home but usually by the end of the month she was broke and had not enough left for her bus fare. Mother too liked to see her and the needful would be found. After a three-year course she gained her certificate in the spring of 1953 and went with her cousin Margaret down to London to see the coronation of our present Queen.

It was during Ena's training that I had my first-ever holiday, a week at Butlin's in Ayr. Ina and I had once been there on a weekend trip organised by the Greeness Mutual. We had enjoyed it so much that it gave Nell the idea. Four Mrs Michies, all sisters-in-law, Nell, Peggy, Ina and myself, ladies with quite different characters, all went on holiday together. "Fit on earth wid ye gyang traipsing awa there?" was Ivan's comment. The Butlin holiday camps were a new concept in holidays, alright for town people but for country folk almost unheard of. I don't remember what it cost but it certainly would have taken much scraping for me to find the train fare, the week's accommodation, and clothes suitable for me to take. I do remember quite well the morning we left Aberdeen en route for Glasgow and hence to Ayr, my memory aided by a photo taken by Ena who had

The four Mrs Michies

come to see us off. I had been able to have a green tweed costume made for travelling and I think I looked quite smart. I was small and slim compared to my three companions who were all ladies of ample proportions. Nell was not with us as she was to travel up from London to join us.

The holiday proved a very happy one and left us many memories. Ina and I set out one afternoon on a three mile walk along the coast to a small village called Dunure. Ina had an aunt who had taught in the school there. This aunt had been good to them as children sending Christmas sweets and toys. When we were so near, Ina thought she would like to see the place. We planned to walk along the coast and come back by bus. There was no path or right of way but, full of hope, we crossed over to the Heads of Ayr and made for Dunure. It was hard going and we were crossing a field of cattle when we realised one was a bull. He gave us an unfriendly look and began pawing the ground rather aggressively. We thought it best to make a hasty retreat. To our joy we came on a railway track and then we made good progress. Like most railway lines it went through a high embankment and the idea

166

crossed our minds that if a train came along, we would never be able to climb out in time. With visions of our mangled bodies lying on the iron tracks we hastily got up to the top. Soon after that we came to what had been the Dunure Railway Station. We just sat down and gave way to fits of laughter; no trains had passed through there for at least 10 years.

We found the village a delightful place. We saw the school where her aunt had taught. We visited the beach and an old ruin of a castle. Tired and thirsty we found a tea room where we had a lovely tea of home baked scones and jam, but alas we had lingered too long and the last bus back to the camp had gone. At least four miles of main road lay before us. Weary and foot-sore we trudged into camp between 9 and 10 o'clock and the first thing we heard coming over the loud speakers was: "Would the two Mrs Michies reported missing please contact the office". We did get into a dither for we thought something awful had happened. We had been due back at camp for dinner at seven o'clock. Nine o'clock had come with no sign of us so Peggy and Nell had reported us missing. We were not amused; we were mature adults not a pair of children.

All was not perfect harmony but we had many more ups than downs. We also had a trip up Loch Lomond. A bus took us to Balloch where we boarded a steamer and sailed right up to Greenwich and then on as far as Helensburgh. That was a lovely day of tranquillity.

My love and interest in Robert Burns was also renewed by visits to the various places associated with him: one highlight was a tour around the farms of Mossgiel, Mont Oliphant and Ellisland where he had for so short a time laboured on the land.

One of the most beautiful memories of all was seeing the sun set over the Isle of Arran.

One evening I had wandered out on my own and, climbing up a little way beyond the camp, I found a seat commanding a view of the Bay of Arran in the distance. Slowly the sun began to sink, casting its golden rays over the shimmering water, a picture of incredible beauty. Straight from where I was sitting was a golden pathway leading to Arran and far beyond, I thought, into heaven. Robert Burns must have seen that scene many times, yet he wrote no poem about it. Down here on the coast, we too sometimes can see a lovely sunset shining over the Bay of Aberdour.

All was well when I returned. A neighbour's daughter, Nancy Wilson, had come over each day and cooked and cleaned to keep my menfolk happy. Often, in the years that followed, Ina and I relived those days, getting laughs and chuckles over the various incidents. It was a long, long time ere I had another holiday though we had the odd day here and there visiting relations, the Turriff Show or the Braemar Gathering. The Mutual Association provided another annual day's outing, but this often coincided with the Royal Highland Show which at that time travelled around: one year in Edinburgh, another in Dundee. Perth, Aberdeen and Inverness were all venues as well. Ivan usually attended. He enjoyed the various agricultural stands and, although he was seldom in a position to buy a new implement, it did no harm to look and dream. Once, in later years at a Dundee Show, he bought a long bogie from the firm of Adams, Old Deer, which gave sterling service and brought many a load of golden sheaves home to the cornyard. It took twice as much in one load as our other carts, and I believe it was later connected to the tractor.

A few times we went to the Braemar Gathering. The setting - marching and music, the colour and pageantry of the Pipe Bands - was a thrill, giving me an uplifting feeling, but the biggest thrill of all was seeing the Royal Family, King George, Queen Elizabeth and the two young Princesses. Beautiful too was the sound wafting down from the hill where lone pipers brought the surrounding hills alive. Having a meal in a restaurant or a hotel on a day's outing was an added bonus, for seldom could we afford the luxury of eating out. One time we went to Braemar I had no money. The bus left Cuminestown around six am. In the hurry I forgot to put my purse in my handbag. Fortunately, Ivan had his wallet with our tickets and a few pounds. The tickets covered the bus fare, entrance money and a meal. Before we entered the Games, we decided to have some breakfast in the village and, while Ivan paid for this, I asked if I could have some money. He pretended not to hear me. Once into the park, we were besieged by people selling all sorts of goods, among them souvenir catalogues of the day's events. I liked them for they contained some good reading, but to get one I needed a half crown. Again I appealed to Ivan and, after fumbling in his pockets, he produced one shilling. I was so humiliated and angry that I turned away and left him to pass the rest of the day on my own, without a penny to spend. Thank goodness the lavatories were free else I might have had to join the pipers away up in the hill.

I still have happy thoughts of one other brief holiday, an earlier long weekend. Ivan's father was still alive and living in the old house that had been my childhood home, in fact my only home till I married. A longing to return to my beloved Mormond had come over me. Leaving Ivan and the other children to fend for themselves, I took Robin, who had not yet started school. First, we hired the car from the shop to take us through Cumninestown and New Byth to meet a bus on the main Banff to Fraserburgh road. We left the bus at Strichen and here we spent the night with an old friend, a lady who had given me my dinner when I was at school and, in winter if the weather was stormy, overnight accommodation. She also made my wedding dress and because I had not seen her since we had left Fridayhill, well over twelve years earlier, we had a lot of news to catch up on. On the Saturday morning I had a nostalgic longing to walk once more over Mormond. There were two ways we could go: up the hospital brae on to the road just past the Burnshangie farms, or the winding right-of-way path through Martin Wood. I chose the latter. Well fortified with food and sweets, we left the Burnshangie farm path to cross Martin Wood and met a track that took us to the foot of Mormond. Climbing up and skirting the White Horse, we made for the 'Hoose on the Hill', a hunting lodge built in 1887 by a former Strichen laird to house shooting parties. It was a ruin even then, but still stands with all four corners up to *"a' the airts the win' can blaw"*.

Here we had a rest and a drink of milk and some food. We had picked wild raspberries on the way and they were delicious. There are few around now, but at one time they grew in profusion and made lovely pots of jam. They had a sweeter flavour than garden reasperries.

Our Robin had proved no trouble thus far. He was a great chatterbox and had an enquiring mind. Knowing my countryside I was able to answer most of his questions. In the Martin Wood, alas no more, we had seen a lot of birds and, to Robin's joy, a squirrel. I was not too knowledgeable about birds, but when we found a nest with four blue-speckled eggs, I was able to identify it as a blackbird's nest simply because I had seen the bird fly off. We were well into summer, so I think it must have been a second clutch. He wanted to have one of the eggs, but I was able to persuade him to leave it. He did find a few creepy crawlies and a cry rose up for a match box. I was no lover of those little beasties, but he adored them, and I had to allow one or two to be put into a hankie. Later, I found they had disappeared but it was not, I thought, to their advantage nor to ours to enquire where.

We enjoyed our half-hour on the top of the hill, sitting beside the house. I mostly recalled past memories and admired the vast panoramic view over so much of the Buchan countryside. Robin played around but was forbidden to climb the ruined walls. I had done it myself but it was dangerous for so small a boy. The rest of the way was downhill and, as we turned to face our destination, part of the Fraserburgh and St. Combs coastline came in sight with the spire of the kirk of Rathen in prominent view. When the heather was in bloom, Mormond was a glorious sight, clad in royal purple.

A small well-trodden path took us through a moss where we disturbed a grouse that got up in a clatter of whirring wings, protesting in its own peculiar way that sounded like, "go back, go back". It gave my son quite a fright. We sat down on a bank among the heather and I told him the story of how his sister too had taken fright at a similar bird on her first walk to school. I also told him that, as a girl, I had known and loved those birds. How thrilled I had been sometimes to find a covey of baby grouse chicks - beautiful balls of brown and golden fluff - which blended so well with the hues of heather that it took a clever person to penetrate their camouflage. Then how angry I had been when the shooters came and slaughtered them. Soon his fright was forgotten as he found some white bleached bones belonging to a long-dead bird. He was determined to collect them, but I would have none of it. Unknown to me, he did manage to hide one. I found it that night when putting him to bed and it lay for years in his treasure box.

The 'old man', as we usually called Ivan's father, and his housekeeper Maggie, had been expecting us and a nice meal was waiting, to which Robin and I did full justice. It had taken us over two hours from Strichen, and the walking and fresh air had given us an appetite.

It was good to be back at the old house. When Ivan's father had taken it over he had built an extra room and now used the old kitchen and living room as a workshop. The garden was much the same. Parts of it had gone wild but there was still the rhubarb patch and potatoes and vegetables along with trees, shrubs and flowers growing in abundance. One big disappointment - my favourite tree was gone. It was an ash tree that stood at the back of the house, towering well above the roof. I really loved that tree and it broke my heart to see that it was cut down. I expect the reason was that the wind might have toppled it and damaged the roof. How often had I climbed in its leafy branches. It had a lovely slender trunk, with all the branches concentrated at the top. I reached the branches by shinning up the trunk and I became quite an expert at this with practice, even managing to take up some planks of wood for a seat. When it was in full leaf I was completely hidden and I often escaped to my tree trunk eerie along with a book. They say hens are stupid creatures and I had a lot of amusement with them from my hide-out. Around feeding time I used to call them and it was so funny seeing the bewildered birds trotting round and round the house in search of food and the voice that called them.

It had been a long day for my son and he was soon off to bed and sound asleep. I slipped out and wandered on my own. The garden held a treasure of memories associated mostly with my grandfather, a presence that I could still feel. My great-grandfather, his father, had taken on the ground from scrub and heather, digging all with fork and spade. His son had followed and made the garden his own. It is from him that I best remember conversations and things from those past days. Not so long ago, while watching the Beechgrove Garden programme, an incident from that time suddenly came to mind. Jim McColl was trimming and cutting branches from a tree and explaining how, when a tree is cut, the sap runs out. To stop this, an elaborate procedure with various liquids manufactured for the purpose was recommended. I smiled to myself and remembered my grandfather cutting and trimming some branches from a tree, taking a handful of earth lying at his feet and rubbing and plastering this into the cut made on the tree. "Fit are ye daein that for?" I asked.

"It stops it bleedin." To this day, if I cut a plant or shrub, I rub earth into it. I passed the rowan tree where I could still see a flash of red-breast and hear the melody of a cheeky robin who had made it his territory. Then I found the track that led on to the hills and for another half-hour I wandered there letting memory take over.

Next day, we were on our travels again over the corner of Waughton, going east and round the foot of the hill to Frosty-nip. There, in a croft, lived my mother's McCrombie cousins. I liked them and I had not seen them since the first year of my marriage. There was more news to catch up on and time went like a flash, and next day we were homeward bound. This time we walked the short distance down to the main road and took the Banff bus through Strichen to the farm road end of Little Byth. Ivan's brother delivered us safely back to Redbriggs in his Austin car.

Ivan's father died a year or so later and I never slept under the old cottage roof again. Seldom do I go there now; it hurts too much. When I was last there the rowan tree was still standing, green and flourishing, but overall it is a complete wilderness with hardly any trace of the garden left. The ground has been commandeered, trees planted and only a few stones of the cottage are left. After the old man's death it was sad to see it pulled down and all the fittings sold, leaving only the four walls standing. It was a corner called 'no man's land' which my forebears claimed and made their own.

Ena qualified and found her first post at Inverurie and soon after that David left home. When he left school he had been persuaded to join the Army Cadets, Mr Hay his teacher being the officer in charge of the Cuminestown branch. David enjoyed getting into uniform, taking part in the various events, and in the summer a fortnight's holiday under canvas. For young lads of eighteen at that time, two years army training was compulsory. David, being in agriculture and working on the land, was exempt but when two of his best friends in the Cadets were called up, David wanted to join them. Robin was growing up and brother Sandy following, both boys being now a big help to their father so we did not hold David back. He joined the Gordon Highlanders and went to train at the Bridge of Don barracks in Aberdeen for a five-year stint in the Army.

The one who missed him most was his faithful pal, Flossie. I wrote before of how she attached herself to David. When at school, one of his jobs in the morning had been to let out and feed the hens that were kept in the wood. Flossie was seldom out at that time, but the first thing she always did was to pick up David's scent and she would go up to the wood, sniff around, come back and only when she was satisfied that he was gone would she go and lie down and content herself till he came home. Although a very friendly dog (and a glutton) she had no interest in any other member of the family. It used to cause a smile that when she lost David, her long mournful face would sometimes appear at the window looking into the room, her eyes searching for him. If he was there she would then go and lie down on the doorstep but if not, the searching continued till she found him. While on his training he often had the weekend off and no one greeted or gave him a more rapturous welcome than Flossie. In between visits, she used to spend long periods sitting at the top of the road looking towards Cuminestown and, I am sure, hoping he would appear.

When his training at Bridge of Don was finished and he had passed out as Private Michie, he was sent to join the 2nd Battalion Gordon Highlanders at Redford Barracks in Edinburgh. He was only there a short time when trouble arose in Cyprus and quite suddenly the whole battalion was sent out to help restore peace and order. He had been due a week's holiday and had written home asking if he could bring a girl-friend with him. He was so quiet a lad that the request surprised me, but permission was given and the pair duly arrived. I was even more surprised when I saw Helen. We did our best, or at least I thought so, to make her welcome, but she was a strange girl and just didn't fit into our way of life. She screamed when Flossie came near and when I spoke to her she never gave a direct reply but mumbled to David and he spoke for her. Robin and Sandy though it a great lark, brother David bringing home a girl-friend and the cheeky pair did not help matters. When the week was up we were glad to see them go, and I think David himself was losing patience with her and looked a bit upset. It was years before we saw David again and Flossie never did.

On the second day after they left, our daily paper headline ran "2nd Battalion Gordon Highlanders air-lifted to Cyprus on active service". David had been lucky that he had been due leave for none of them were allowed to communicate with relatives. David had not even said goodbye to Helen. They were allowed to write letters, but those were only posted after they had gone under a cover note which explained the reason for the secrecy and urgency. With David going to Cyprus the romance seemed to fade out.

To me, Cyprus was only a name on a map. It may have been a jewel of an island in the blue Mediterranean, but for David it proved no paradise. The uprising that the Gordons had been sent to quell became a nightmare to those young lads. There was no face-to-face encounter with the enemy. At times a few were flushed out and captured, but mostly they were themselves ambushed, shot at, their vehicles blown up by land mines and they never knew the moment when some of them might die by a sniper's bullet. David was privileged in a way. He had, during his training, taken a mechanic's and driver's course and was given the post of driver to a colonel. This may later have saved his life.

Towards the end of the campaign a terrible disaster occurred. They had thought Grivaise, the leader, was surrounded in the Troodus mountains, but he knew the terrain much better and was able to slip through the net. David's platoon was caught and trapped in a forest fire which, without a doubt, had been contrived by the enemy. Only a few got out, most of the young lads dying a terrible death. It was hard that they had to die so far from home, in a cause that concerned them so little; many of them belonged to this corner of Buchan. One was Ian Grey, the youngest of the boys from the Greeness Shop, a school friend of David's and almost the same age. Ian had just gone out in January that year and the massacre had taken place on June 15th, David's 21st birthday - one he was not likely to forget. At the time of the fire, David had driven the colonel further up the lines and was thus out of its range.

Soon after that, Archbishop Makarios, the Greek Envoy, signed an agreement with the Turks and the Gordons came home, this time by boat. It was dark December and the sea journey was rough. Continual bouts of sea-sickness made even the prospect of coming home fade; "Give me flying anytime" has been David's motto ever since.

The troopship was due to berth soon after Christmas with the boys home for the New Year but it must have been either the 2nd or 3rd of January when David came marching home. I remember that New Year. Ivan had gone to visit his friend Jimmy Bruce in Byth and

174

the boys and I were alone. We sat around a peat fire, I was knitting and the boys were playing draughts. Sometimes I joined the game but I was determined to finish the garment I was knitting before the New Year came in. It was a pullover which I wanted to be ready for David coming home. It was finished well before midnight, and before we went to bed the boys and I toasted in the New Year of 1957 with ginger wine.

Two days later the phone rang and it was so lovely to hear David's voice saying he was in Aberdeen and would soon be with us. He looked little different but we soon realised that he had come through some terrible experiences and that his nerves were in shatters. The three boys shared a bedroom and the other two did not understand. They were amused that if one of them made the slightest move during the night, David would be up and shouting, "Who's there?" Often he could not sleep and I would hear him go downstairs in the early hours of the morning. He would go out and wander about and it was always such a relief when I heard him come in again. One of the saddest tasks after he came home was to visit the Grey family and speak of Ian. He had brought back a photo of the grave and some of Ian with himself and others taken shortly after he had gone to Cyprus.

He had about a month at home before he had to rejoin his regiment in Kent. His five years were up and in a few weeks he was demobbed and returned to Redbriggs. He missed old Flossie for she had died about six months after he left for Cyprus. I am sure she knew that he was gone. She went no more on her vigils to the top of the road and she lay about showing little interest in anything, often she had to be coaxed to eat. She stayed in the house a lot, lying beneath the table where David had usually sat. Nearing the end, I had to bring her up from the barn where she slept and take her back at night. One morning she lay as if sound asleep, but there was no wakening her.

David found many changes had taken place in the five years of his absence. There had been the phone, his sister had married and his mother was a grandmother. Robin had left school and become his father's right hand. The old International tractor, the bane of David's life, was gone and a David Brown was in its place. There were switches and bulbs in plenty all over the house and steading, although no electricity. The rest of the Howe, except Charles Wilson and us, were all enjoying light in dark places by the flick of a switch. But the biggest upgrading of all was that father had become a Bonnet Laird.

In 1942 when we had come to the Teuchar Howe, it would have been almost inconceivable that twelve years later, in 1954, we would become the owners of Redbriggs. The war had caused so many changes. Those who we had thought wealthy and who owned big estates and stately homes were finding that, due to heavy taxation, they were unable to keep going. With successive Labour Governments in power, many of the good traditional ways of life were going by the wayside. The Hatton estate, of which Redbriggs was a part, was finding it difficult to meet the demands of State and part of their land had to be sold. The tenants were given first option and easy terms were arranged.

In this changing world, money was beginning to be more available; most goods could now be bought by hire purchase and this had begun to be the accepted way to buy. I still kept a little financial world moving on the income from the poultry but our bank balance remained on the debit side though other possessions multiplied. Our stock had more than doubled, crops were beginning to be reasonably good and I now could spend a five pound note without too much soul searching and a guilty conscience - yet it was hardly conceivable that we would be able to buy the farm on this alone. It was made possible by money being more easily borrowed through hire purchase, insurance companies and other agencies. It was a big commitment on our small resources but we were able to purchase 84 acres of land with house and buildings. It cost us £900. We ourselves raised £300, but the rest came through a life insurance policy in Ivan's name. The solicitors handling the Hatton estate, Stewart and Watson of Turriff, made the arrangements and throughout the years that followed they have continued to handle all our affairs.

Redbriggs covered seventy-two acres but another twelve acres of woodland for which we had grazing rights, were added. Land is selling now for over £1000 an acre, yet only thirty-seven years ago Ivan became a Bonnet Laird for the sum of £900. (This name was given to any one who worked and owned his land.) Only seven years later, we resold Redbriggs for £4,200 and last year it again came on the market and fetched £84,000. It is more than I can take in.

In 1953 electricity came to the Teuchar Howe. A year earlier, men had come around the property, measuring and marking out where the poles and lines were to go. Four poles were to be on our farm, lying along the burn side. Ivan objected until he understood he was to be paid, then he gave permission for their erection. The Hydro Board also offered contracts to supply electricity but Ivan still viewed it suspiciously, as did our neighbour Charlie Wilson. When first asked to sign a contract they both refused. I was furious and argued till I was blue in the face but Ivan stuck to his stubborn policy. I had long envied the Rankins at the school house, for they had been enjoying the benefits of electricity for years. This was supplied by an engine that the Parents' Committee had provided for school use but being clever, Mr Rankin had incorporated it into his own house and Mrs Rankin enjoyed the use of a cooker, iron and lights.

Sometime prior to this I had acquired a gas cooker called a New World of which I was very proud. It had indeed opened up a new world for me. A firm called Rural Gas had been giving country folk the benefit of their services for years. They had a mobile van for demonstrating their appliances. On a visit to Greeness we gave them permission to set up their outfit in our corn yard which was next to the main road. When they moved on, by way of payment, they offered us the latest, most up-to-date cooker for half price. It was one of the happiest and proudest moments of my life when the lovely cream enamel model was set up in the kitchen at Redbriggs. They supplied the gas in bottles. That cooker came with me to Bankhead and it was some years before I was persuaded to change to electricity. My New World cooker still stands in a corner of the back kitchen and when we have a power cut it comes into its own. I believe I could still purchase spares and we still can buy bottles of gas.

Soon after the electricity contracts had been signed, poles and cables arrived in the district, followed by a squad of men who soon completed the grid, and in no time all but the Wilsons and Michies were enjoying the benefits electricity brought. The pair soon regretted the folly of not signing and when the Board again came round offering to connect they both willingly signed. The others were connected free but our two culprits were charged an extra fee. The Hydro Board did the work of connecting the wires to the farm buildings but we had to supply all the wires and fixings for the inside. This had been completed some time before they actually came round to connect us and we were in this position when David returned from Cyprus.

One day a few years before this, completely out of the blue, this small Baby Austin arrived at Redbriggs. This was one of Ivan's big surprises. Except for the Greys at the shop and the Rankins, we were the only others in the immediate corner to have a motor car although his brothers at Little Byth had an old Austin. Ivan had bought it without my knowledge. It cost around £100 and was Ivan's first deal in hire purchase, a method of payment I have never approved of. Ivan thought it great and I was never able to convince him how much more the goods actually cost. I had, of course, to find the payments out of my egg money.

However, hire purchase and all, I began to love that little car, and almost from the very first day of possession was determined to drive it. Ivan already had his driver's licence but I had to pass the test before I could drive alone. I could drive with Ivan beside me but this was not a success. I got one of the boys from the shop, Alfie Grey, to take me out sometimes and in between I discarded the L-plates and practised on my own. I soon became confident and it gave me no qualms that I was breaking the law. Even the local policeman used to turn a blind eye. One day I had driven down to the garage at Cuminestown and he was there, tinkering with his own car. He looked up and smiled and as I passed he softly said, "You've naething tae fear, I'm aff-duty the day." He had spoken to me before saying that he knew I had only L-plates but that did not bother him, but if by chance anyone came along and reported my misdemeanour to him, he would have to take action.

I made up my mind to take a driving test and then I failed. The examiner told me I was quite a good driver but he could not pass me as I had no confidence in traffic. Determined to remedy this I booked classes in Aberdeen at the Mannofield School of Driving. Ivan thought this a big extravagance: my day's outing cost me ten shillings for my bus fare, the same for an hour's tuition, and five shillings for a meal. Having finished my course of lessons and full of confidence I again took my test, but much to my disappointment I again failed. This was a bitter pill to swallow. What went wrong I never knew but

178

from the moment the examiner entered the car I could feel a hostile atmosphere. My misfortune may have been due to the time of day for, immediately after lunch, perhaps the poor man had indigestion.

Again, I got another learner's licence and carried on much as usual but seldom were the L-plates seen on the car. We had had the car for over a year and the older it got, the higher the repair bills were. Ivan decided to replace it and yet another hire-purchase agreement was drawn up. The next car was a grey Singer, a bigger model, and I found it easier to drive. When we went out together it was usually Ivan who took the wheel but I went out more often on my own. I had been lucky driving around, never having been stopped or had an accident, but I knew that one day my luck would run out. I had given little thought to the fact that I did not have a proper licence but the thought of having failed my test kept nagging me and at last I resolved to have another go. I applied, telling no one not even Ivan. My test was to be on the day we went to Turriff together. To avoid traffic we were in the habit of parking the car at the railway station and walking the short distance into town. I thought Ivan would notice but no comment was made when I took the car right into Turriff.

This time it was a ten o'clock appointment and I think I was the first on the list. The examiner, a younger man, greeted me quite pleasantly and I felt relaxed as we set off. All seemed to go well. The test over, he criticised a few points in my driving but I could hardly believe my luck when he handed me the coveted certificate. Ivan was, as usual, late in getting back to the car but got in, never noticing that the L-plates were missing. It's doubtful if he had even noticed they were there in the first place. All the way back I was gloating over my success. I was really bursting to tell all, but hugging the secret made me feel good. Then, on reaching home, I drove right into the back of the garage, denting the bumper and knocking a few boards off the shed. That took me down a peg. It was a week later, with Ivan standing beside me, that one of our neighbours casually remarked, "Oh, I saw you in Turriff last week. How did it go?" When I showed the bobby my licence a delightful grin spread over his face. He gave me a pat on the back and said, "Weel done lass. There'll be nae mair lookin the ither way."

CHAPTER ELEVEN

REDBRIGGS -
THE LAST YEARS

OUR TIME at Redbriggs was coming to its close and I wasn't sorry. It was not unkind and it did repay us for all the work and toil we had lavished on it; possessions we now had in abundance, but no money. When we left the croft we had about a hundred pounds in the bank. That was used up taking over Redbriggs and we have never had a penny of our own in the bank since. That first hundred we borrowed from Ivan's brother grew into debts of hundreds, then thousands, till now the sum is beyond my comprehension. Borrowing is now an accepted way of life. All the ideals and high standards of the past have disappeared. To farmers in those days it was a disgrace to owe the banks money. I would not go as far as that but I still think the old way of life was better.

I spent a lot of unhappy days at Redbriggs, the continual struggle of making ends meet and the ever more distant relationship with Ivan being mostly the cause. I could never rid myself of the feeling that this land resented us. Ivan gave so much of himself to those dour acres that I am sure it changed him. The bouts of black withdrawal that I could not fathom became more frequent. I had accepted them at times, but at other times I fought to find the cause and ended in blank despair. Matters we had to discuss became quarrels, which I hated. For my survival I had another world to which I could escape - a world of books and fantasy.

There were also times of achievement and quiet contentment. Possessing a car gave Ivan great satisfaction and I too enjoyed the benefits it gave. Many a Sunday afternoon we set off, the two boys, Ivan and I, going where the fancy took us (my special delight was old castles). Sometimes I packed a picnic basket but, more often, we had tea out in some restaurant or hotel. This was a special treat for all, but more so for me. It was so nice to be served a meal I had not cooked myself and afterwards have no washing up. On one of our excursions we discovered Aberdour beach and I found Dundarg. We had been exploring along the beach towards Rosehearty and I decided to leave the others and climb up to the top. There, to my surprise, lay the house with its grounds and ruined castle. The others were not long in joining me but, as the house seemed to be occupied, we were wary of exploring. Out came a lady and said we were welcome to look around but to, "Please be careful, it is rather a dangerous place for adventurous little boys." There were huge holes all over the forecourt. The lady explained they had been dug up recently by Aberdeen University students, under the late Dr Douglas Simpson, searching for clues to the castle's early history. The castle itself lay on a peninsula jutting out to sea and was reached from the forecourt only by a narrow piece of land. We spent quite a while wandering around and I found lots to fascinate me, little thinking that one day I would come to know it well. At that time I knew none of its history, not even its name. I would have liked to talk again to the lady who had greeted us, but the large door remained closed and had a look of "don't approach me". One morning soon after, I opened the daily paper and there was a picture of the castle with the excavations in the foreground and, alongside, the sad story of the lady having gone out at dusk to feed the birds and fallen to her death in one of the holes. A short history of the castle followed with pictures of the findings of the archeological party.

Another old castle we visited was Slains. Ivan had for a time worked on a farm called Earlston, in the Cruden Bay district, and had expressed a wish to go back. A map was bought, the route planned and, with a picnic basket packed, we set out. The first attraction was a magnificent roofless building with an 84-foot tower. It was built in 1899 in the best of Scottish baronial style by the Great North of Scotland Railway Company as a hotel for the wealthy golfing

181

fraternity. It was sad to stand and look at this building now. Its most conspicuous feature was a massive battlemented square tower flanked in each corner by turrets. It had over one hundred bedrooms with bathrooms attached. It had also contained large coffee and breakfast rooms, drawing and dining rooms and a writing room with a billiard room attached. There was a grand entrance hall with a handsome staircase and passenger and luggage lifts as well. A railway line from Cruden Bay station was also laid on. The 1914 war had been its downfall and shortly after our visit it was completely demolished.

We saw Slains from a distance and the nearer we got, the more remote it seemed. Like Dundarg it was built on a rocky and precipitous peninsula jutting out to sea, the walls of one of the towers like a continuation of the perpendicular rock. The older castle dates back to 1308 and the present structure to 1836. It was the home of the Hays of Errol. We had our picnic but did not linger long. If Dundarg was dangerous for small legs, this castle was much more so. The atmosphere was eerie and I, for one, felt evil things had happened there. It fascinated me though and, although I have never returned, I read all its history.

I have an obsession for those old places. As a lone child, I often let my imagination take over and played many games of make believe, though as childhood things were put behind me my attitude to everyday matters was, I think, sane and sober. It was only in those places associated with past history that my imagination ran riot. Another such place is the old ruin of the Castle of Gight, the home of Catherine Gordon, mother of Lord Byron. At the back of the braes of Gight, to reach the castle, you have to climb up a long and winding road and then suddenly you are looking down on the castle. Somehow, I knew before we even reached the final bend that this was so. I had only to shut my eyes and it appeared as it must have done in years long past. Scenes came to life, and the strange feeling that I had lived there and been happy took over. Yet the castle has a tragic history: three men died violent deaths which had been strangely prophesied by Thomas the Rhymer:

At Gight three men a violent death shall dee
After this the land shall lie in lea.

182

First was Lord Haddo in 1791, who fell from his horse. Some years later, a servant on the estate met a similar death. And then, around 1856, when the estate had fallen into decline and the home farm buildings were being pulled down prior to the land being turned to grass (lea), one of the workers was crushed to death by a falling wall. It is uncanny how so many of the things the bard Thomas prohpesied came true.

Another relating to Gight has a connection with the Bard of Auchmedden:

When the Heron leaves the tree
The Lairds of Gight shall landless be.
   and the other:
There would be an eagle on the crags
While there was a Bard of Auchmedden.

Catherine Gordon, descended from the Earls of Huntly, owned, at her marriage to the Hon. John Byron, the castle and all the lands of Gight, but soon after the estate was sold. A family of herons, which at that time occupied a tree near the house, left their abode and went to the wood near the House of Kelly on the Haddo estate. Strangely enough, it was Lord Haddo who bought Gight. Both estates are still under their management and there are still herons around, for quite recently I saw one standing motionless by the Ythan waters.

The connection with Auchmedden is this: to the east of Pennan, rising to a height of almost three hundred feet, lies the magnificent rock called the Red Head and here a pair of eagles were wont to nest and bring up their young, but when the estate was sold they completely disappeared thus fulfilling the prophecy. The land had been bought by the same Lord Haddo who owned Gight. When one of them married Christine Baird of New Byth, who was of the family of Bards of Auchmedden, we read in the statistical records of the Church of that time, that the eagles returned to their eerie on the crags, only to disappear again when the estate changed hands once more.

Like all the others, Auchmedden estate and its lands have been sold. Farms and crofts are now owned by individuals. One of those crofts is occupied by a family bearing the name of Baird and eagles have again been seen around the red craggy rocks at Pennan.

Surrounding us at Redbriggs not more than a stone's-throw away, but unknown to me were, or had been, numerous relics of the past. It was only when I found that gem of a book on Buchan by John B. Pratt that I became aware of the fact. A few yards up the road where the Teuchar Howe ended, lay the farms of Keithen, Brownhill and Lendrum. In this area a terrible bloody battle had taken place in the time of Malcolm Canmore. The Thane of Buchan had fought with one Donald of the Isles whom Pratt believed was Donald Bane, brother to Malcolm Canmore. At one time, a huge cairn locally known as Donald's cairn had stood on the farm of Keithen, but farmers regarded it as a nuisance and an eyesore, and it disappeared under the plough. It is such a pity that those stones and cairns have vanished in this way. Another cairn called the 'Woggle', which lay on the East border of Keithen, has also disappeared. Even in our time, I remember seeing parts of barren land on the farms of Brownhill and Lendrum thickly studded with mounds and small cairns. When those were ploughed, many pieces of corroded iron and other evidence of a battle were found. Pratt wrote of other cairns: 'Charlie's Houff', 'Grove' and 'Eiger's Glen', but I have never been able to locate any of those places, though there still is a farm of the name Eiger's Glen.

Lendrum may not be known for past history and ancient battles, but it is now famous for its white cow. Once we had the car, I had all sorts of jobs given me: up to Huntly for parts for the binder or to the knackery with a dead calf or to the smiddy to get something welded. One day on a visit to the blacksmith's, where there were usually a few others gathered, in the general conversation the Turra Coo was mentioned. Immediately, a picture came to mind of my granny's kitchen dresser on which stood an ornament: a white milk jug in the shape of a cow. On one side the words 'From Leek to Lendrum' were printed and on the other side, 'The Turra Coo'. My interest was aroused and soon I had the full story.

The years have passed so quickly. Before David returned from Cyprus, Ena had married and was herself a mother. The two younger boys were at Turriff School with Robin ready to leave. As a result of his experience of guerrilla warfare, David came back with shattered

184

nerves and it took him some time to adjust. In fact, he was never the same placid lad that he had been before.Having been chauffeur to a Colonel he thought he would like a driving job, but his applications to bus companies were not successful. When each of the children had gone to school they had opened a Savings Bank account, paying in small sums each week. When David joined the army, he made me a weekly allowance out of his pay which was doubled when he went abroad on active service. I had added all this to his bank account, along with a bonus he had been paid upon discharge and it all came to a useful sum, though not enough to start him up in a business. He was now too old to start an apprenticeship to any of the trades; farming and army life were all he knew and, with the latter, he was rather disenchanted. Perhaps if Robin had not taken his place on the farm, he would have settled into his old routine. It was suggested that we might try for a bigger farm, but nothing came on the market. Eventually, he found a tractor driver's job locally, bought himself a second-hand car and met Isabella. Later, when they were married, he joined her on the payroll of Tait's paper mills in Inverurie where he has been ever since.

I would have liked it very much if at least one of the boys had tried another way of life. At that time, like most mothers, I thought that a school teacher, doctor or minister had a much better lifestyle. And yet did he? My own ambitions had come so abruptly to an end, yet now I would not have any other way of life.

Robin never seemed to have any doubts about what he intended to do. After he left school, he applied for a grant and for two years attended the Agricultural College at Craibstone on a daily basis, with an occasional fortnight or three weeks in residence. Robin's first love was sheep. We had only a very small flock, about thirty ewes, consisting mostly of Greyfaces, a breed between the Blackface and Leicester, but we were not fastidious on pedigree, and it all happened from a very haphazard and humble beginning. We started with a pair of 'sickies' that I had reared and from which I would not part. They had done a bit of wandering, getting into a neighbour's field, and they got themselves pregnant. A ewe and a pair of lambs were added out of a travelling flock of sheep that used to come around in the spring to feed on surplus turnips, and a few more from a consignment of lambs bought at the market for feeding purposes - among them some Shetland ewe lambs. From such beginnings, a flock of just over thirty ewes was built up. At this time, all sheep were just sheep to me but, once I got interested, I did a lot of reading and questioning until I could distinguish between ewes and tups, gimmers and hoggs and shearlings. Then there was all the confusion of the different breeds and crosses required to produce a small compact lamb which would provide succulent chops.

How lovely a sight it is to see, on a bright spring morning, a green, lush field filled with ewes and those gambolling, white, fleecy lambs. Not such a pleasure, however, caring for ewes having lambs in a snow storm and digging the poor creatures out of huge snow drifts. Most sheep owners had an organised lambing season but ours were just left to nature and our lambs often began to arrive in January, a month which mostly brought big snow storms. During January, the Teuchar Howe was notorious for snow blocked roads, and for all the eighteen years we lived there I cannot remember a single year when we were not cut off several times, often for two or three weeks at a time. I am almost sure our climate is changing, for the present winters bear no semblance to my childhood memories. I do remember those snowstorms through the eyes of a child; I recall snow piled high on walls and pathways which were dug to the peat stack and chicken house, and a shovel kept in the porch just in case we had to dig ourselves out.

The biggest storm I recall occurred in the winter of 1942, just before we came to Greeness. It took April winds to disperse the last of it. Memories still remain of other storms of the 1940s and 1950s, with long weeks of blocked roads. Ivan and the boys would go off to fetch food supplies for man and beast, and that was when Daisy came into her own, hitched to a sledge, while the tractor stayed put in the shed. There were weary treks over snow-covered fields to feed poultry and up to meet the postman, who trekked up to the shop making sure the mail got through. There are sad memories too: a neighbour, Mrs Skene, died during one of those storms. The funeral had to be postponed for more than a week and only then took place after the coffin was pulled down through the fields to the main road on a sledge.

Other, happier memories come to mind: long evenings toasting our toes before a roaring fire, a purring cat seated nearby and a dog stretched her length in deep contentment beside our feet on the fireside rug. Ivan would be in his armchair, perhaps asleep, and the two boys would be enjoying a game of draughts, or perhaps squabbling over a jig-saw puzzle. I have nostalgic memories of a fast and furious snowball fight. As few pupils could make it through the snow, Mr Rankin usually closed the school at mid-day and, dinner over, our two boys disappeared outside and took up positions fortified by piles of snowballs. Coming out from his dinner break, Ivan had walked into the firing line, but he decided to enter into the fray and give them some of their own medicine. Later, when I emerged on my way to the byre for dinner-time milking, I encountered the crossfire. I could see Robin's cheeky face peering round the end of the milkhouse with an arm extended. The snowball found its target right on his father's forehead and knocked his bonnet off. About the same time a snowball hit the back of my neck with some force. A split second before the ball hit Ivan, he caught a glimpse of me and, thinking I had thrown it, floundered through the snow and proceeded to rub my face in it, and push more down my back. Much to the boys amusement, I then managed to plonk the milk pail over Ivan's head, though it soon got thrown off. With squeals and shouts of laughter,the battle now took on new dimensions, the boys on one side and Ivan and I on the other. The boys, more agile and with stacks of ammunition, were soon on the winning side. Edging down towards the byre, I was glad to find myself near the door and quickly stepped inside. They must have moved round to the back of the barn, for soon the noise died away and, shortly afterwards, Ivan quietly slipped the milk pail into the byre and disappeared. On my way back to the house I found his cap still lying trampled into the snow. I knew he had been back to the house for another one, for Ivan would never be outside without a bonnet.

The fields of Redbriggs gave the boys gentle slopes to sledge on, but the favourite was down the road, past the house and, nothing daunted, to the bridge where they sometimes landed in the burn. All sorts of objects were commandeered for sledges, but the favourite was a kitchen tray. Robin got friendly with one of our nearest neighbours, George Blake, and, whenever he was lost, we knew we could find him up at Ewebrae. George was very good to the little lad and very handy with his hands, much more so than Ivan. He made Robin a small barrow which became one of his most treasured toys and, when he was bigger, he made a sledge for him which travelled with us to Bankhead, though Robin was long past the age for sledging.

Those interludes of snow were a break, but it was always a relief to get back to the usual routine. When the snow came in the short days of December and January, one could enjoy a long cosy evening by the fireside but, once the longer days of March and April came, there was an urge to get moving and I longed to see the snow disappear. Yet in a way, long periods of fields covered in snow did the ground good, protecting it from the frosty winds and, in the spring, crops seemed to grow better.

The land on Redbriggs was slowly improving and responding to Ivan's care and hard work. We were able to graze a greater number of cattle and the corn yard had expanded, often being full with ricks built in odd corners of the fields. We were well fed and clothed but had no money in the bank; the struggle to make ends meet was still with us. We owned the farm and improvements to the buildings were becoming a necessity. With the increase of stock we found the barn a bit cramped. The door which a horse and cart could use were too small for tractor and bogie. Newer and easier methods of rearing cattle were also coming to the fore making the old type of building obsolete. Most houses as well as having water inside, had new bathrooms. Grants were being given by the government to allow those improvements and our thoughts began to turn to other things as well: an extra cattle court, or a large storage building with bigger doors would be handy. My ambition was to have hot water and plenty of it, for so far I had not got round to dreams of a bathroom. All the paraphernalia of application forms were filled up and our hopes were high when in due course an official came to inspect. What went wrong I don't know, but we were turned down. Maybe the fact that the farm was unable to show enough profit to justify the extra expense was a deciding factor. Although a grant of between 50 to 95 percent was given, the farmer had to provide the rest and carry out all improvements to a certain standard. In our circumstances, it would have been a hardship but we had overcome greater ones and had been prepared to take the risk. Our dreams were put away and we did what we could. An extension where more sheaves could be stored was built over the end door of the barn. The outside door ran the full length, a decided improvement enabling the tractor to reverse in and tip the load. Visions of a back boiler, which would have given me an ample supply of hot water had to be discarded, but an electric geyser was fitted over the sink. With this I had to be content. I did, however, get new fireplaces in both the living and front rooms.

At this time, my own health began to cause me some concern. Since the birth of David, when events went so drastically wrong, the two subsequent births and being into my forties, age began to make itself felt. Nearly all my life I had been subject to backache and can remember Dr Tommy saying rather scathingly, "Oh you women - your sore backs," so that when I did see him, I never mentioned I had a bad back. The attacks became more frequent and for days and sometimes a week at a time, I was laid out flat. I often found it a struggle to keep going and my interest in things began to flag, but on the whole the workload had dropped considerably. Some Christmas poultry, such as cockerels, turkeys and geese we hand-reared, but the chickens were now bought as day-old pullets and even sometimes at 'point of lay'. No mashes had to be mixed now, all we fed was corn and pellets. The boiler was still put on for the pigs, but only once or twice a week. The biggest labour saving was in the calf rearing. Two or three cows were now used, each rearing four calves throughout her lactation which greatly reduced the hand-milking. The tractor made life easier for Ivan for the boys used it to do the heaviest work. I still hoped to persuade Sandy to stay on at school, but farm work was all both he and Robin seemed to be interested in.

On one occasion I'd had a particularly bad attack of backache, and the doctor had been called in. He decided that an operation might perhaps put things right and I was put on the hospital waiting list. Here again something went wrong. Time passed with no call. I admit I was often depressed. Then one day Dr Tommy was passing Redbriggs and remembered. He never knocked on doors just walked in, took a look at me and suddenly said, "You've never been to hospital have you"? I shook my head and he came across and plonked me into Ivan's armchair, made a perfunctory examination and shaking his head, told me I had been a bad girl. When I had been feeling like this I should have gone down to see him. He had no idea what had happened to the hospital appointment. He said he would see to it immediately and within a week I had a summons to attend. Ten days was all I expected to be away but it was six weeks till I saw the farm again because after the operation I had a relapse. It was my first time in hospital but I found it quite enjoyable and made a lot of friends. I had to take a lot of teasing for one night a doctor dressed in his pyjamas had appeared by my bedside and given them a thrill, but it was a thrill I missed out on.

At home they had muddled along pretty well without me. Our neighbour, Mrs. Wilson had been good to them - cooking and taking their meals over. Robin had left school and, it being the summer term, Sandy had been at home too. No one ever said so, but I got the vague impression that I had been missed; it was really nice to have some VIP treatment. I who always hated getting up in the morning, was now allowed to lie a-bed and was provided with a cup of tea, a habit that Ivan began and faithfully carried out for many years. I had no breakfast to get, no early morning milking of cows, nor calves to feed, and only the afternoon feeding of poultry. It took some time to get back to my normal routine, and I took full advantage of it. It seemed to be a period of standing still, a peaceful interlude when time itself stood still. Ivan and I started to communicate again. I let things slide and lie dormant and there were no arguments. Those black moods of Ivan's that overshadowed our lives were less in evidence. I read a lot and around this time sent away for a correspondence course in history. I'd had a previous one which had given me great pleasure and I had also enjoyed one on Greek mythology and bible knowledge. Another correspondence course, in English, had helped Ena when she first started her nursing career. There are now so many facilities for people to broaden and improve their status but at that time, except for evening classes, there were few ways to improve your education. This course led me to much more and deeper reading. My passion for local history has brought much colour and pleasure into my life. Lying around somewhere are boxes of written material, for always I had to get a story's facts down on paper. Someday I must have a big bonfire.

Television entered our lives around the year 1957. Few of our neighbours had sets but there was one up at the schoolhouse. Ivan had been in league with Mr Spence of Turriff again. He had supplied our first wireless and it was he who supplied our first television. I misfitted Ivan over this and went 'uppish'. I went 'ben the hoose' and refused for a long time to come through and view. With Ena being married, we had a spare bedroom for visitors. The bed in the front room was taken down, a new wallpaper put on the walls and after careful saving I was able to get two new armchairs and a bed settee which would still come in handy if another bed was required. A rug was bought for the hearth and here the television was installed. This meant that Ivan had to take off his boots and put on his slippers. He did not approve and called it a lot of nonsense. I can also recall being annoyed at the boys who, when they came home from school, pitched their bags into a corner beside the dresser, took off their boots (they would not have dared do otherwise) and made a bee-line for the other room. The set was switched on and down they sat, eyes glued to the screen and all their chores forgotten. It is now all taken for granted, but what a marvellous thing it is, taking people and places into our homes right from the other side of the world.

On one occasion our neighbour Mrs Wilson came across to watch the Christmas day broadcast. When it was over we had a quick cup of tea and the boys and I then got into the old grey Singer car and set off to Little Byth for our usual Christmas day visit. Ever since we had got a car this had been our routine. Ivan had the cattle to feed and cows to milk so it was seldom he was able to join us; it was just a little treat for the boys and me. Presents had been carefully selected and wrapped; we always tried to get something for each of the family and something for everyone to share (usually a box of sweets, and a big current loaf which was Porter's the Cuminestown bakers' Christmas speciality). Ina always had a table laden with good things, especially her home-baked sausage rolls.. A week later, two or three younger members of the Little Byth family cycled up to Redbriggs to have their New Year's dinner. The menu never varied much - broth, chicken stuffed with oatmeal and served with vegetables. A dumpling was next, followed by 'tipsy trifle', a sweet made of sponge, fruit and jelly with some sherry, or perhaps something stronger, poured over it. New Year was always a holiday and a time for absent members of the family to get home. Parties were held with music and dancing and on the stroke of midnight drinks were served, toasting the New Year in. Then it was away on first footing expeditions, getting merrier as the night progressed. Morning usually found them asleep in someone else's house. Then they would wake up and often the high jinks began all over again. For those who, like us, had animals to attend to, there were problems but often the women folk had to tackle those jobs. The New Year dinner suffered too for often after a night of gambolling there was little appetite.

This year, I had prepared most of my New Year's dinner the day before. A dumpling was placed at the fireside bink to keep hot. The young folk from Little Byth had arrived, and when our neighbour John Gorden came to call he found Margaret, Ena's cousin, seated in the armchair beside the fire. Mistaking her for Ena he began to tease the lass but he spied the dumpling and suddenly snatching it up he made for outside. I followed shouting for him to come back, but making their way up through the courtyard, man and dumpling disappeared between two ricks. Sad to say, that was the last I saw of my dumpling. It was all such innocent fun but now those Hogmanay capers, like my dumpling, have disappeared and Christmas is celebrated more - celebrations and present-giving that to me have gone all out of context. It used to be a happy time, especially with children, giving small simple presents to mark with joy our Saviour's birthday. The true spirit of Christmas has now almost vanished, commercialised by shops and families competing with each other for the most expensive toys.

Although Redbriggs was, in one sense, an alien place to me, looking back many blessings were given us. Our children grew up there, an ordinary, healthy, well-balanced lot, giving us much happiness. The land, which we now owned, was producing more than double its output of former years, but as the nineteen-fifties were coming to a close, the urge was upon us to move on. Getting another and bigger farm did occupy our thoughts for, though we had no spare money, it could be borrowed. We were well stocked but our biggest asset was that we had two young lads keen and eager to have a go.

Ivan was easy, but their mother was determined they should have a chance. Many farms came on the market, many places were visited and many offers were made, but someone else always made a better offer.

At the end of 1959 Sandy left the school and our endeavours to find a larger farm intensified. We visited many far and near, at Corsegight, New Deer, one at Strichen and another at Badenscoth in the Auchterless district called Linnshie. I had greatly liked that one and we made an offer but much to our disappointment the owner decided not to sell. Another farm, in the district of Easterfield near the distillery of Glenrothis had been on the solicitor's books for some time and we were offered it at a bargain price, about £7000. After a visit we agreed on a price and an offer was made. Somehow, nothing was definitely settled and as the weeks dragged on, extras were added and the price moved up. This happened twice and then, realizing we were being led up the garden path, we withdrew our offer. It was not sold till almost two years later.

Also in late February 1960, the farm and lands of Bankhead and Waulkmill in the parish of Auchmedden came on the market. Here the Michie family had a connection and we knew the farm. I recalled a visit we had made in the first year of our marriage to a cousin of Ivan's, James Laird. He had talked of his boyhood on the farm. Particulars were sent for and a visit arranged. Ivan drove the big blue Zephyr. Robin had been unable to come but Sandy and Ivan's brother Cecil were with us. We came through the village at Aberdour and took the road down towards the sea, a road I had often been on with a carload of children on our way to picnic on the beach. Turning left at the Mill farm, we left the main road and took a narrow hidden road leading down into a den, not much more than a glorified horse track. We crossed the small bridge which spanned the Dour and then proceeded to climb upwards. Here Ivan began to lose his nerve and suddenly, coming to a double bend like the notorious Devil's Elbow, the engine of the car stalled. Although he had never driven the car (he was only fifteen), Sandy came to his father's rescue and managed to bring us safely up to the farm, climbing all the time. Viewed from the bottom it looked very high up indeed but the farm lies only about two hundred and fifty feet above sea level. Accustomed to Redbriggs which was situated on a main road, we'd had little or no experience of such roads. At first it did cause us some concern but as we got used to it, it became a family joke. The old road had once been part of a main road between Fraserburgh and Banff. A milestone can still be found about half-way denoting that you are eight miles from Fraserburgh. A stage coach carrying the royal mail had run here and it was also used by the Pennan people to carry their dead for burial in the nearby kirkyard of St. Drostans.

Arriving safely at the farmyard close, we were welcomed by a very large man. Brownie was one of the ugliest I have ever seen but he proved to be one of the nicest people I have ever met, a gentle giant with a heart of gold. He seemed pleased to see us and first took us to a spot in a nearby field where he said a part of each field on the farm could be seen. By the way he talked, I could sense he loved the place very much and some of it, even on that first day, gave me a feeling of enchantment. The men then set off to view the steading and tour the fields while I was taken to the house and handed over to Mrs Brownie. She was seated at a nice fire in a room which they were using both as sitting room and bedroom. She did not look very pleased to see me and seemed annoyed when her niece asked her to show me over the house. It turned out to be a pure farce. First I was taken through into the front hall, and opening a door on the left but keeping hold of the door, she allowed me only a brief glimpse inside, just long enough to see a bed and two windows, one of which had the shutters closed. She quickly closed the door and moved over and opened the door on her right. I edged in front of her and was able to have a better view. It was quite a big room but empty. She again shut the door, making the remark that they never used it and turning round she went back down the hall and up the stairs. Here on the landing were four doors. The procedure of downstairs was repeated. She opened two of the doors and let me have a peep in. One room was completely empty and the other had a bed and a chair. I learned later, that during the lambing time Mr Brownie took up his sleeping quarters here and brought the ewes into the garden which was surrounded by a large stone wall. Outside the window he pegged up a light which lit all the garden. All he had to do was get out of bed, switch on the light and from the window he could see if all was well.

If there were any lambing problems he could go out; if all was well it was lights out and back to bed.

After she had shut the door, saying only that the other two doors were a small bedroom and cupboard, she went downstairs. Naturally, I expected to be taken over the rest of the house, but she went back to the sitting room and her niece came in with tea. There was little enchantment here, for it was badly neglected in terms of creature comforts and decorative art, but I was not dismayed for it was a fine old building which held all sorts of possibilities. Later when I complained, the menfolk pointed out that the house did not bring in any money.

The visit led to an offer of purchase. The land was good, providing both heavy cereals and grass crops. The road was a big drawback and one part next to the sea had high dangerous rocks forming a part of the boundary, which was a hazard for cattle and sheep. Few things are perfect and as the saying goes, "there's aye a something".

Mr Brownie had come to Bankhead as a tenant and about the same time as we had bought Redbriggs, he had become the owner. When asked about the price he refused to comment, saying it was up to each individual to decide what it was worth. A date was fixed for offers and none was to be opened till twelve o'clock on that day. Then, providing the person who offered the biggest price was suitable, it would be his. Thus all were treated alike. Well I remember the day it was to be decided. Ivan and I set out for Turriff, left the car at the station as usual, and walked up through the pleasure park to the town. It was ten o'clock and we had two hours before we were due at the solicitor's office but I had no interest in the shops that day and kept with Ivan. It was nearly twelve o'clock and we were on our way to the solicitor's office when we met Ivan's brother Alec who greeted us with the words: "Fit a drop. I've just heard a fermer fae Byth has got Bankhead". It was still not twelve o'clock and I was rather sceptical. Oh, but he was sure as he had heard the farmer himself say he had got it. As we continued on our way to Stewart & Watson's, Ivan got a bit despondent but in the back of my mind I was almost sure that Bankhead would be ours. It was barely twelve o'clock when Mr Purdie burst into the waiting room, beaming all over, and vigorously shaking our hands said: "Congratulations - we've got it."

195

CHAPTER TWELVE

TO THE FERMTOUN - BANKHEAD

IT WAS the month of May, apple-blossom time, in the year nineteen-hundred and sixty when the Michies came to Bankhead and made it their dwelling place. Never in our wildest dreams had Ivan and I dreamt we would own a large farm and three hundred acres. We had come, in twenty-eight years, from the cottar house at Fridayhill to this - a place of delight and full of history going back to 579 A.D. when Drostan landed on the shore of Aberdour Bay. He and his monks taught the Picts how to dig and grow food. I like to believe that the farm had its beginnings then.

It certainly goes back to 1702 when John Gordon, a respected elder of the Kirk, held the tenancy and in 1834, one Robert Walker donated a hundred pounds to aid the poor of the parish according to 'The Church of Aberdour', by the Rev Wm Crammond writing on the statistical accounts of the St. Drostan Church.

Reading the stones within the precincts of the old church, I was able to piece together some more of Bankhead's history. A family of Murcars had followed the Walkers. Both Walkers and Murcars were also connected with Waulkmill. That was once a woollen mill with a croft of a few acres of land adjoining Bankhead and lying down near the shore. From around 1722, perhaps earlier, the croft and mill were run by the Walker family. First mentioned was James, who died at Waulkmill in 1800 aged ninety-three. He had a brother called George who died four years later. Both left sons, James and Robert respectively. James was followed at Waulkmill by his son Peter who was born in 1782 and died in 1869. A rather quaint epitaph describes Peter: "He lived in single blessedness at Waulkmill for nearly seventy years, a pattern of contentment, admired and loved by all who knew him." The Mill had been a thriving business and a big asset to the Aberdour district. One of its best customers must have been the Rev Andrews Youngson who was the Minister from 1766 to 1800. He was twice married and had a family of eight sons and one daughter.

Bankhead as it was when we moved in

In 1784, when Peter was only two, a terrible disaster took place at Waulkmill. A family of the name of Torrie lived there, and Thomas was employed as a dyer. The winter of 1783-1784 had come early, with successive days of wind and rain followed in January with snow throughout the whole month. Back came the rain in February causing the landslide. At ten o'clock in the morning of 8th March 1784, all the workers in the mills were busy when the first rumble occurred. (Mrs Walker, busy with her household chores and attending to baby Peter, may have heard it, but being accustomed to the sea and the noise of machinery payed no attention.) On rushing out, they were confronted with falling stones and rubble. At once all eyes were drawn to the hillside where the Torrie's cottage stood; nothing but a big black mound of earth met their eyes. In those days they had only spades, shovels and manpower, so it took hours to dig through the high mound of earth only to find Mrs. Torrie, the baby and a young maid-servant dead. It is thought that when the first fall took place they had come out to see what was happening and had been caught in the avalanche. There is now no trace of the cottage and no one can tell where it once stood.

The woollen mill must have closed during Peter's lifetime and both he in Waulkmill and Robert in Bankhead were followed by people of the name of Murcar. By coincidence, Robert's second wife was a Murcar though where the connection came in, I am not sure. I am told that the tenants of both places were brothers and between the Walkers and Murcars they totalled up more than two hundred years of farming. Next, in this century, came the Lairds who were related to Ivan through marriage and by then both places were joined together and the mill house at Waulkmill was used for a cottar house to Bankhead. They stayed into the late 1930s and were followed by a Bell from Tyrie Mains who farmed only for seven years. John Bell was in turn followed by Brownie, a shoemaker from Fraserburgh. He, as a boy, had often come to the farm on holidays. Being about the same age as one of the Laird boys at Fraserburgh School, they had struck up a friendship. He had loved the farm and when the chance came, he sold his business and took over at Bankhead. Here he laboured for eighteen years, never losing his love for the land and in 1947, when part of the Auchmedden estate was broken up, he became the owner. He had no family to follow and only ill health and advancing years made him give up. On the day that the offers closed, he came on the phone to us at Redbriggs and said how pleased he was that we were to take it over. Of all those who had made him offers, he had thought we might be the best. This in itself was a compliment, and in all the transactions that followed we found him a gentleman to do business with. His name was George Brownie, but all and sundry called him Brownie, a name I think suited him. He was no great talker but once

198

you got him going, he was well-read and could converse on almost any subject with a delightful and singular sense of humour.

It was almost the end of March when the purchase of Bankhead was complete, so we had only weeks to organise the flitting and the sale of Redbriggs. A few came to view but there was no flood of offers. In fact we only got one genuine offer from one of our neighbours who wished to add it to his farm. During the coming summer, a nephew of Ivan's was to be married and his brothers decided they would buy it for him. They only offered £4000, the same sum as our neighbour, but beggars can't be choosers and we accepted. Twelve years before we had purchased it for £900. We had now bought Bankhead for £10,000.

Ivan enjoyed an outing to a roup, more so if he was able to get bargains. I very seldom went to one, for seeing what had been gathered together by hard work scattered far and wide, was heartbreaking. In the spring before a roup took place, the seed for the cereal crops had to be sown and when the crops were ripe they were valued for the new occupier. The work finished, all implements were cleaned, repaired or given a coat of paint in readiness for the great day. The roup at Bankhead was held one day at the end of April. Anything for which it was difficult to get a bid was often knocked down to the incoming owner and Ivan acquired quite a lot of odds and ends. Our first priority was stock. When coming from the fertile land at Millbrex to the poor soil of Redbriggs, our stock had been ample but here at Bankhead it was the other way round. With the extra acres that grew heavy crops, we needed to more than double our stock. Ivan was able to purchase four cows with calves at foot and a few ewes and lambs, but when the items of machinery were added to them it came to quite a sum of money. I was horrified and angry words were exchanged, but it all ran off Ivan as water from a duck's back.

We were not entitled to move into the farm till the 28th of May but we did have access to the land. Again it was worked on a seven-year rotation. The field due to return to grass had to be undersown with grass seed by us. Soon after the sale, a bogie was loaded up with implements and the boys went down with a tractor to get the potatoes in. They had to be fetched home at night and this required courage on my part, but putting the car into first gear and going slowly I was able to negotiate the braes and bends without mishap. Brownie told me that I would get accustomed to it. Being used to the good road at Redbriggs, however, it did take some time.

The flitting took us about a week. When Brownie left, a good week before the term, our boys moved in. The cattle and sheep came down first, joining the ones that had been bought at the sale. At that time we had only about a dozen cows suckling calves and just two hand-milked cows, Whitey and Rhonie. Whitey was an almost white Fresian with just a few black spots and was the calf I had bought from Douglas Panton for ten shillings. Rhonie was a cross Shorthorn. Both cows were real characters, very good milkers and very affectionate. Rhonie had a bad habit: if a cow calved in the field beside her she always went and claimed the calf, making a real nuisance of herself. On the morning she was to be taken to her new home, Whitey disgraced herself for, when being loaded on to the transport, she did her best to escape. Finding herself cornered, she then lay down on the ramp and no amount of coaxing would get her up. She had to be lifted and manhandled on to the lorry. Daisy, our one and only horse, also decided not to leave Redbriggs. Ivan coaxed her with tit-bits but to no avail. She snatched them but refused to walk the plank. In the end Robin put a sack over her head, then hauling with a rope and pushing from behind, it took several men to get her loaded. Neither animal had ever been in a float.

There were another thirty cattle and forty sheep to be transferred. Robin had gone down with the first load of twenty animals and later told how the driver reacted when he came to the Mill farm and was directed down the narrow road into the howe. He said, "Nivver!"

"Oh, aye", said Robin, "that's the ferm at the top o' the hill." Seeing there was nothing else to do, he proceeded to take the motor down into the den and then climb up the steep hill. He reached the farm without saying a word and Robin directed him into one of the grass fields, which he negotiated successfully. Robin immediately got out and went round to the back of the lorry to help the driver open the door. No driver appeared and Robin, going back to see what had happened, found him very sick, slumped over the wheel. Taking the lorry up the road had been too much for him.

The last of our stock were the 600 hens and their houses. Giles from Fyvie, who had been our grocer and was also a poultry dealer, came to transport the birds on his lorry which was fitted with open net boxes. The hens were going to be housed in a brand new deep-litter shed. It had become the thing to keep poultry in that way before battery cages. Electric lights were fitted to go on and off at certain times; extra hours of light gave the hens the idea it was always summer and they provided eggs all through November and the winter months. This kept our income steady all year round. When the snow was on the ground and the howling winter winds blew from the North, it was certainly far more comfortable for woman, man and hens when it came round to feeding time. Water and automatic feeders were also fitted and only required filling once in two days though the eggs were collected daily. It really was the beginning of the end for small poultry farmers. Firms began to expand into very big units and from the deep-litter system; the houses were fitted instead with cages for each individual hen. Here the hen lives out her miserable short life, automatically fed and watered, laying her eggs on a conveyor belt which transports them on to a collection point. To me, to keep hens that way was a horrible practice. I still keep a few hens in the old deep-litter house, but they have the freedom to come and go as they please. It's a delight to see them around the farm, scratching away happily and keeping us and a few friends in eggs.

I had arranged by phone that the lorry drivers and all who were helping were to get a mid-day meal at the Beach House, which at one time had been the manse, but had recently been turned into a hotel. I returned to the bare and desolate kitchen, all empty except for a box standing on the floor which was to hold the breakfast dishes, a teapot and a small brown enamelled kettle, and a box of bread which, along with the tablecloth, was, piled on the windowsill. The lorry for the last of our furniture had arrived early and taken us by surprise. I had still had a few items to pack and would not be able to join the men in time for their meal, nor was I particularly wanting to do so. I could still manage to make myself a cup of tea but I had no cooker or electric kettle, just the brown one which I could boil on the fire. That was still burning and with a little more kindling I soon got the kettle on the boil. As I sat on the box enjoying my last cup of tea, you might think I was feeling sad, yet after eighteen years at Redbriggs I felt no regrets at leaving. I was filled with happy excitement and a feeling that I was going home. I'd had the feeling from the very first contact that we belonged together, Bankhead and I.

The big blue Ford Zephyr was standing in the close, packed full, but I hoped I would get this one last box into the boot, and then I had to find two cats which were coming with us. I had a sack with string handy. They were usually around the door, though with all the steer of the last few days they had grown scared. I knew where I would find them, however, down in the byre and I had little difficulty in getting Blackie and Darkie into the sack. They did protest rather loudly at the treatment from one who usually handled them kindly. As I came back to the car I looked back and saw our other cat, a big black and white Tom, seated on a bank in the small field below the steading. A faint twinge of guilt passed over me for he was being deserted - no more would he be finding dishes of food or creamy milk awaiting him in the byre. He had been a stray that had come to the place some time ago and taken up residence. We soon learned he was a considerable thief and when he came around the house door, he was usually greeted with the sweep of the brush.

Twice at least he had brought my wrath down upon his head. Some friends had been coming to supper and, before I had gone down to milk, I had laid the table, opened a tin of salmon and put portions on each of the plates. This was to have been a special treat for we very seldom had salmon. No-one was in the house and I carefully shut the door as I went out. Half an hour later as I opened the door, the big black brute shot past me. I could not believe my eyes when I saw the table: nothing was touched except the plates and each one of them was clean and polished with not a scrap of salmon to be seen. The other time, the fishman had called and I had bought a fine big yellow Finnan haddie, a favourite of mine which we seldom had. Coming back in, I met the black cat coming out carrying my lovely fish in his mouth. How he got into the milk-house was a mystery. Hoping he would drop it I gave chase. No such luck. He disappeared in below a railway carriage; I could see him quite well guzzling my lovely haddock but all I could do was hurl abuse at him.

The couple who were taking over Redbriggs were to be married in June but not taking up residence till later, as a bathroom was to be added along with some other alterations. Tom therefore would be on his own but he survived quite well, as I was later told of some more of his thieving escapades.

I managed to pack the bags with the two cats into a small space in the back seat of the car. Before I locked the door I had a last look round but there were no lingering goodbyes. I was ready to go. On opening the car door I was greeted with plaintive mews. I spoke to them and gave them a pat or two but then to my dismay the two began to fight. Can you imagine the confusion that can be caused with two cats fighting inside a bag? I had no idea where I could find another sack - then I had a flash of inspiration. Packed into the car were the blankets, sheets and pillowcases from our bed; a pillow slip would do. With some nasty scratches and a great deal of patience I was able to get Blackie into the pillow slip. I cut the string in two and it served both bags. I learned that day never to put two cats into one bag.

The weather was lovely, reminding me of the day when Ivan and I first set out together for our new home at Fridayhill. I liked being in the car alone, for sometimes my family were a bit critical of my driving and it was nice to be able to put my foot down and feel the power without being told I was going too fast.

Down the Teuchar Howe, up through Cuminestown and New Byth then away towards the sea. The road leads up through the Den of Glasslaw and on towards Cowfords, then it comes to a long stretch of road that does something to me.

It happened that day. Down went my foot and the car picked up speed. It was not that road I saw before me, but another winding over the hills. I started to hum a few bars of an old tune then broke into song:

White in the moonlight, the long road lies
that leads me to my home.

There was more but I can't remember it. It was over in a minute and I was back on the real road but feeling very happy. There I met Giles' float returning with empty crates and knew my flock of birds had been delivered safely. Soon we passed through the village where several people were standing around in the street. Some would be beginning to recognize the blue Zephyr and would be saying, "There goes the wifie from Bankies."

Turning left at the church, round the corner, there spread before us was a lovely view of the sea. I can well remember the first time I saw it. I was but a child of around twelve and had come to the school picnic; for most of us it was our very first sight of the sea. It was also the first time the school children had travelled in a bus for such an event. At that time, the road down to the sea shore was little more than a track, and the bus could go no further than the church at the top of the street. We all scrambled out and our disappointment was great when we could see no sight of water. Once we were organised into lines and marched round the corner, the Bay of Aberdour lay before us in all its sparkling beauty.

I was now almost home, for the road to Bankhead turned off at Mill Farm, and just as I approached the bend, I looked up and saw the lorry with the hen houses climbing up the brae. They must have stopped at the Beach House for a meal and were only now delivering. I drew the car into the side and waited. That would allow a clear road for me to get up. Watching the lorry climb up the brae it did look very steep, and loaded with hen houses it looked so top heavy that it could easily topple over. I began to understand why the young lad had been sick.

When I arrived, the lorry was being manoeuvred into the dam park where they were to unload the hen houses. None of the men saw the car but the dogs did. They had been down with the boys for the last few days. Just before I stopped the car I had caught a glimpse of pink flowers on a tree, and back I went to view it. My reward was the lovely sight of an old apple tree covered in pink and white blossom. To this day I always think of this season as apple-blossom time.

It may have been apple-blossom time outside, but here in the kitchen at Bankhead it was winter indeed. When last the uneven rough cement floor had seen a scrubbing brush and water, was anyone's guess. Uneven walls, plaster broken with big holes and distempered in a depressing shade of brown, made me shudder. The fire was out and in the sink were the boys' breakfast dishes and those of the night before.

The gas cooker was fitted and my old dresser, along with the meal girnel, was up against one wall. In the middle of the floor stood an old table with some chairs that Brownie had left and I wondered where my own table was. Looking at all this, some of the joy of the morning departed but then I looked up and saw the rafters and all else was forgotten. They were oak and, although black with age and smoke, they were beautiful. I learned later that they had come off a boat, a wreck that had been taken in for breaking up. They had been there for at least two hundred years. The kitchen and four other rooms had once been the original farmhouse and the front part had not been built till the late 1890s. Looking up at the beams, I thought how lovely they would be if they were polished but alas that ambition has not been fulfilled. It is strange that after all this time salt marks still appear on the wood in between. I was once told that if I had these rafters taken out and sold I would get enough money to pay for a new kitchen.

Both front rooms were packed with furniture and boxes. Our bedroom had the furniture in but the bed had still to be put up, which reminded me I had our blankets in the car and I'd best get them unpacked. I found Blackie had got herself out and was now seated on the pillow slip, grooming herself and showing no signs of being in unfamiliar surroundings. Still, I would have to find somewhere to shut them up till they settled down. Cats and dogs are so different. A dog is happy to go where its master is, but cats are not so attached to humans, it is the place they adhere to. I had not been through the steading yet but I soon found a place for my cats. It had once been the shelt's or the clip's house.

The cats disposed of, I unpacked the car. No menfolk had yet appeared so I plugged in the kettle to get hot water for the dishes. I have always hated having dirty dishes lying around. Later, I thought I'd get the fire going; it would be lovely having hot water on tap. The geyser I'd had at Redbriggs had been a Godsend, but it only gave a limited supply. Soon afterwards the men appeared and of course needed tea - I was glad I had washed up for at least I had cups. There were two from the Michie family at Little Byth and our neighbour, Charlie Wilson. He had come down with one of the lorries and now needed a lift home. The others were going much the same way so offered him a lift which he gladly accepted.

Little more was done that day. The poultry had to be fed but the sorting was left for another day. The cows had to be milked and I had to get used to the new byres. Our bed was put up and the bedroom put to rights. I always remember that, as there were no curtains for the window, Ivan had, to my horror, closed the shutters. They completely covered the window. He got away with it that first night, but I made sure before another night came round that curtains were up.

We had a picnic supper and by this time I had my own table in its rightful place in the kitchen. I was in no mood to do any more. Supper over, Ivan and Sandy disappeared outside but Robin stayed in and he and I went for a tour over the house. First it was up the back stair. It led directly off the kitchen and was part of the old house. The boys had decided that this would be their quarters. It was a wider stair and easier to negotiate than the one at Redbriggs. Many of the steps were quite worn but the landing was spacious with plenty light from a skylight. The rafters were open and the walls bare but what a surprise awaited me on opening the bedroom door: I found quite a big room all lined in a lovely varnished pine wood. What a nice room it would have been if there had been a window with a view down to the sea. The boys had been sleeping there for the past two nights and they had just taken the furniture in and dumped it. To my astonishment, they had acquired a nice big wardrobe. Robin explained it had been left in the room as Brownie thought it was too big to get through the door. We have never put it to the test. I made up their bed and said I'd come back next and put their room to rights, and perhaps find a rug.

I liked the fireplace in the kitchen. It was modern, built into the granite surround, with a back-boiler which gave us plenty of hot water. The oven came in handy to store kindling and many's the chicken, baby duck, turkey chick and even sometimes a lamb, was brought back to life in there. In a recess on the left side was the hot-water tank which was filled by hand. There was also a curious granite stone about two feet high. It stood at the side of the fireplace. I presumed it was a seat but I was told later it was used by the menfolk as an aid to tying their boot laces, thus saving their backs. On taking a closer look I could see that one side of the stone was well worn where the boots had rested. Other such stones were found outside the kitchen or bothy doors. The menfolk at Bankhead believed in tying their 'pints' in comfort.

The house had two back doors: one in use, the other part shut. The one now used for an entrance was actually the door of another building which was attached to the house. The Bells had converted the house to hold two families and had a married cattleman living in the old part. To give them more accommodation, a door had been taken out between the kitchen and this building, which must have been a washhouse or a store, for it had a large loft on top where the water tanks are now kept. The lower room was divided and one part was lined and used for a bedroom. Another small room was also added on the other side of the kitchen, below the back stair. The farmer and his family used the other door, which was fitted into a corner where the milk-house was joined by a small passage to the main building. The family had the other four rooms with the three upstairs bedrooms. When the house reverted back to one family, the old door was closed up and the other used for an entrance, but it was in a straight line with the front door, creating a wind-tunnel.

As we went through the narrow passage from the kitchen, Robin's attention was drawn to a board high up on the wall. It took us some time to figure out that this must have once held bells to summon servants. Another surprise was finding a hatch for passing food from the kitchen to the dining room. That evening I also found another room off the front room - long and narrow, about four feet wide, it had once been a 'ben 'e hoose pantry'. It was lined with shelves for storing food and dishes. The other opening was on the wall of the staircase, a few steps up, but as it had been covered with paint and paper it was some time before we found it. The pantry is now our bathroom. Ah, that bathroom. As we went through the rooms, Robin and I spent a lot of time discussing where it might be. There were two spaces above the small bedroom, and quite a big space between the back of the front bedroom and the wall of the boys' bedroom. To reach this space we had to crawl through a hole in the back of the cupboard. If there had been a window it would have made an ideal bathroom. The floor was all covered with cables and electric wires for it was through here the electricity supply came. We also found a big enamel basin that had been put there to catch drips; we found later that when the wind and rain were in a certain airt, water came in, appearing on the ceiling of our bedroom below. We also found a lot of wires attached to the rafters. Robin made me go downstairs to watch the bell board and right enough, when he pulled, there was movement in the one marked 'bedroom no. 2'.

There were fireplaces in two of the upstairs bedrooms but the last fires there must have been lit by those maids that answered the bells - long, long ago. All the newer parts of the house were well-built and the walls and ceilings very good, but all were in need of paper and paint. I knew that money for this would not be forthcoming and I would have to budget for it myself out of the egg money. I was not too despondent about the state of the house; I loved it and felt that in time I would be able to put it right. I was dismayed by the state of the lobby. From the massive front door to the kitchen were flagstones, some quite broken. How would I ever keep them clean? It would cost a fortune to have them covered, and with what?

The other two had now come in and we all had a cup of tea around the kitchen table, a little conversation, some questions asked and answers given, then the two lads went off upstairs and Ivan went through to his bed. I tidied up and put things out for the breakfast but I felt I must have one last look around.

Quietly, I slipped outside to find it was a lovely evening, that gloaming hour that I loved so well. How sweet and fresh the air, and I could hear the gentle murmur of the sea breaking in waves upon the shore. I disturbed the dogs which were shut up in a house nearby and they set up a crescendo of barking. I called to them by name and told them to be quiet which they instantly obeyed. It was all so lovely and peaceful, and I had a contented feeling that I had now come home. I gave thanks for that which had been given me. Suddenly I was startled by a loud hoot, a sound that I had not heard before and there, quite near on the garden wall, was an owl. I had never seen a live owl but there was no mistaking its round face, short pointed ears and beady eyes, which contemplated me without fear. It was quite near and stayed like that for some time and I was able to admire its feathers. Then, with another eerie hoot, the wings unfolded and, very gracefully, it flew to another part of the garden. I have never seen one again so near but we often heard them around twilight, mostly when we were in bed. Lately I have not heard them at all.

Darkness had now crept in, a few stars twinkled up aloft but still

I stood leaning on the old garden dyke, reluctant to leave that enchanted spot. But tomorrow was calling with all its commitments and I would need my bed. Back then to the house. As I was sure Ivan would be asleep, I did not put on the light, but just as I crawled in beside him, he turned and said, "Far hae ye been? I was thinkin ye was tint".

"Oh, I was just ha'en a look roon", was my reply.

Then in a short interval came the words: "I think we've deen wrang comin here."

I was flabbergasted but all I said was, "Fit wey?"

"The beasts will be fa'in aff the cliffs an gettin killed, an the loons will be coupin the tractors on thae affa braes an gettin killed an a." I had known he was unhappy at leaving Redbriggs but I had never dreamt that he did not view Bankhead as I did. Some of my joy seemed to melt away and a feeling of disquiet took its place. I told him he was an old fool, and then as his arms crept around me, some of the old magic returned and I felt that at least as long as were together all would be well. I slept with the thought that soon he would come to love Bankhead too, but I'm afraid he never did.

CHAPTER THIRTEEN

BANKHEAD -
EARLY DAYS

WHEN WE moved from the crofting community at Millbrex to Greeness, it took us some time to adjust to our new surroundings. We had now climbed another rung in the social ladder and entered into a community of bigger farms. I still had nostalgic memories of our croft and the dear people who had been our neighbours and companions, but the move to Bankhead was the fulfilment of a dream: Ivan's dream, which had become mine.

In a way, we were isolated up on the top of a hill. I had the feeling that we were almost in a world of our own. Our northern boundary was the Moray Firth with a panoramic view of cliffs and a sometimes blue ocean that stretched far into unknown territory. To the east we had the Mill Farm, our nearest neighbours. We could see the fields of other farms and knew when they started to hoe the turnips, or cut hay, or when their fields were ripe for harvesting. Beyond these were Bonnetonhill, Quarryburn, Egypt and others. Still further back was Darra and the village of Rosehearty. This was quite a view, but it was distant and remote.

Coming round to the south we faced a hill, 'the Knocker', at the foot of which was the farm of Warelands. On the skyline, the church and the houses of the north end of New Aberdour were silhouetted. How lovely and pleasant it was on a Sunday morning, to hear the church bells pealing across the valley that lay between us, calling and

210

summoning us all to worship. This last year or two they have been silent, which is such a pity. Further to the south and west, two other farms, Towie and Clinterty, formed our boundaries, but both were completely out of sight. Towie was the more remote; the road to Clinterty went up past the bottom of our steading and the family moved up and down quite frequently. In fact, they lived in Fraserburgh and commuted to the farm daily. They did have a sitting room, bedroom and kitchen which were partially furnished and, when necessary, like at lambing and calving time, they stayed overnight. I think Mrs Buchan must have taken up the same attitude as Mrs Brownie did at Bankhead. She said it was fine to come to visit on a bonny day, but she disliked it at other times. They had two sons, the youngest about the same age as Sandy, but farming was a mere sideline to them. They were more concerned with the fishing and had a fleet of lorries for fish transport.

Mrs Black, who later became a dear friend, occupied the Mill Farm. Her husband had died a few years before and she now, with the help of a grieve, carried on the farming business. It took us some time to get acquainted. We often saw her as we passed and would stop for a chat, but it was really butter that buttered our friendship, lovely home-made, creamy butter churned from our own cows' milk. I loved it, but was seldom able to indulge; our milk was all fed to the calves. Some folk reared their calves on skimmed milk, but the finished animals were no match for ours which had swallowed pailfuls of rich creamy milk. When I found out that Mrs Black made butter, I persuaded her to let me have a supply each week and made a point of collecting it myself. Slowly we got acquainted and our esteem for each other grew. It took years to get to know the other neighbours, the Irvines of Warelands and the Bells of Towie.

When new people moved into a district, it was the custom that the minister called and when a farm had a new owner, there was usually a visit from the banker. No one seemed concerned for our souls or our money, for we saw neither for some time. It would have been almost the end of summer before we had a visit from the Reverend Hannah, but we later became very good friends. Although I had gone to the Monquhitter Church quite regularly and the bairns had all attended the Sunday School, Ivan and I had never been members, for Ivan still adhered to his church at Old Deer and would not be moved. When I explained this to Mr Hannah, he understood and said that we would be welcome any time we wished to attend communion at St. Drostan's.

Judging by my attendance at church, some would say I was not a very good Christian, and it is difficult to talk or even write about my beliefs. In my inner heart I knew God was there, and life would have no meaning to me if it were not so. When I think of all the ills that beset mankind in the present day, a great sadness often fills my thoughts. If people would only turn to Christianity and obey its commands, life would become a paradise or as Robbie Burns says: *"man to man the world o'er would brothers be for a' that"*. But, unlike Robbie, I cannot see it coming.

It was nice to be up on the hill all alone, but I did miss the vans. There was only one which still came, a grocer from the village. Being so near a main road at Redbriggs we'd had many more of them than we needed. At the time we came to Bankhead in 1960, the village was very well supplied with shops: there were three grocers, two of whom went out with vans - a butcher and a baker - and there were at least three sweet shops which also sold various other goods. There was a post office, a policeman and also a bank run from Rosehearty which opened on certain days. Now, all but one shop is gone and there is not even a policeman around to protect our interests. There is still a school but it is reduced to junior status and the church survives, but I wonder for how long.

The grocer had been established for some time, was very obliging and could supply almost everything, but having been accustomed to so many vans it was difficult for me to adjust. I did not like having a supply of bread only once a week, nor did I like the postman bringing beef from the butcher, as had been the custom. The grocer came on a Tuesday which was not a handy day to have weekly books and papers delivered. (Ivan had had his daily paper delivered by post ever since we were married.)

I did some thinking and planning. First, I arranged for the grocer to come on a Saturday which took care of our papers. Then I tackled the butcher and baker. Kennedys, the butchers, had quite a big shop in the village and two vans going out and around the countryside. One day, I walked into the shop and asked why he couldn't come up to Bankhead with one of his vans. The road is not all that bad for cars, so I could not see why his van could not do so. He took me by surprise by saying that he had never been asked before. "But if you want me to come to Bankhead, I'll come." So, for many years a supply of good quality beef was delivered to Bankhead twice a week. Filling the bread basket was not so easy. The three grocers in the village all sold bread, but I wanted a fresh delivery twice a week. When I approached the owner of one small shop, I found he was trying to build up a van round. That was fine and I persuaded him to call. He was far from reliable, was often out of bread and it was only a short time before he packed it in. Another took his place and he too soon gave up, but not before he put me in touch with Mitchell and Muill, the bakers who at that time had shops and vans all over the country. For many years their vans made twice-weekly visits up the winding braes to Bankhead.

Selling my eggs was no problem. Brownie had been a member of Buchan Poultry Products and he passed on his membership to me. I supplied ten to twelve boxes each week. They were lifted one week and paid for the next, much in the same way as Giles had done at Redbriggs.

One fraternity did not fail us: the agricultural and commercial travellers. Some were new but several of the old ones found their way up the hill, and numerous cups of tea were still produced and drunk in the farmhouse kitchen. Few travellers now come around, and both vans and lorries have long since ceased to come.

That summer of 1960 must be put down as a good one in the records, for I have memories of many sunny days, especially the first weeks in June. The mornings were usually misty but mist soon gave way to balmy sunshine, full of sweetness, and the earth was full of green growth. Hanging out the washing on a bonny breezy day has always been a task that gave me great pleasure. The sheer joy of that first Monday washing day is still with me. The green lies at the back of the house on an elevated position, looking down to the sea. The rocks below, the cliffs towering above and the sparkling blue sea with tufts of white foam combined together, yielding a beauty that is hard to describe. I had never seen anything so lovely. Well, maybe I had

213

once, for another scene comes to mind: January with snow lying over all in panoramic beauty, a scene I have already described.

Just down from the green is a small field usually used for ewes and lambs and at the foot of this is the woollen mill at Waulkmill. There are a few trees, a rowan and some willows, growing on its banks. The same morning, something drew my attention and I wandered down to have a look. To my surprise and delight, my eyes encountered an enchanting sight. On the bank, a huge patch of wild hyacinths grew, mostly in shades of blue, dark and light and intermingled with white and pink. They still grow there in profusion and the area is now more than twice the size it was when I first saw it, though it is beginning to be spoiled by ferns and brambles growing up through it. Around the end of May or early June I gather bunches of them which I put in vases. In England they are known as bluebells and cover many a small wood. Our Scottish bluebells are called harebells, but they are a quite different type of flower which is not found in woods but on waste ground and by the roadside. We pick them on Bankhead from late June to early July.

It was in our first weeks at Bankhead that I saw my first cuckoo. There had been cuckoos in the wood at Redbriggs but I had never seen one, only heard them in the distance. One morning, quite early, I was out with the ashes and up from the den where the bluebells grew came a loud clear 'cuckoo'. I threw down the ash pan, slipped quietly down the side of the fence and I was able to see it sitting quite unconcernedly on a branch of a willow tree. It was a small grey-blue bird about the size of a blackbird, but of slimmer build. I stayed motionless and was able to observe it for a short time before it gave a few more calls and then flew off. I have caught glimpses of others since, but that was the one and only time that I had such a close view of the elusive bird.

I saw other birds that I had not seen since I left Mormond. Out for a walk with the boys on the Darder Hill, quite a few curlews were to be seen flying around, their plaintive calls awakening memories of how I had watched them swooping low, skimming over the heather giving that mournful call which filled you with sadness. It made me think of some lost soul debarred from the gates of heaven. Those birds, along with the lapwing (tuchats), now seem to have completely disappeared from the countryside. They were, I believe, related to the

214

corncrake, another bird that I have not seen for some time.

I well remember my first walk along our northern boundary. The supper dishes had been washed; the boys said they were going off for a walk and asked was I coming with them? We made our way down through the field towards the sea. At the foot of the second field, if you are making to the west, you have to go into a very deep den before you begin to climb the Darder Hill. This area is a nature reserve trail, for a lot of rare plants grow there, though some have been destroyed by the grazing of our cattle and sheep. Some years there are foxgloves intermingled with yellow vetch, yellow iris, memuls, buttercups of course and, down by a stream that flows through the bottom, large and smaller celandines in abundance.

Up to the top, and just across from the border on the Clinterty side, is a stone denoting that this is the highest point on the cliffs. From here on a clear day, the hills and the outline of the Caithness coast are visible. The scene takes your breath away, that is if you have any left after climbing this far. There is the sea, miles of it in all its various moods and colours, and a panoramic view of rocks and towering cliffs. And turning your eyes to the east where the sun rises at the back of Dundarg, you see the houses and buildings of Rosehearty nestling on a point.

I certainly was 'puffed' ere I reached the top. The boys' main interest lay in inspecting the wire fence which was in need of repair. The cattle and sheep had to be protected from falling off the cliffs. There was a pathway between the rocks and the fence for people walking, and during the summer months they were numerous and often not too careful. Some broke the fence and those with dogs were a menace, for if startled, our animals were likely to bolt, not inland but over the cliffs. We never lost any cattle this way, but we did lose several lambs and a few ewes.

That first year, a pair of sheep wandered out on to a narrow ledge, stayed there and would not move. A rescue operation had to be organised and our farm and pictures got into the newspapers. The animals had so little space to manoeuvre but had they reversed back - a thing a blackface ewe is very good at - they could have quite easily got back. Robin, who was in charge of the flock, had done all he could to tryst them back to safety. Eventually one escaped, but when the

215

other was still on the ledge a week later, something had to be done. First we contacted the police and they in turn called the coastguards. They decided to climb up the cliff-side and throw a net over her. I was not down to see the operation, but it was successful and when she was released she went off quite happily to nibble grass, seemingly none the worse for her ordeal. Afterwards, the rescue party came up to the farm and had a cup of tea. We shared a happy interlude, the coastguards telling stories of other experiences and a lot of banter and teasing went on.

The sheep were not the only ones that had to be rescued from the rocks. Those rocks and towering cliffs were also the happy nesting and breeding grounds of a huge colony of gulls and around this season, eggs were to be found in their hundreds, mostly in dangerous and inaccessible places. Adventurous boys were tempted to climb and they often found themselves in difficulty. They too had to be rescued by the coastguards and police. They often fell, causing serious injuries and I can recall one who fell with fatal results. Some people, though not very many, like to eat those eggs and others deemed they were excellent for baking, but though I did try them, I didn't like them. To me the taste of fish does not compliment the egg flavour. Brownie told us they were excellent feed for hand-fed calves, but we never tried them.

I have digressed but now return to our walk. Having reached the farthest point of our western boundary we turned east, skirting along the top of the Darder till we came to the end of the pathway. We had then to negotiate a very steep decline into the Caird's cave which, on a lovely summer's day, is delightful. There is a waterfall there and it is an ideal spot for a picnic. It is now known as Jock's cave. Jock - or to give him his proper name, David Reid - made it his home.

Where he came from, no one seems to know but he suddenly appeared just after the First World War. He had a slight Irish accent but, though he was a great talker, he never referred to his past private life, only to say that he had sailed all over the world in cargo boats. He liked to be called Captain or Skipper. Each week he collected a small pension from the village Post Office which he eked out by snaring rabbits, catching fish and collecting heather which he made into scrubbers and sweeping brushes to sell. He came around the farm and had become very friendly with the folk of Bankhead whose tenant he really was. He did not seem to want employment, but did accept food and did the odd job in return. He often took in pails of water and peats for the women folk, made ready a chicken for the pot or gave them a present of a rabbit. Once a week, a boiler was filled with potatoes for pig and poultry food and his delight was to tend the fire. In return he accepted bowls of soup, cups of tea, milk and eggs or oatcakes and scones. I liked a story told me by a Mrs Coutts, the youngest of the Laird family and at that time a girl at school - about how he attended church on most Sundays and on his return journey came up past the farm, coinciding with their lunch hour. Sunday dinner usually had broth on the menu and he was always offered and accepted a bowl. His seat was the old stone by the fireplace and he never started his meal before first removing his cap. I am sure he must have been a strange but delightful character, staying in his small cave right up into the late thirties at least. The Laird family who were in Bankhead often tried to get him to come to the farm in the winter months, where he could have had a bed in the chaumer, but he would have none of it. The small den is indeed a delightful place on a lovely summer's day, but quite the reverse on a wild winter's night when the roaring of the wind and the noise of the waves dashing on the rocks are an awesome and terrible sight and sound. But never once was he known to seek shelter.

I once met him at a school picnic. It was my very first visit to Aberdour shore and he was living in the cave at that time. The teacher took a few of us to visit the hermit, as he was then described, but the cave was shut up and Jock was nowhere to be seen. We will never know what made him forsake kith and kin to make his home in so lonely a spot. He must have stayed over twenty years before he fell ill and was taken to Maud hospital where he died a few weeks later.

We did not linger in Jock's cave, but made our way on sea level, scrambling and slithering over rocks, passing another two small dens which are named on the ordnance survey map as Muckle Kip and Little Kip. You can only do this part of the walk when the tide is out; at other times you have to walk along the top. We rounded the last of the higher rocks and before us lay Aberdour Bay.

Mostly it is full of life, but this evening only one man could be seen taking his dog for a walk. Here, a wire fence divides the land and sea. We climbed over the fence which surrounds a small field where a woollen mill once carried on a thriving business. All that can be seen now is the outline stones of the building with one solitary gable-end of the dwelling house still standing. The mill also had a croft attached and when the mill was closed down, the buildings and the ground were added to Bankhead. It later became the cottar house.

Another story lies here: the incredible heroism of one woman who single-handedly saved the lives of fifteen seamen. She was a cottar wife, Jane Whyte, whose husband was foreman at Bankhead.

At the ruins of the croft we came to the end of our walk for there, only a few yards away, was the small stream called the Dour flowing into the sea. It formed our eastern boundary and also gave Aberdour its name. Our walk was over and we made our way up through the fields back to the farmhouse.

That first summer passed quickly as, I am afraid, did the successive years. We had lots of visitors and one of my first priorities was to get a bedroom ready to receive guests. Friends and relations from the towns used to come to the country for their annual two weeks' holiday.

We first removed the fireplace - a rusty old grate - but to our shame we broke up the surround. It was comprised of lovely red tiles which would fetch a good price today. Somehow, things then considered old-fashioned and worthless, have become fashionable for the younger generation. We boarded up the holes and then came the job of tackling the walls. I have seen walls with layer upon layer of old paper that had to be removed, but here it was easy for there were only small patches of paper left and I could only count two different patterns. The woodwork only needed washing down before painting, but the roof was quite a difficult undertaking. I had tackled many difficult walls, but this was my first experience of papering sloping walls and roof. It would not go on straight and more and more batter was slapped on as I hoped for a miracle. It got very wet and I got more frustrated. I had made a start one Saturday afternoon and I finished at about four o'clock on the Sunday morning. I shut the door in disgust on what looked an awful mess and wearily went downstairs to bed. It was late afternoon before I could find the courage to climb the stairs and open the door. Glory be! A miracle had taken place. To my delight the room looked a dream of pink flowery perfection. All the wet bumps had dried out and become flat. I could scarcely believe that such a transformation could have taken place and I soon had the room in order. Nothing very grand: an old square of lino from Redbriggs covered part of the floor and the wooden surround was varnished. A new rug and curtains were bought and also a new wardrobe from Maitland's, but the rest had been my mother's.

When we came to do the other room upstairs, it was much the same but here, along with the sloping walls, were fixed wooden frames to hold the beds and I had to get a joiner to remove them. The room in the middle also had a frame for a bed, but we kept it and many a little girl and boy came and loved the room. They thought it grand having a room of their very own. These same children have grown up and now their children occupy it. The very first person that used the room was not a child, however, but a friend, related through marriage, who came that first year to help Jean. She was a young widow with three small boys to bring up and this she had tackled with no aid from Social Services, doing odd jobs at Turriff School. When the school closed for the summer holidays, she was glad to get the boys out to the country, away from the streets. She proved a blessing to me, for having visitors and trying to make the old house comfortable that first year, proved no mean task.

Although we had ample hot and cold water in the house, we had no bathroom. Our mortgage had stipulated that a bathroom would have to be installed and, if this had not been the case, I am sure it would have taken us years. Ivan would most likely have dithered and dallied for, to him, a bathroom was quite unnecessary and the old arrangement quite satisfactory. As to lavatories we were quite well off. We had two outside houses: a workers' one and one for the 'ben a hoose' folk. They were both situated on the gable end of the kitchen premises, very compactly, with one seat in each and a pit in the middle. I am sure that the people who lived here when the house was built must have been very tall. Inside in the front hall are rows of pegs fixed on the wall for coats, etc. They are so high that I have to fetch a chair and climb up before I can get them satisfactorily hung. The box and seat for the lavatory was never meant for the bum of a dainty lady such as I. Before I could get comfortably seated, I had to climb up and was left with my feet dangling more than a foot from the floor.

When you are dealing with the County Council - and where a grant is involved - things do not progress very fast. Although proceedings were begun soon after we arrived, it was almost a year before a bathroom was fixed up. Would we build, or use the accommodation we already had? Would it be upstairs or down? Upstairs was best for the bedrooms, but would benefit visitors more than the family. Finally it was decided to use the old pantry. Access was through the front room, but that door could be sealed up and an opening made through the back wall, giving an entrance from the scullery at the old back door. This was next to the pantry, which we called our milk- house, and it was pointed out that it was not hygienic to have a bathroom next to it, but a wall almost three feet thick divided the two so this could be overlooked. Unfortunately, when the plans were almost completed, Mr Ogilvy, the Fraserburgh Sanitary Inspector, took ill and was replaced by a young man from the Aberdeen office.

The day he arrived to inspect the plans and give his final approval, I was doing some cleaning in the kitchen and had moved the cooker out beside the other small sink, in the passage way of the proposed bathroom. From the moment he arrived I had the feeling that we were not compatible. He was full of his own self-importance and I almost think he had come prepared to wreak havoc with the plans. After numerous questions and a casual look around, he said we could not go through a scullery to reach a bathroom. "Nonsense," I said, "and it's not a scullery, only a temporary arrangement." He made no comment and did not even listen but if he had explored just that little bit further, he would have found our milk-house and pantry which would have put the cat amongst the pigeons properly.

In the other passage he saw the door of the small room that lay below the back stair. It had once been fitted with a bed, but I had put cupboards in the recess and it now held brushes, cleaning materials, old coats and other objects. Opening the door and looking around, he said, to my astonishment, that this would make an ideal bathroom. "Never", I replied and went on to explain that the other inspector had already explored the possibility and it had been turned down. The water cistern and all the pipes were on the front wall and it would mean a much bigger upheaval, including moving the back stair to allow for a bigger window. All my arguments fell on deaf ears; I might as well have gone out and talked to the man in the moon. He took some measurements and left saying he would be back with another plan. Some weeks later he appeared complete with a new plan which I turned down. Many letters and visits followed, but my mind was made up and I was not having the bathroom installed in this room.

Months later, Mr Ogilvy's health improved and he was able to return to his office. He soon put matters right. It was the spring of 1961 before we had the pleasure of turning on a tap, decorating the room and laying tiles on the old 'ben a hoose' pantry.

Another delight that awaited us at Bankhead was the coming of the swallows. They had been here on our visit in the spring for I can remember one evening, collecting the boys from work, coming into the close and stopping with Mr Brownie to watch the birds darting to and fro the old cart shed. It is a miracle how each year, when winter begins to approach, those small birds fly thousands of miles across land and oceans to find food and warmth. When spring returns they are back to their own special place to breed and rear their young. It was always a delight when someone came in and said the swallows were back.

Just the other day, I was in the sitting room with the door open. The sun was shining and to let the fresh air in I had left the front door open. I heard a slight whirring noise and to my surprise a tiny bird flew into the room. This had sometimes happened before and the birds - usually sparrows but once or twice robins - became very frightened. If you opened the window quickly, all was well, but otherwise they would dash and hurl themselves at the window in distraction, making it very difficult to catch them. This stranger did not seem so frightened and landed on the window sill and quite easily, I was able to hold it in my hand. To my great delight I found I held a swallow. I had never thought they were so small. Seeing them in flight with their great wingspan, you assume they are bigger. I looked down on a beautiful bird of perfect symmetry with jet black feathers and on its head and here and there glinting specks of blue, green and gold. I could but marvel anew at the miracle of migration;

it could surely only have been the hands of God that guided it safely back. I took it to the open door and gracefully the wings opened up and it glided away towards the steading where, for the past few weeks, the swallows had been gathering twigs and feathers to build their nests.

Over the years, we have planted trees and bushes which have attracted and given cover to many different species of birds. As I write, I often watch a pair of blackbirds busy building a nest. They are a cheeky pair but delightful company and so amusing. How they chatter and scold when one of the cats appears. It is surprising how many different varieties there are, many which I have seen for the first time. There was the owl, the cuckoo and that lone heron who stood motionless down by the stream. Once I thought I had an eagle sitting on a post quite near the kitchen door. It was a lovely gold and brown colour, but later I realised that it was a buzzard.

At one time a pair of peregrines nested down on the rocky crags beside Jock's cave and raised a family of three. The female peregrine is the falcon and its mate the tercel, which is the bigger, more dominant bird and the provider of food for the mate and family. That was the only time I have seen them, but I am told they sometimes nest further along the coast nearer Pennan.

Our next unusual and far-travelled bird was a glossy ibis, a rare bird from the Greek-Turkish border area which has been spotted in Scotland only twice. I have a newspaper cutting dated November 14th, 1986 which confirms this. I was at the kitchen window and my attention was drawn to an unusual-looking bird, stalking around on very long legs, only a few feet away. It resembled a curlew but was bigger, dark purply brown in colour and it had a shining green iridescence over its back. I watched it for some minutes then called Fiona my grand-daughter to come and look. She was much more knowledgeable about and interested in birds than I was. She asked if it could be a curlew but as I knew those birds well I told her it wasn't. Thinking we might get a closer look, we quietly opened the door. It immediately took fright and flew away.

A few days later, opening the newspaper, I was confronted by a picture of the very same bird that we had been watching. There was no mistaking it and, reading on, I learned it was now at the nature reserve at Strathbeg only a few miles distant. It had been there for a few days and was raising considerable interest, but the experts were concerned that it would not survive typical north-east weather. I folded up the paper to reveal only the bird and when Fiona came in I showed her saying, "Ever seen this bird before?" She only needed a glance to say, "Gosh Granny, that's the bird we watched on Saturday." I never heard of its fate or whether it stayed or not.

I had been some months at Bankhead and was out for a walk to the top of the Hill Park one evening, when I had a view of my beloved Mormond Hill. But now a great sadness filled my heart. The Mormond I had known was no longer there. Large tracks had been turned up and put to the plough. Other parts had been planted with trees and on the highest point was a monstrosity of iron girders and pylons: an American-based radio station. It was an early-warning system, and if a nuclear war was started it would perhaps save a few lives, but what for?

On the side where my homeland lay there was a more pleasing sight - acres of trees planted by the Forestry Commission. Their foliage covers all my old haunts and secret places which have now all disappeared: nooks and crannies where the bell heather bloomed and where treasured clumps of white heather grew; places only I knew. The banks where the small, succulent heather berries could be found. You would be lucky to find half a cupful but they tasted like nectar.

The 'auld hoose' that sheltered me is away too, but I have memories that stay with me strong and clear, dear memories of my grandfather, whose teaching guided me through all my years. There were so many other crofts there in my time but the hill has taken them back. Even some larger farms have disappeared. One croft in which I have more than a passing interest has not yet gone back to heather: the one my great-grandfather reclaimed from the heathery, stony slopes of Mormond. From where, or how he came to the foot of Mormond and rented the piece of land is a story that will never be told. All we can tell, is how David Skinner laboured on the land which was in the Philorth estate belonging to Lord Saltoun of Cairnbulg Castle. He paid rent for it and broke up most of the ground with pick and spade. He dug ditches and put up fences, some of which were dykes built with the stones he had taken from the clearance of

223

the land. He also built himself a three-roomed cottage, a stable, byre and barn and a few other outhouses. Crofting was a very hard, penurious life and David, I believe, was no great farmer, but was more interested in books. As a young lad, he had hoped to enter the ministry and had studied towards this objective, but just about the time he was ready to enter the university his patron had died and there was no money for him to go forward in his studies. He was well versed in Latin and I know he taught his son, my grandfather, Latin and to read and write. This would have been around the 1840s and few children at that time could read and write as there were very few schools. He must have spent many years on the croft. As others did at that time, he used his horse and cart during the fishing season at the Broch to cart away offal, getting manure for the land and earning a few shillings besides. One year, his horse died and he was unable to replace it. He fell behind with his rent and was put out of his croft by Lord Saltoun. When a tenant was put out, even if he had put up all the buildings and taken in the most of the twelve acres, he recovered not one penny. David took the laird to court and failed only because it was proved that he had used more clay than lime in building. His contract had been to use lime only. Desolate and broken hearted, he had to move out. If I had been in his place, I think I would have demolished the buildings and taken what I could of the materials, but he had perhaps moved out before the court case came up.

He moved only a few fields away to an empty croft house. Near the dwelling, the estates of Philorth and Techmuiry met forming a small triangle. For some reason, neither of the estates claimed this corner; it was designated a no-man's-land. David Skinner took it over and made it his own. It was about half an acre of land and he again dug up the ground out of the heather and built himself a cottage, surrounding it with a garden. Up one side a stone dyke was built and round the other two sides trees were planted for shelter - rowan, elderberry (boultry), some laburnum that in summer was so pleasing to see and one solitary ash on whose branches I built a tree house. When he died, his wife Jean stayed for a time but when the time came that she was unable to stay alone, my grandparents came and took up residence. It thus stayed in the family up to about 1938. Around that time, Ivan's father took it over and lived there till he died in 1947. The family could not sell the ground, only the cottage and as no other occupant was found, it was taken down, much to my sorrow. All that now remains are a few stones surrounded by trees and to a stranger those stones would be difficult to find. But my memories can trace all that was my happy childhood home. I seldom go back now; I prefer to remember it as it was.

The first ten years at Bankhead saw many changes in our way of life. I still found my way to the byre but only occasionally milked a cow. Whitey was still the principal milk cow. Rhonie was given a couple of calves to rear and joined the rest of the herd. At first we had only about thirty cows but from this the herd was built up to over one hundred. A Friesian heifer was bought to replace Rhonie as our intentions were to have one cow calving about April or May and the other in November or December, thus keeping up our milk supply all the year round. It did not always work out, but over the years we have bought very little milk.

Whitey, the calf I bought for ten shillings, survived almost twenty years, having a calf each year and once she had twins. When she stopped breeding I did try to persuade the menfolk to retire her but was not successful. With Ivan, sentiment played no part in farm life and poor faithful old Whitey was put on a lorry and sent to Aberdeen mart. That morning I kept well behind closed doors.

Daisy, the best of our gallant and lovely Clydesdales, did not share the same fate but lived out the rest of her life in idleness. Whether she was content I hardly knew for she was such a different character from our first horse, kind gentle Gyp. Daisy was haughty and arrogant and thought nothing of taking a bite out of you and giving you a kick if she felt inclined. She had only been in harness for a few years before the tractor arrived and after that her duties were light. In the winter months, if the ground was wet, she came into her own carting home turnips and she also did some scarifying and shimming, but once she came down here I do not remember her ever being in harness. Our visitors used to pet and admire her and the younger ones loved to have a ride on her back but she only allowed this with Sandy's supervision. I was the only one she showed any affection for and this I think was cupboard love, or in her case, nosebag love.

She was very partial to a handful of oats out of the hens' feeding pail. Although I did not love her as I had done Gyp, I did have a good deal of affection for her and I often thought she must have been a very lonely animal with only cows for company. There was no stable at Bankhead, it had been converted into a cattle court, but in the worst weather Daisy had a bed in the byre. One autumn, just before the cattle came in for the winter, on a horrible day with cold north winds lashing everything with icy rain, I pleaded with the boys to go and fetch her indoors. Daisy was growing old and was prone to rheumatism. "Oh, she'll be alright", they said, and did not heed me. I donned a raincoat and set off across the fields to fetch her in myself. I found her in the farthest away corner of the field standing with her back to the elements. With the wind in my back it had been easy crossing, but to get back I had to turn right into it. She refused to let me put on her halter but I slung it round her neck and the ungrateful hussy refused to turn. I coaxed and pleaded to no avail, turn she would not and I had to return home without her, to be laughed at for all my pains. Sandy and Daisy shared the same year of birth, she in April and he in September, so there was no argument about her age. She was into her thirtieth year when she died. It was a pity we were unable to breed from her. We had tried several times before we left Redbriggs but we were unable to get her in foal.

Over the years, many Clydesdales have given loyal service to Bankhead. I have one photograph taken around 1900 showing seven of them: three pair of horse and an orra beast. It must have been hard work indeed for the horses at Bankhead, the carting work in particular. There were no motor lorries then to bring home the supplies and goods, all of them had to be hauled up the steep brae by horse and cart. I have been told it often needed two to pull up one load. What a lovely sight, in the brown and tinted yellow colours of autumn, to see a ploughman guiding a pair of these stately animals over a field, striding out so precisely, pulling the plough to leave behind a tight furrow of black mould. Gulls wheeling overhead and the soft lilt of a favourite tune, maybe Bonnie Mary Morrison or Afton Water, whistled blithely by the ploughman. A few horseshoes lying around the farm - I have two by the garden gate - are all that remains of those noble and lovely animals.

A big ugly monster of red, green, yellow or brown - they come in all colours - now parades the fields, doing in one day what took the horses weeks to do. The gulls still hover and wheel, but no lilting ploughman greets the ear, only the roar of a combustion engine and filthy fumes float behind. The tranquillity of farming life seems to have vanished. It was hard work, sometimes drudgery but there was more contentment, lots of laughter and none of this ever-searching quest for amusement or something new.

Ivan and I on the day of our Golden Wedding

CHAPTER FOURTEEN

THE PRICE
OF PROGRESS

TIME PASSED so quickly and changes came so fast. We had only a few years of the old harvest routine - cutting with a binder, stooking and the cornyard full of bumper crops - before that all vanished. Harvest had always been a welcome break from household chores. Meals were prepared the night before and eaten next day in picnic style. When horses pulled the loads, the work was harder, but now I only drove the tractor around the field, stopping and starting for the men to fork and build the loads. It was a wonderful feeling of achievement to see the cornyard filled with rows of neat stacks, knowing that man and beast were again provided for in the winter. At the beginning, people were adamant that the combine would never take over from the binder; our climate would not allow it. But the prophets were wrong. At Redbriggs we had grown no barley, only oats, but here at Bankhead, Brownie had one or two fields in barley and we followed suit. Oats had gone out of fashion and barley was now much more profitable. Oats were best cut when not too ripe and matured in the stook. The straw was then of more value for cattle feed. With barley, the straw has little nutriment and handles best when very ripe, and thus suited the combine better. Our first combine was hired around 1967. I very much regretted the passing of the oats, for it was the main bulk of the feed for the poultry. I had considered it better than barley. However, it was not long after this that the poultry followed the oats.

I did not regret the passing of the steam mill. At the croft, having our own small mill, we had no need of its services.Then at Redbriggs, most of the crop was thrashed in the barn but with the bigger acreage we did need a day of the mill in the spring to thrash the surplus. This gave Ivan a few quarters to sell and provided the seed for the spring crops. That was but one day; here at Bankhead it was four whole days, two in the autumn and two in the spring. Having two consecutive days of the mill was hard work for me and domestic help was not to be had. There were always sixteen or so men to feed: a mid-day meal and a snack forenoon and afternoon. Tattie soup, or mince was the favourite dinner followed by milk pudding with fruit or a dumpling. The piece was usually tea, with bread and jam and home baked scones. The last year we had the mill, the workers - Ivan and the boys included - were fed down at the hotel, at least for their mid-day meal. It was a happy sight to see them from the sitting-room window all going down the road to be fed.

Hiring a combine was unsatisfactory and in 1971 we bought a second-hand Massey Ferguson from Neil Ross in Ellon. This survived for a couple of years but under pressure from our neighbours to cut their crops too, a bigger combine, this time a New Holland, was purchased. It only took a few days to cut our own crops. Demand for hiring was increasing and there was a temptation to earn extra money to cover the expenditure and upkeep of the combine. Extra acres needed a reliable machine, not one that broke down and needed expensive repairs. In 1978, a brand new combine from Italy, a Lavada, trundled up the Bankhead road. The boys were very proud of this purchase which cost £18,000. By this time our carefully planned budget had completely been thrown over the garden wall. In eighteen years our farm was worth ten times what we had paid for it. The land had always been well farmed and grew good crops, but we had concentrated on growing more grass and increasing our livestock. We now had over a hundred breeding cows, with their followers mostly sold at a year old but sometimes kept into their second year to finish. The sheep flock was still around a hundred breeding ewes.

Up to this time, I kept the books and sorted the transactions but it was very difficult to adjust to rapid changes in money matters. The books had to be done each month, for the work entailed was prodigious. As Government came in with more rules, more and more forms had to be filled in. A farmer out all day, perhaps putting in ten to twelve hours in byres and fields, was not fit to tackle bookwork. I did it as best I could. Each month, a detailed statement of expenditure and income had to be completed and at the end of a twelve month period handed over to an accountant who analysed it and forwarded it to the Inland Revenue. I never totalled the expenditure column; I preferred to be in ignorance.

Both the banks and the government encouraged heavy borrowing and our overdraft, like the farm's assessments, went up at least ten times in value, and kept on rising. Grants on buildings were easily available and that encouraged us to invest further.

We started making silage because it was easier managed than hay; it was extremely good for young cattle. Our first building was a covered silage pit, followed by an Ascott building with cubicles for the cows.

The wintering of cattle outside had begun to be common and anyone with rough grazing - a wood or a den giving shelter - was encouraged to take up this method. We had over one hundred acres of rough grazing in sheltered dens, stretching along the side of the Dour on our eastern boundary. Long before we arrived, these dens were known far and wide for the lovely big black juicy brambles that grew there. Baskets of them weighing hundredweights must have gone to the village alone. The village people were therefore not too happy about cows wandering around and poaching on ground they regarded as their preserve. I too enjoyed many an afternoon across in the den filling a basket with brambles. It was so sheltered and peaceful. An odd cow would approach, and then disappear. With the sound of the burn tinkling over the stones all the world's cares seemed far away.

Brownie told me how a friend of his got trapped in bushes while gathering berries. The relating of it was amusing but for the poor woman it must have been a dreadful experience. She had come up to the village from Fraserburgh by bus, making her own way to the den and, once her basket was full, she was to come up to the farm for Brownie to take her home in his truck. Six o'clock came and no lady appeared and later, when there was still no sign of her, he decided to look for her. In all probability, he thought, she had found other transport and gone home, but just in case there had been an accident, he thought it best to have a look. Accompanied by his constant companion, a brown and white spaniel, he spent some time searching and had almost given up when he heard a faint cry. At the same time the dog began to wag its tail and made for a nearby bush. He came upon her basket, almost full and then he saw the lady herself, half-way up a steep slope, firmly held by long tendrils of bramble bush wrapped all around her body. The best berries were often to be found in inaccessible places and, seeing a fine clump high on the slope, she had climbed up to the branch. In doing so she had been caught by a branch; her woollen jumper was an ideal garment for the thorns to get fixed on. The more she struggled to free herself the more firmly she was held.

By the time Brownie found her, she could neither move an arm nor a leg and it took him some time to cut her free. She was a good sport, Brownie said, for once over at the farm and fortified with a cup of tea, she was able to have a good laugh at her mishap. Later on I read in a newspaper of another incident where a young lad had slipped and fallen into a quarry. His life was saved by a bramble bush for he would otherwise have plunged to the bottom into several feet of water.

There are still a lot of brambles in the den but the bulk of them have disappeared, along with many other wild plants. Our cows have seen to that. Long ago a lady called Mary Wilson gathered plants there to make cures for all the ills. Mary lived in the time when witchcraft was still practised and her grandmother had been burned as a witch. She lived in a tiny cottage of which you can still find traces by the side of the burn on the Wareland's side. Stretching up from this towards the main road is a deep ravine still known as Mary's den.

For the first few years we out-wintered our herd of cows but, although there was ample shelter from the cold wintry winds, if snow came or successive weeks of rain, the sheltered places got into a mess of wet and mire. This usually happened in early spring when the animals were calving, resulting in great losses among the newly born calves. Cows took staggers and got bogged down in the muddy mess

231

and much manoeuvring was needed to drag the poor animals out and bring them home. Some never recovered. Two consecutive severe winters brought a lot of snow; the continuing losses and the difficulty of getting the cattle fed made the boys think again.

Our first cubicle house was the byre where in days gone by the farmer had finished cattle. It was an outside pen in the close with a concrete floor surrounded by gates and pillars of wood called tombstones. A bigger door gave the cows access to their food which was placed behind the barriers. They were able to come out and feed and then go back to shelter. This method worked very well but the shed only held about twenty cows with the bulk of the herd still outside. Beef calves were getting scarce and prices were rising. The government was encouraging upland farmers and those with waste or rough ground to put these acres to the plough, giving them subsidies to cover the purchase of grass seed and fertiliser along with a yearly payment. It began with almost £10 for each cow and also a payment on calves reared. Very generous grants were also given on buildings, up to 75 percent. We decided it would be profitable for us to have one to hold about seventy cows and their calves. An Ascott cubicle building was erected. We called it the 'bed and breakfast'. Later, an extension was added bringing the number of cows it held up to 100. It made life more comfortable for both man and beast but, ironically, there have been no severe winters since and snow is now seldom seen. One of the advantages is that when the cows do go out in spring, they find fresh green grass where before it was all muddy and took weeks to recover. A few are still wintered outside: heifers carrying their first calves and late calvers.

With the coming of the combine, straw had to be handled differently; there were no more rows of stooks to be built. A baler followed the combine, picking up the straw and packing it into neat bales. For their storage another building was needed with just a roof and open sides. Many such buildings were to be had cheaply; old hangars and storage sheds from the discarded aerodromes. We acquired one of those and erected it at the back of the old feeding byre on ground that had once been part of the cornyard. The baler also made the old way of hay-making disappear. Once cut, the hay had been built into coles to dry and mature and, although the forking and stack building were hard work for the men, for us other workers it was a day of sheer delight. Our job was to bring in the coles. Sometimes they were lifted by horse and cart, and in later years by tractor and bogie but, before the tractor took over, the common method was with the horse and rope. The rucks were in a corner of the hay field and the rope was manoeuvred around the cole. It was then dragged by the horse across the ground to where the men were working, one building the stack and the other forking up the hay. One person could easily keep up the supply. When we first came to Bankies, the method was still used and with a tractor, but it is of Redbriggs days that happy nostalgic memories of hay-making linger on. Daisy was backed into the cole and the rope was fixed around it. We then flopped on top - it was nice to sink into the soft sweet-smelling grass. Then, with our feet holding the rope, we whipped up the reins and guided the horse smoothly across the field towards the stack-builders. There were mishaps of course: sometimes the rope slipped and you arrived with only half a load; at other times you were left lying in the field, the horse going gaily on without you. Dragging hay with a tractor was quite different but a young boy would have preferred that to a smelly old horse. I have dragged hay with the tractor but all the joy and charm of the job departed.

Some years before we had come to Bankhead, Brownie had turned the old stables into a loose cattle court. The old method of keeping cattle tied up in stalls with chains round their necks was over. It was beginning to be considered cruel. Cruel? I don't think so, not to those who have ever worked with cattle. I can still remember seeing rows of stalls filled with placid contented cows chewing away at their cud, tied but lying comfortable and clean in straw, looks of pure enjoyment on their faces. Today, I can see cattle battering and punching each other for a place at the feeding trough, their hoofs in wet muck with hardly a dry spot where they can rest. Another way which came to be popular was to keep them on slats - a floor of open planks with a pit below. The animals have to walk and lie on those with no straw or bedding of any sort. Having no comfortable place to lie down seems to me most unkind and I was glad when the boys agreed. Nearly all our buildings have now been adjusted to rearing more stock, but we still have one byre with stalls which accommodates twenty tied cows and pens for calves. In winter, the two milk cows occupy one stall and the others are usually filled with cows suckling two calves. They all seem happy and content.

With the increase in the number of cattle, much more straw had to be bought and this caused storage troubles. The first baler delivered square bales which packed into a building well, but unfortunately they were easily wet and very difficult to dry out. To combat this, a baler producing round bales came on the market. They were twice the size of the square bales and not so easily wet, but they were difficult to store. The usual method was to store them together in a corner of the field until they were required.

I loved the old farm house and still do, and have no great ambition to change it. My dream of having the old oak rafters polished has not been fulfilled but they still adorn the kitchen roof and are my delight. Very few old farm kitchens now remain. The modern craze of having streamlined kitchens, where everything is packed neatly away into cupboards and the cooker and washing machines are fitted into small spaces, never has appealed to me. For a time I struggled in vain to have a big bay window fitted into the back wall. That would have given us the morning sun and a lovely view of bonnie Aberdour Bay. In the room above the kitchen, where the boys sleep, there is only one skylight and it faces the wrong way; a new staircase was also badly needed. However my first attempts were thwarted by the scarcity of tradesmen willing to do small jobs. All were so busy building new houses and putting up farm buildings, with government-grant aid.

Then, at last, I thought my efforts were to be rewarded. The boys got involved and a scheme for renovating the kitchen premises got under way. I was to have my big window and a new fireplace with a boiler for central heating. Also, part of a kitchen unit was to be installed, along with another window upstairs and a new staircase. A grant of about 50 percent was available but a qualified surveyor and architect had to be employed to draw up the plan. As might be expected, he and I disagreed, but he did concede a few points and so did I and a full plan was drawn up which the government officials would accept. These plans were talked over and discussed, but before a final decision was made, the boys had a change of mind. Somehow, plans for covering the dung court had come to the fore and both could not go forward. That building would bring in more money, my kitchen improvements none. I was upset, but as usual my disappointment had to be hidden. The plan for a new fireplace and the radiators went ahead, but the dream of sitting on a broad window-seat looking out at the blue water or the white storm-crested waves of Aberdour Bay has still to be fulfilled.

The old fireplace had a broad granite surround and to take it out, the whole gable end of the house would have been destroyed. Former owners had covered it with coats of black varnish and black-lead but I thought, if cleaned, it would be lovely. This was achieved with a great deal of soda and hard work with a scrubbing brush, but it did come up nice. A smokeless-fuel burner with a back-boiler, one that heated up to five radiators, was installed by a plumber and around it the boys built a fireplace consisting of granite blocks in three different shades of Aberdeen grey, intermingled with red polished granite supplied by a granite merchant in Aberdeen. My fireplace is now very much to my liking and, I think, complements the oak rafters.

When we arrived at Bankhead, there was a row of almost derelict small buildings across from the kitchen door. Only one had a roof, some had doors and in one were the remains of an old boiler which I expect had once been used to boil potatoes for pigs and poultry. Most likely it was the same boiler Jock the hermit had loved to attend. Brownie had used an old truck for transport but he had had no garage. We liked to have our car under a roof so we decided to adapt those small ruined buildings into a garage. All were attached to one well-built back wall. One end was left open for a nice big door and with a side door further down the front wall we had a nice big garage with part of it a coal house, and just yards from the back door. The boys did the work and our only outlay was a roof, a door and a few bags of cement.

I remember later how indignant I was at it being classified as a double garage. The farm house and a garage came under the rating system but all the other buildings were free of charge. The inspector noticed the new building near the house. Not giving it a thought, I said it was the garage. It went into his book as a double garage and was taxed accordingly. I did try to tell him it was also the coal house and with the door being at the end of the building it could not house two cars, but I might just as well have saved my breath.

My old dream of having a pure Aberdeen Angus herd had by this time almost faded away. Ever since we had come to Bankhead we had used an Aberdeen Angus bull. Ivan found it very convenient to attend the cattle mart at Aberdeen. He could get a bus from the village and there were few Fridays that he did not find his way to Kittybrewster. He met so many cattle dealers, some honest, some not, but Ivan could never resist having a banter and making deals.

We were looking for a bull and one Friday Ivan returned from Aberdeen saying he had got one. The float duly delivered it, but anything less like the lovely sonsie black calf of my dreams one could hardly imagine. The boys had reared many a better-looking yearling stirk. His birth certificate showed that he bore the grand name of Excalibur Enterprise of Rannochie and had been bred on a farm near Buckie. He was two and a half years old and big for his age, but he lacked conformation. Ivan had to bear many a sarcastic remark, the only consolation being that he was cheap. The bull was kept in the background and not shown to visitors.

A few weeks went past and he began to improve. They say breeding will show and so it was with Excalibur. In six months you could not have recognised him as the same animal that had first arrived. He grew quite big, filled out with massive fore legs and good back quarters, but best of all he proved to be a good stock-getter. His calves fetched good prices and took prizes at the sales, but I am afraid our Rannochie lived up to his name. He was an enterprising bull and became, over the years, a legend in our district. He had no regard for fences or gates and if some cow was in heat he would wander far and wide to find her. All our neighbours had his services free and some of them did not like it. Their own bulls resented him and fights ensued. Rannochie did not always triumph and sometimes he returned a sorry sight. One year, our nearest neighbour was grateful for if our bull had not visited, he would have had few calves as his own animal had lost all interest. Mind you, our boys did say that our bull was to blame in the first place as he had terrorised the other young animal. He was provoking, but when a call came, which it often did, to fetch him he was docile and came home willingly - yet in ten minutes he could be off again. Our neighbour Mrs Black from the Mill farm, on her way to church one Sunday, found him wandering on the road and sent her grieve to phone us. He was fetched back to the field beside the shore and the fence mended, but the boys were only back for an hour when they had another phone call; on coming out of church, Mrs Black had again found him outside, just a little late for the morning service.

We had him for many years and he would have been about ten years old when he was sent to market. This is the side of farming I like to forget. His enterprise finished him. We returned from market to find that he had broken out of his pen and made his way round to the barn where feed and cake and bruised oats were kept. He had forced a door open, found the cake, and of course gorged himself. This had made him thirsty so he had made his way to the dam and drank his fill. This caused the contents of his stomach to ferment and swell and when we found him, he was so bloated he could hardly breathe and was foaming at the mouth. The vet was summoned and by probing his stomach and letting the wind and gas out, saved his life but he never regained his old vitality.

He was replaced by another likeable character. He was bought through an advert in the Press and Journal and had been the stock bull from a small Aberdeen Angus herd owned by the Thompson Brothers of Loggan, near Dufftown. His name was Excalibur also, but to us he was always Charlie. He had no roaming instincts and broke no fences or gates. I often came across the field and found him lying down, chewing away at his cud, and I could sit down on his back, tickle his ears and scratch him. His calves too proved their worth and he sired

With black cattle at Bankhead today

237

two champions. It was indeed a proud day when a silver champion-ship cup from the autumn sale of suckled calves came home to Bankies. And it was a sad day when one morning, after five years, they went out and found Charlie had died in his stall.

By this time, the menfolk had begun to attend the Perth bull sales and were beginning to get acquainted with the various pure Aberdeen Angus herds. When one year Robin and Sandy returned from the Perth sales to say that they had purchase two pedigreed heifers, my delight knew no bounds.

The thrill of seeing those two animals step from the float out on the Bankie's close is with me still. They were Eva and Pinky Pride, both about one and a half years of age. Photos were taken and proudly shown on screen later. A new bull was needed and the best price they could afford was paid. If I had been told years earlier that the boys would one day go down to Perth bull sales to buy one, I would have dismissed it as moonshine, but off they went with a banker's order allowing a price of over a thousand pounds. They bought a bull of Irish blood costing 920 guineas, and thus in 1978 our pedigree herd of Aberdeen Angus was begun. Unfortunately, a Bankhead herd already existed, that of the McLaren brothers in Perthshire. With Bankhead we had the croftlands of Waulkmill, and I was for calling our cows the Waulkhead herd but the name Millbank was chosen.

Establishing a pure herd not only takes time, but expertise and judgment. Time from their other duties was something the boys had little of. Their father had the time but not the interest. Sales had to be attended, herds visited, catalogues and pedigrees studied. Since first I had seen and fallen in love with the black Asleid calf, I had read and become well versed in the history of the Aberdeen Angus breed. They had become known around 1879, called after the two counties in which they were bred, and the first known pedigree herd was owned by William McCombie of Tillyfour, North Deeside. William not only bred good cattle but was also a good publicist. He took cattle to the then European Show in Paris where he took all the top prizes. No less a personage than Queen Victoria came to take tea with him at Tillyfour where he paraded his famous cattle in front of her. The Aberdeen Angus with their black skins and polled (hornless) heads usually look all alike and the story goes that, in order to make it look as if he had more cattle than he really had, he made the cattle go round and round the house, and when out of sight behind the farmhouse new leaders took over the same cattle.

During the late 1950's and early 1960's the Blacks really came into their own. They had had worldwide success and the Perth sales were full of Stetson hats from the States and Canada and ponchos from Argentina and Brazil. In 1964 a bull called Envalise of Lambertie's fetched 60,000 guineas. Sad to say, those high prices were the worst thing that ever happened to the Hummle Doddies, as they were affectionately called. At that time, all the high-priced bulls were wee short-legged dumpy animals and everyone in the breed jumped on the band wagon and tried to breed export bulls. In doing so, they forgot their bread and butter, which had been and always will be, the farmers like us who breed commercial suckled calves for the fattening trade. Suddenly, the overseas demand dried up as the breeders there realised, before Scotland did, that when you stopped weighing you stopped paying. A new system of weight recording was brought in and they were found wanting.

When we entered the market in the 1980's, top prices only ranged from four to six thousand pounds; on average, a bull cost from one to two thousands pounds. By then, they were beginning to breed much bigger bulls for they now had to compete with Charolais, Simmental, Limousins and other exotic breeds. The Irish had been more sensible and had kept and bred their bigger stock. Importing Irish stock and semen from Canada made a big improvement. Will they, I wonder, now veer towards too big bulls and again spoil the Aberdeen Angus image.

Our herd has not progressed far, but it is established and has paid its way. Eva and Pinky Pride were later joined by another two heifers Pesselqua of Fordhouse and Erica of Asley. Three other cows culled from a dispersal sale came into the herd, but two of them were a complete loss for one was only home a few days when we found her dead of staggers. A few months later, the other got stuck in a gate and was found strangled. The third cow was not a success either. She did supply one or two bull calves, which were sold as stores and then a promising heifer calf - one the boys hoped they might breed - but that promise was not fulfilled. She was a big heavy cow and when the calf was only a few days old, she lay down on top of it. She was sold shortly afterwards.

Pinky Pride and the Fordhouse cow are not with us now, but both have left stock and Eva is a grand old lady of fourteen years. She has three daughters and three grand-daughters in the herd. Two of her bull calves have been registered and sold for stock bulls and another son and two grandsons are in the pipeline. Erica is also around, with a daughter in the herd and a bull calf sold for breeding. Having Eva and Erica in the herd is now providing us with a headache as their calves have to be registered with a name beginning with the letter E. Two of the daughters are called Eva 1st and Eva 2nd of Millbank, leading to more confusion.

Our stock bull is now mostly used on the commercial herd. AI is used on the pedigree cows. This was obtained through the Aberdeen Angus Society and the bulls we have sold have been bred from Canadian stock. Our cows and heifers can also claim well-known bulls as their fathers. It has been disappointing for me and for the boys not to have seen some of their more promising stock in the sale ring at Perth, but to do so takes time, time the boys have not got. At an early age the show animals have to be haltered and taught to do the cake walk, to show off their good points, and near sale time they must be washed and groomed.

It was through the Aberdeen Angus that I came to visit the Castle of Mey and have tea with the Queen Mother. She is a patron of the Aberdeen Angus Society and an enthusiastic and knowledgeable breeder. A small herd is kept and maintained at her farm at the Castle of Mey in Caithness. Soon after the Millbank Herd was formed, we became members of the North East Aberdeen Angus Breeders and through the Society an open field day was arranged to view her herd at the Castle. It was August 1983.

I do not think people realised that they were to meet the Queen Mother (we certainly did not), and a bus party that had been arranged had to be cancelled owing to so few coming forward. We were a small party, about ten, and we travelled in our own cars. Only Sandy and I went and we took a friend, Mrs Pittendreigh, with us.

We stayed in a hotel in Wick and went next morning to Thurso where Sandy wanted to attend sheep sales. Mrs Pittendreigh and I had an enjoyable couple of hours wandering around and then Sandy joined us for lunch before we set off for the Castle a few miles distant. We were due at two-thirty and were the first to arrive at the entrance gate where two policemen were on duty. All cars had to be checked and the occupants' names and addresses taken. There were questions to confirm our identity and, after a list was consulted, we were let through. When the Castle came into view I recognised it instantly from pictures I had seen. We were directed to park the car in a field at the back, facing the North Sea. A very high wall surrounded the garden, protecting it from the cold north winds, and we were free to wander round. They say Her Majesty had much to do with the planning and laying out of the garden and it was an absolute dream of loveliness - roses bloomed in profusion. From a pink rose tree growing on the wall, I managed to take a small piece, putting it safely away. It was planted here at Bankhead in a sheltered spot in my garden. It seemed to take and all through the winter it was carefully nursed and when spring arrived, to my joy, a small bud appeared from which two leaves sprung. Alas, they withered off and died, much to my disappointment. I have plants from many parts growing in my garden, but none from the Castle of Mey.

At the hotel in Wick, when all the party had dined together, we had been told that the Queen Mother was in residence and was expected to appear at the opening of the Field Day. Still, it was quite a surprise and a delight that, as we wandered around, two ladies appeared at the front door, accompanied by a few Corgie dogs. Although I had never seen the Queen Mother she was easily recognisable.

We had bright sunshine most of the afternoon but, occasionally, wisps of fog from the sea drifted in, blotting out almost everything. This annoyed me when I had the camera at the ready, but they only lasted a few minutes and I did get quite a lot of good slides.

As two-thirty approached, the atmosphere of expectancy in the crowd could be felt, but the Queen did not keep us waiting. Promptly on time the castle door opened and she stepped out with her entourage and walked down the driveway. One could scarcely believe that she had celebrated her eighty-third birthday the week before. She was dressed in her favourite blue - hat, frock and coat all to match. The

President of the Society, Will Maitland of Balhaggarty, came forward and bade her welcome and with no further fuss she mingled with the crowd. There is something very special about the Queen Mother's personality that she can bring a gathering of ordinary people up to an extraordinarily high level. She makes herself just one of the crowd. Several people were introduced to her and I too could have had that honour, but somehow a shyness came over me and before my time came, I slipped behind another and manoeuvred myself out of the company. I don't know why.

We saw the Aberdeen Angus herd and the pedigree North County Cheviot ewes. The cows and sheep were in the field adjoining and several were penned for demonstration purposes. There was a marquee where teas were to be served, and several other small stalls selling plants, flowers and souvenirs. In the garden were collection boxes with all proceeds in aid of Scotland's Garden Scheme.

An hour or so after our arrival, we gathered at a point outside the marquee where a table had been set up to accommodate a few guest speakers. Will Maitland was in the chair. He introduced Her Majesty who, in a clear sweet voice, bade us welcome and gave a short speech. I know I thought it was wonderful but not a word do I remember. What I do remember, is my amazement when I felt a tap on my shoulder, and on turning round found Her Majesty's equerry standing behind me holding a chair. "Madam," he said, "Her Majesty thought you might like a seat." I gladly sat down. Noticing that I had been looking tired and sending her equerry with a chair, was a most endearing gesture from the Queen Mother. Later on in the marquee, where they were serving teas, she moved around quite freely speaking to anyone. There were piles of home bakes and just like the rest of us, she helped herself to a cup and a cake. As she drank it, I almost stood next to her and I could easily have thanked her for the chair, but I was far too shy.

It really was a marvellous day. We left shortly before 6 pm. The day was to conclude with a ceilidh in the Pentland Arms in Thurso, but though it would have been most enjoyable, we decided to come straight home. A few years before, I had been in the district and I wanted to revisit the Conisbay Church where the Queen Mother worshipped when in residence. This church had a special interest for me as it had also been founded by St. Drostan. We also had a look around John O'Groats before heading for home. Once on the way, Sandy hates to stop, and except for one call of nature, we didn't stop till Nairn. I was a bit grumpy for my tummy kept rumbling. When we did stop it was too late for a meal, but a big surprise was awaiting us.

Since we had left John O'Groats, peculiar noises had been coming from the car, sometimes just a small squeak, at others a most weird wail. None of us could think what it was and I think it was this, more than hunger, that caused Sandy to draw into the car park in Nairn. Under the bonnet was a very small black and white kitten wedged in the engine. It took Sandy some manoeuvring to get the poor mite free. How long it had been there none of us had any idea but it seemed to be none the worse for its ordeal. Mrs Pittendreigh, evidently no lover of cats, thought it would be best just to let it go free, but it was a tiny little thing and I gathered it into my arms and kept it safely there for the rest of the journey. Mrs. Pittendreigh had to be taken home first and it was well after midnight when we arrived back at Bankhead. No cup of tea awaited me, as all had gone to bed, but I found some milk and both the kitten and I had a hot drink. I put it in a box and carefully shut it in the office.

I was well rewarded for bringing home that small kitten. It took only days to settle in and became a much loved cat. It was such a pretty thing with distinctive markings and, as it also had a very dignified and aristocratic manner, we named it Lady Elizabeth.

Where it came from has remained a mystery. All that afternoon the car had been parked in a corner of a field far away from habitation. In the forenoon, it had been standing in a back street in Thurso and it might have come from some of the houses, but I myself think it came from the hotel in Wick where we had stayed the night because about a year later I spent a night in the same hotel. In the morning, we had to go round to the back to board a bus, to the same place where our car had been parked. As we waited for the bus to leave, I noticed a black and white cat come out of the kitchen premises. One of the staff came out and fetched her in, but in no time she was back. She reminded me very much of Lady Elizabeth. If it had not been that we were just leaving, I would have gone and had a chat with the kitchen staff and perhaps solved the mystery of our unusual passenger.

The cat was not the only surprise we had from that trip. Next evening the phone rang with Mrs Pittendreigh on the line. She was very excited. "Did you see the six o'clock news on the telly?" she asked and sounded disappointed when I said we hadn't. The BBC had been giving the news of the Field Day, showing pictures of the Castle of Mey and the Queen Mother. Among the views was a picture of us three, she said. She herself was more in the background, but it was very good of Sandy and those who knew me would have no doubts as to the identity of the lady seated in the chair. I knew the BBC had been filming that day and could remember, just after the incident of the chair, a bright light striking us, but had forgotten all about it. The cameramen must have noticed me being given the chair.

That same year, a film on the life of the Queen Mother was being made and surprise, the clip from the Castle of Mey was again included. Much to my disappointment I still have not seen it. I had a friend staying with me when it was being shown, and both being fond of the Queen, we were looking forward to viewing it. Somehow we forgot and it had started before we switched on. Little did we know that the purchase and restoration of the Caithness castle was at the beginning of the film, and that the picture of me at the open day had already been shown; most of my relatives and friends recognised me and told me how good it was. I was dressed that day with a white blouse, a Forbes tartan skirt and jacket which had blended well with the surroundings. I always hope it will be repeated sometime and I will be able to have a video-tape of it.

As I write, another Aberdeen Angus heifer has been added to the Bankhead Herd: Pink Primrose of Kinellar. She calves in January 1992 and will be three years old in March: PERTH HERE WE COME!

CHAPTER FIFTEEN

A MIXED BUNCH

BANKHEAD WAS no jewel in Ivan's crown. He had had a slight limp since childhood, one of his legs being slightly shorter than the other. Before he left Redbriggs, the leg had caused him trouble and he had a great deal of pain in his hip. That increased at Bankhead caused, he said, by all the braes he had to climb. He was fit otherwise and did manage to get through a good deal of work, but always in pain. This, I think, was the reason that he disliked the place. He never settled. Ivan was so difficult to understand. The black moods had gradually disappeared but in their place came bouts of depression, and we all suffered from his fits of bad temper. Looking back, it must have been awfully frustrating feeling fit, yet being unable to do the jobs he liked doing. Visits to the doctor and numerous pills did little to help.

At that time, they were beginning to experiment with hip operations and when it was suggested to him that he go into hospital to have one, he readily consented. A year later he was allocated a bed in Stracathro Hospital. He had never been in hospital, never had a serious illness of any kind, yet he was quite determined to have the operation. His keenness waned somewhat, however, when the time came nearer. I can smile now at the excuses and capers he got up to the week before he was due to leave. Bathtime the night before, clean garments and getting him into the car for the journey, were nightmares. From here to Stracathro takes about three hours. As he was due at the hospital in the early afternoon, we left mid-morning, stopping in Stonehaven for a meal. All the way down it had been a continual argument and by that time I had given up and left it to Sandy. After our meal, he was all for going back and Sandy had great difficulty in getting him back in the car. But after a half promise to take him back, a promise he had no intention of keeping, Ivan was once more seated in the car and the final miles of the journey were accomplished in record time.

After being booked in, it was suggested that before we left, we might all have a cup of tea together at the canteen. When Sandy or I made a move to return home, Ivan was determined to get back into the car and come with us to the top of the drive; he would walk back, he said, but Sandy was not risking this. Finally, we bade him goodbye, leaving him standing at the entrance steps, a forlorn figure. It made my heart turn over, for I did love him despite all his shortcomings. I can still recall the big sigh of relief I gave as the car drove out through the gate.

Early that evening the phone rang; it was the nursing sister from his ward. He had been scheduled to have his operation next morning, but they would have to be postpone it as they had found a sore on the back of his neck that would have to heal before they could operate. They were thinking of sending him home until it healed. I interrupted saying, "Oh no!"

"You don't seem to be happy at the prospect of getting your husband home." she said.

"Neither would you," I replied, "if you had known all the trials and tribulations I went through to get him down to Stracathro. I just could not face going through that all over again." After some more talk she agreed to keep him and try to get the sore healed quickly. The operation took place the following week.

Today a hip operation is simple; the patient is up and about in a matter of weeks. In the 1960s it was more complicated. A steel pin was inserted into Ivan's hip joint to fix it together. It took months to heal and get him mobile again. Once the operation was over, Ivan settled in well and enjoyed hospital life. In the bed next to him was another farmer from Premnay, a Mr Smith. The pair became great friends and on our visits to the hospital, I met Mrs Smith and we formed a friendship which lasted for many years.

I tried to get down to Stracathro on a Sunday each fortnight and with other members of the family going on the Sunday between, he had visitors each week. Ivan entered hospital late in February and came home at the end of April. The operation was not the success we expected. It did ease the pain and with the aid of a stick he was able to get around for a short time. In a year or two he was back in hospital, this time at Forresterhill, and the pin was removed. It had slipped, they said, but had done the job it was supposed to do. Once home, the hip got very stiff and it was only with considerable effort that he managed to get around. He gallantly soldiered on. The other leg served him well, and it was surprising how many jobs he managed to do now that he was free of pain. The operation had at least saved him from a wheelchair.

The year after Ivan had his operation, Robin decided to get married. This upset matters somewhat as there was no second house on the farm and in any case we were not in a position to run two households and pay wages. Robin left Bankhead and took work elsewhere. At that time, casual labour and agricultural contractors were available from the village and Sandy managed to keep the work going. That year a dog called Nellie and I helped with the lambing - a spell of work I enjoyed. It was into March when lambing started and the weather was exceptionally good, otherwise I might not have been so enthusiastic. We missed Robin most then. From an early age he had taken an interest in the ewes and from then on had been the shepherd.

One afternoon, I had gone for a walk round the sheep and Nell had come with me. Ivan always had a few dogs around him and, although Nell was a favourite with him, neither he nor anyone else had ever bothered to give her any training. Much to my surprise, she answered when I gave her a command. Later, I took her, following closely at my heels, on an early morning round . It was sheer delight to breathe in the fresh air, feel new growth awakening all around and see a pair or perhaps three newly born lambs. She obeyed my commands beautifully, rounding up the sheep and holding any that needed attention. I had to fetch Sandy for any ewe in trouble lambing, for over the years, with all the various jobs I had tackled, I always kept away if it was killing a chicken, lambing a ewe, or calving a cow. I got told off many a time, but it made no difference; nursing the little lambs and the sick calves I excelled at. Just don't ask me to go near a birth. I had never had a dog that worked for me before and have never had another. I trained our first dog Lassie, but when we moved over to the croft and Ivan was at home, she deserted me and attached herself to him. At Redbriggs, Ivan usually attended the Tuesday mart at Turriff and I would go out at dinner time to get the cows in for milking. When Ivan got them in, all he did was open the field gate and Lassie did the rest. When she came with me, however, and I told her to fetch the cows, she paid no attention,

A new lamb above Aberdour Bay

gave me a disdainful look and walked off. All the other dogs I tried did the same, so it was quite a thrill having Nell working so well for me. Strange to say, she never worked for Ivan or the boys. She was timid, lovable and gentle, but had one bad fault: along with the other dogs she used to go poaching, often staying away all night. This troubled us very much; we were afraid the dogs might land themselves in trouble and so we began to chain them up.

One day, Nellie broke her chain and went off with it still attached to her collar. The other dogs came back but not Nellie. We were almost sure she had got caught in some bushes and had been held by the chain. We went out often in the evening to call her. We thought if she was trapped in her own territory, she would hear us and bark in return, but not one bark did we hear and after a week or two, we gave her up for dead. It was at least three weeks later when, to our joy, a very thin, sorry and dejected Nellie returned home. She had no collar or chain. How she had survived we never knew, but as she got thinner she must have been able to pull her head out of the collar. Her delight at being back was obvious, and she soon recovered and never roamed

248

again.

Robin was not happy and soon got tired working as an employee, so a way had to be found to establish him back at Bankhead. A short distance along the coast road, just above Dundarg Castle, there was an empty croft house. The owner was willing to sell the house, along with about two acres of ground, at a very reasonable sum. The house was in good repair, with water and electric light, and Robin would have been very happy to move in. It had been standing empty because a demolition order had been placed on it by the District Council, prohibiting anyone living in it until a bathroom was installed. The previous tenant had wanted a council house in Fraserburgh and to get one, had had to have his present house condemned. It was best to observe the rules and in the meantime another cottage, not nearly so good, was found in the east side of the village. Robin moved in with Anne and their baby son Robert. It took more than a year to have the order on the croft rescinded and a kitchen, living room and bathroom added. The name, Bridestonefold, intrigued me. Dr David Murison, an expert on place names, suggested it might have connections with St. Bride or Bridgit. I think the simple explanation is that someone came to this stony place that still has big boulders lying near, built himself a house for his bride and called it Bridestonefold.

During the time that Ivan was in Stracathro, I too had trouble with my leg and hip. After an examination in Aberdeen Infirmary, it was arranged for me to have a course of electric treatment. Throughout that summer I went twice a week for massage at the Fraserburgh Clinic and it helped greatly. In the years that followed I was fortunate to be able to get domestic help. The girls of a family living nearby, although still at school, were keen to earn some money. They came each Saturday during the school holidays, first Sheila Bannerman and then her younger sister Monica. Both girls gave service over several years.

I now marvel how I managed to look after and feed all the visitors I had, including my own family. I remember one particular weekend I fed and bedded twenty-two people. I had no freezer, only vans to supply me: a baker and butcher twice a week; sometimes a fish van and the grocer, Grant Gauld from the village. Numerous nieces and their friends came for holidays and my two grandchildren - Ena's

Robert and Aileen - always spent their holidays at Bankhead. There was never a dull moment.

Other visits I enjoyed were through the Young Farmers movement. Sandy had joined the Strichen branch and become a prominent member. He persuaded me to board various visiting members from overseas. From a peanut farm in Australia came Pat Moore and from Sweden, Bengt Kowlands, sturdy, charming and fair-haired. We also enjoyed a pair of sisters from Switzerland - Verena and Elizabeth Gerber and two lovely boys from New Zealand - David Anderson from the North Island and Peter Cook from the South. Peter did not have a lot of Scottish connections - he thought his forebears came from England - but David had many Scottish ancestors and I was able to help trace them. They came from Ross-shire and left at the time of the clearances. Both kept up a correspondence for years and hoped to persuade Sandy to make a return visit, but he would not be moved. In later years, Peter came to a conference in London and was able to visit for a weekend. He again did his best to make Sandy return with him, but by this time Sandy was suffering ill-health. He had been unfortunate in picking up Brucellosis from the cows. He still suffers some effects of it and we were never able to persuade him to travel to New Zealand.

Another visitor was Marie Claude, a delightful lass from France. She and my niece Elizabeth had become friends through a school correspondence and one year when Elizabeth was visiting, Marie Claude too came for a holiday. She loved Scotland and made many repeat visits. Later, the Swiss girls came and somehow they all managed to persuade Sandy to make a return visit to France and Switzerland.

He decided to take the car and, as there were two spare seats, Auntie Win and I were asked to join them. Robin and Anne would be working with Ivan on the farm and Mrs Duguid, an old friend, came to stay with Ivan to keep him company and cook meals. That year the weather had been good, letting the boys get the spring crops in early. Even the turnip sowing was almost completed. Gone were the days of back-breaking work when weeds had to be gathered and dung carted out, all of which took weeks to accomplish. The work is now mostly mechanised and over in days.

Sandy and Marie Claude on Daisy

We left in the middle of May on a lovely morning. The car was packed and clothes laid out the night before so all we had to do was get up, have some breakfast and be off. Ivan and Mrs Duguid were not to be disturbed, but she appeared to wish us 'bon voyage'. After the long weeks of planning, I remember the delight I felt as the car slipped quietly down the Bankhead road. There before us lay the shimmering dew-covered grass and the air felt so fresh and sweet. We had lunch at Moffat with another Young Farmer friend and after a brief farm tour (they had a dairy herd and grew potatoes), we were on our way to Manchester where Auntie Win lived. We stayed the night and left next morning for Leigh-on-Sea, near Southend, the home of another niece, where we stayed the next night. It was an experience to pass through the Dartford Tunnel and to see the flat, green fields of Kent, then on to Dover. The hustle and bustle of getting the car and ourselves aboard the ferry was all new and exciting, but in no time the boat pulled out to start the crossing to France. I recall looking up and seeing those majestic white cliffs and humming the words *"see those blue birds over, the white cliffs of Dover"* which were so popular after the War.

They say the crossing can be very wild but it was like sailing over

251

a pond. Soon the shores of France appeared. We disembarked and then had the thrill of setting foot on foreign soil. We soon left Calais behind and headed north into Flanders where all the bitter fighting of the First World War took place. We stopped for the night at a small hotel at Bethune. The French I had learned at school served me but little; I could neither speak nor write it, but I could read it quite well and this often helped. From Bethune, we drove through the Somme valley to Peronne and hence to Caen, again travelling through a First World War battlefield. We stopped to visit the British cemetery of La-Ville-Aux-Bois. It was beautifully kept but filled us with sadness. We looked for the Scottish regiments and were standing near some Gordon Highlanders' graves when a man who had been working nearby came and spoke to us. "Excuse me" he said, "but I could hear you were from Aberdeenshire. I come from Keith." What a pleasant surprise. We talked awhile. During the war he had been billeted with a French family and had fallen in love with their daughter. They were married and he had got a job in the British Cemetery. We had another stop, in Rheims, to visit the Cathedral; I wanted to see the rose window.

We reached Marie Claude's home that evening and were welcomed by Mr and Mrs Jacob who lived in a flat above the bank where Mr Jacob was manager. We stayed a full week and were treated like royal guests. I think a show was put on for our benefit, for I could hardly believe they lived like that all the time.

I shall never forget that first night - the table and the meal that followed were beyond belief. Before we sat down, I enjoyed my very first glass of champagne. The table was beautifully set with a silver candelabrum and lighted candles, but no flowers. Mrs Jacob and Marie Claude brought all the food through from the kitchen and we each helped ourselves from the serving dishes. The first was cold lamb in a sauce and thinking this was the main course I took a generous helping. Variety, they say, is the spice of life and that night we had it in abundance. Three, if not four meat courses were served, followed by the same number of vegetable dishes, and all off the same plate. Seated beside me was a young niece of Mrs Jacobs. After each course she carefully cleaned her plate with a piece of bread and I followed her example.

As dish followed dish, my confusion mounted, for although only one plate was used, it was not so with the glasses. On a side table next to Mr Jacob stood an array of wines and glasses and from this, as each new dish appeared, he very graciously replaced and filled our glasses, giving us very little chance of refusing. The vegetables were followed by a sweet course consisting of several different dishes, but for this we exchanged our plates for smaller ones. To finish, we had cheese and biscuits with the choice of a liqueur or coffee. Sweets and fruit were also on the table and towards the end I had to refuse many of the dishes - how I managed to drag myself from the table and stagger to bed is quite beyond me.

I wondered how Mrs Jacob had, single-handedly, been able to cook, arrange and present all this fabulous food, but I realised later that much of it had been bought ready for the table; there were many delicatessen shops selling the dishes we had been served. The meal in itself took over two hours. Marie Claude said it was usual for French families to sit down together each evening for their meal, enjoying each other's company and discussing points of interest and any family news.

Breakfast was a simple meal in the kitchen, of grapefruit, cereals, bread and some delicious buns. Win had coffee, but Marie Claude made tea for Sandy and me. We went out each morning and came back in the late afternoon. Marie Claude had taken leave of absence from college and Mr Jacob a week's holiday to take us around. Mrs Jacob never accompanied us, but was always there to welcome us when we returned. Except for a small snack with wine or coffee, we never ate out. We usually returned in plenty of time for a rest and a wash before our evening meal at seven-thirty. Before we went through to the dining room, a pleasant half hour was spent chatting and enjoying a glass of champagne. Each night the meal followed the same pattern, though perhaps not quite so elaborate as the first. I had now become wiser and missed out what did not appeal to me, but I always rose from the table having consumed far too much.

The weather was good, dry and warm each day and we were able to go out, but one night there was a dreadful thunderstorm which kept us awake for most of the night. The morning papers reported a lot of damage, not that we could read them; Marie Claude did. Her parents knew only a few English words and we knew fewer of French, but when she was present, communication was always very good.

Time moved on quickly and we reluctantly said goodbye, for we were now due to join the Gerber family in Switzerland. Our route to the border lay north-west and we planned to spend a night at Ponterlier quite near to the French-Swiss frontier. It was well towards evening when we arrived.

The day had been long but pleasantly warm and we were all tired and hungry. Although supplied with ample wine and food for the journey, we had eaten little. Our first priority was to find somewhere to sleep. We found a secluded spot and while Win was getting the meal ready I found a bottle of wine in the boot of the car. It was good and I had two glasses. During the meal I had another and, lo and behold, when I made the effort to get up, I found my legs were not there. I felt light and bubbly and immediately began to giggle. Win and Sandy thought this most amusing and had to help me to the car to head back to the boarding house. Getting me upstairs to bed was hilarious - Mother was drunk and all on a 4s 6d bottle of wine.

The next morning we had to be on the road early and I did not feel too good. The frontier was only a few miles up the road. There were two sets of Customs - the French and the Swiss. We passed through with no bother, just a quick look at our passports and a check over the car. We hoped to reach Berne that day and the Gerber's farm was in a village only three or four miles further on.

So far, we had travelled in very flat country, but now the road began to ascend gradually through a pleasant wooded valley, turning and twisting all the time. The scenery was very attractive, with views of lakes and mountains. Sorry to say I was in no mood to appreciate it; the movement of the car going up and down was making me feel sick. At mid-day we stopped at Neuchatel. Win and Sandy enjoyed a lunch from some of our leftovers, but all I wanted was a drink of water. Somehow Win managed to persuade me to have some brandy, assuring me it would settle my stomach. It did the opposite, and before we reached Berne I was very sick. We had to stop for over an hour, but once on the road again, Sandy was able to pass through Berne and find the village. He showed some people the name and address of our hosts and found we had stopped right in front of the Gerber's house.

We had a wonderful time, for Switzerland is such a beautiful country. France has its attractions, but one has to remember that France has twice been ravaged by world wars fought on her soil. Switzerland has never been invaded and, seeing her terrain and boundaries, one does not wonder why. Our stay in France with the Jacobs was delightful, but the Gerbers were more our kind of folk. The food was completely different and all cooked by Mrs Gerber herself with potatoes, milk and veal frequently on the menu. No wine was served, but coffee and boiled milk. Milk has always been a favourite of mine. I was not particularly fond of it boiled, yet it fitted in fine; their coffee was very black and strong which pleased Win, but to me it was almost like poison. If I put just a small drop in my cup and filled it up with milk, however, it was a very acceptable drink.

The first day, Elizabeth showed us over the farm and round part of the village. What a contrast to our untidy yard and farm buildings - not a single straw, piece of paper or even a single feather floating around. All had been miraculously swept clean by the men, using brushes. The midden, well it had to be seen to be believed in its conception and appearance.

They kept about twenty Simmental milk cows in a large cow shed, summer and winter. The milking was done by machine, all up to date and hygienic and, would you believe it, in the byre they had a long trough filled with flowering geraniums on a window recess.

They reared few calves, only some heifers for replacements. Most of their calves were sold at a few days old and killed for veal. They had a bull with the cows and their other young heifers grazed during the winter in a long orchard. When spring arrived, they were moved up to the hills. Compared to our farms theirs were small, with only about thirty acres in cultivation: a few acres in wheat and maize and the rest in grass which was cut as silage and hay, several crops being taken off each field. I have always been interested in flowers and I soon noticed the yellow dandelion heads in the crops. On closer inspection, I saw that there were several long plants - in fact I had never seen such big healthy specimens - all through the grass crop. Dandelions were just weeds to me, although I remember that we gathered them as children and fed them to our pet rabbits. I pulled some leaves and tried to make Mr Gerber understand that I was surprised at them growing there, but he just shook his head and said "cow good" and rubbed his stomach. Elizabeth explained later that they were grown profusely in some grass mixtures and were high in nutrients.

All the farms had their homes and buildings in the village, with their cultivated ground well outside. They also had access to vast common grazings away up in the mountains and hills that surrounded the village. Most were dairy farms and they had their own creamery in the village. The milk was taken there twice daily and was measured and recorded before the farmers took back their own supply of milk and cream. They also had butter, cheese, yogurt and ice cream. It was all a marvellous piece of organisation and all village affairs were conducted in the same way. Each village was complete in itself; the schools and road repairs were also in local management.

The family rose very early, having breakfast about five o'clock but we were told ours would be ready at eight o'clock. The children started school at seven am but were home, finished for the day, at twelve-thirty. It got very hot after mid-day and after their mid-day meal most people returned home for a rest and did not start work again till around four o'clock.

Most days, Elizabeth took us out in her car. One day we went up to Lake Lausanne for a cruise, another day we were taken on a train journey high up into the Alps and visited a ski slope on the Agra. We went through tunnels deep into the mountains, seeing marvellous waterfalls and awesome cauldrons. Our last afternoon was spent visiting Berne, doing some shopping and seeing the famous bears.

Like the rest of our holiday, our days passed quickly and soon it was time to move on again. Sandy had promised the Young Farmers that he would assist them at the Highland Show which was at the end of June, so we would have to be in Edinburgh then. We thought it would be nice to see some more of France and with a map, we planned our route. We travelled north, visiting Geneva, then crossed the border into France and spent the night in the ski resort of St. Moritz.

Now, for the first time, we saw snow-clad mountains. The village was charming and full of big hotels. I was beginning to think it would be nice to have one night in a posh hotel and Sandy even offered to pay the whole bill, but Win would have none of it so we had to find accommodation in a smaller establishment. Next day we walked around and watched the cable cars taking skiers off up the mountain. Sandy would have loved to join them, but not so his companions. Soon after lunch, we left for Paris hoping to stay the night somewhere and see some of the sights next day.

That night we almost slept in the car, for it was very late before we found beds at an isolated boarding house for woodworkers. It was Saturday night and most of the boarders were away home. To our surprise, we found our hostess had once worked as an au pair girl in Aberdeen and could understand us. We spoke of our desire to visit Paris, she explainedthat, it being Sunday, there were no trains and advised us to go to St. Denis. But nowhere could we find any bus tours, nor any English-speaker to direct us. We were only ten miles out and Win was keen to see some of the sights so, much against Sandy's better judgment, he consented to have a go. A long autoban surrounded Paris with at least five or six routes going each way. It proved an absolute nightmare. We could not understand the signs and Sandy had no idea which route to take. We came quite near to the city and could see the Eiffel Tower but we could not find a way in. Sandy began to have a horror that we could be driving for the rest of the day till our petrol ran out.

Wemanaged at last to get into a petrol station and found that the attendant understood English. We had given up hopes of visiting Paris and just wanted to get out. The man gave us directions on to the north route which would eventually lead us to Calais. Here my slight knowledge of French came to our aid, and by recognising the word 'north', I was able to guide Sandy out. What a delight to leave the cars and fumes behind, stop our car and get out; I almost danced with joy. By checking on our map the name of the first town we entered, we found no difficulty in taking up a route to Calais which took us another two days.

I have many happy memories of our trip, but our biggest source of amusement was the toilets. There were no two alike and it was often difficult to puzzle out how they worked. There were a lot of primitive ones with just a hole over a drain - no seat or water. Win was horrified, but I viewed them more complacently for I had been brought up with an outside toilet and no water.

257

Many of those toilets were to be found in towns, usually in the middle of a square. They were round, built of iron with a wooden door and consisting of six to eight cubicles. The doors were hung with an open space at the bottom and if you saw feet on the earthen floor, you knew not to go in. They must all have disappeared long ago. In the countryside we often saw a man standing by the roadside or on a bridge, having a free pee.

Another amusing thing was that the hoteliers were all determined to make us sleep, if not in the same bed, at least in the same room. Win and I usually went together to negotiate, leaving Sandy in the car and a difficulty always arose trying to get him a single room. We began to take him with us but it made no difference, and often to get a single room we had to pay for a double.

We arrived at Calais the day before we were due to sail home, and after booking in for the night we went to visit Dunkirk. We found no trace of the holocaust where so many of our kin had lost their lives. My brother, Win's husband, had been one of the lucky ones that had been taken off the beaches, but now the whole area was a vast expanse of hotels and holiday homes. We did find a quiet secluded spot with marked graves of many British soldiers and seamen, their bodies laid to rest.

Next day we crossed a calm and placid channel again to the white cliffs of Dover. We headed north, first to Manchester to take Win home, and next morning we left early for Edinburgh, spending a few hours in the Lake District on the way, having a lunch break beside the dark, deep waters of Lake Coniston.

I had known Edinburgh for a long time; my niece Agnes and her husband Jim lived there and through them I had come to know and love that old grey city, known affectionately as 'Auld Reekie'. It had also been my mother's second home and, although she was a Buchan lass, she loved Edinburgh more. That love passed through her to me.

The night we arrived I phoned home and found all well. No-one seemed anxious for our return, but we had now been away five weeks and we were both ready to get back. Sandy had three days to put in at the Royal Show-ground first, helping to set up the Young Farmers' stand, then acting as steward. I spent one day there and enjoyed looking round, but it was very hot and dry, and I soon tired. Agnes persuaded us to stay an extra night. As a treat she had booked seats at the Picture Theatre where the first showing of 'The Sound of Music', was taking place. Watching the lovely scenery of the Austrian Tyrol, I never thought that one day I would see it for myself, but I did.

It had been a great holiday, but it was good to be back and to see again the green braes and winding 'loups' of Bankies. As the car covered the last mile home, I thought how fortunate we had been having no trouble with it, not even a burst wheel; the fan belt broke at the Mill Farm the very next day. Although we got no rapturous welcome, I think they were all pleased to see us back, safe and sound. On the table I noticed, with pleasure, a vase full of fresh flowers but I knew well it was not Ivan's idea.

CHAPTER SIXTEEN

TIME FOR LEISURE

WHEN BANKHEAD was bought, a full partnership was drawn up between father and sons and my name was also added. Ivan had always seen to the business side of the farm, such as ordering supplies, interviewing travellers, consulting the bank and signing cheques, but when he went down to Stracathro to hospital, I had to take over. On his return, Ivan was content to leave matters as they were, but gradually the boys began to take over the responsibility and I was more than happy to shed mine. It left me free to pursue my other interests. One of those was my garden.

They say you are nearer to God in a garden than anywhere else on earth and that has been so very true for me. Working away in the garden, pulling out a few weeds, feeling the earth slip through my fingers and seeing the wonder and beauty of new blown flowers, many a rebellious thought has vanished and peace and solace restored my troubled mind.

Of all our abodes, Bankhead was the only one with a real garden. When we arrived it was far from promising though it was ideally situated. It lay in a half acre of terraced ground which sloped away from the front of the south-facing house. Fifty years before we arrived it had been beautifully laid out with boxwood paths, trees and shrubs and many apple and plum trees which provided an abundance of fruit. The old walls hold ample proof of this for there are still numerous nails which held their branches. One very old apple tree remained, the one that had drawn my attention the day we arrived with its lovely profusion of pink blossom. One bush of flowering currant and two very tall, old and ugly holly trees also survived. Some of the branches

Bankhead and the garden from the air

still bore a few green leaves but most were weathered. Later on we trimmed them and the birds love to shelter beneath their prickly green leaves. Nests are often built in them and cheerful chatter can often be heard though it rises to a crescendo of fearful shrieks when the white cat appears. She is an expert bird stalker but her colour proves a hindrance. The garden is now a haven for small birds, for it is again filled with trees and shrubs.

Among all the bustle and hustle of moving to Bankhead I managed to plant two treasured rose bushes: a pink one called Queen Elizabeth and Victoria, a yellow one. They had been at Redbriggs and were planted each side of the door. Beside them some Tom Thumb seeds were sown, the only flowers I had successfully grown at Redbriggs. They gave a nice display around the front door. From there, there were steps into the garden proper, where the remains of a path going east to west could still be traced. Another, going down the centre, had a gate opening into a small field which had been used as a sheep pen. Neither Ivan nor the boys showed much interest in the garden and shared the former owner's view that it was more use to hold sheep.

With a great deal of coaxing from me, the old pathway was covered with shingle and between it and the wall a herbaceous border was dug; the garden soil at Bankhead is rich and loamy and easy to

261

dig. A clump of pink lupins which had struggled to survive at Redbriggs were the first plants to grow and flourish but, alas, they were no longer a pretty pink but had reverted to their natural blue. Someone suggested I buy a packet of Russel Lupin seeds. This I did and I got a marvellous display in all colours which attracted admiration for many years. Lupins do well by the sea for my neighbour, Mrs Black, also had a lovely display. Since then I have planted several clumps of paeony roses: cream, pink, pure white and a lovely deep red rose which grew from a root I dug from a long-deserted garden in Pennan.There are now several clumps of Pennan paeony and they are, I think, just about the most beautiful flowers in my garden.

All summer, veronica bushes bloom profusely in the herbaceous bed and even in autumn there is still quite a bit of colour: some silver and golden variegated privet, a few clumps of mauve Michaelmas daisies, some very large mauve and white autumn crocii and always the glossy green leaves of the veronicas.

The first spring after we came to Bankhead, when no spring flowers appeared, except for one lone bunch of snowdrops, I was very surprised that no-one had planted daffodils. I thought of that garden of my childhood: first there had been snowdrops, aconites, then crocus followed by the daffodils. I decided to remedy this and one year made a pilgrimage to Mormond with my friend Chrissie. Armed with spade we dug up daffodil bulbs from my childhood garden.

Along with the lupins brought from Redbriggs were blackcurrant and gooseberry bushes. Robin was very proud of those for he had grown them from cuttings while still at school. After over thirty years those bushes still flourish and bear a lot of fruit. Later I planted a pear tree, an apple and a plum tree beside them. The apple tree is so lovely when in blossom and, when the winds allow, produces good apples. The pear tree has also done well but the plum, though it has grown and flourished, has never once even blossomed.

Beside the wall where Mr Brownie had grown his vegetables I planted strawberries. Since the days of my childhood it had been my dream to own a strawberry patch. I have many memories of a garden where I scrambled up and down searching out those succulent red berries, filling up a brimming basket. Many more berries found a home elsewhere in the process. How often on the way to the 'wee hoose', a handful was plucked and, seated on the throne, eaten and enjoyed. I was determined to bring back those early joys but my strawberry patch at Bankhead never flourished. My grandfather planted the one in the garden at home long before my time and never once did I know him dig it up or replant it, but all the coaxing of runners I tried at Bankhead never gave me what I aimed for. The plants often bloomed in abundance and my hopes were raised, but the flowers soon faded. Some said there were no bees to fertilise them but reading up on the subject, I realised my plants were hybrids and like hybrid pullets, only produced for one or two years. Visitors often enjoyed strawberries and cream, but the pots of jam I was able to make were few and far between. A new crop of weeds also seemed to come up each year and when buttercups took over, and more yellow flowers than white appeared, I dug the lot up in disgust.

Most gardeners get great satisfaction from their success in growing vegetables, but my interest has never been in that. Ivan liked his potatoes and cabbages, but those were grown in the turnip field so supplies were plentiful. Brussel sprouts, carrots, cauliflower and peas were all grown there. They might have been safer in the garden for at times the cattle broke out and the vegetables disappeared like magic. Deer also played havoc and I have known badgers to eat all the carrots. Once I grew a super row of beans for their lovely pink and red flowers; I found they were much easier to grow than sweet peas. My feathered friends, the sparrows, had often foiled my attempts to grow sweet peas by digging them up and eating them.

For flavouring soups and stews I like to have some kale, parsley and chives in the garden. Chives have lovely flowers which I have used many times in flower displays. Leeks were never grown in the field, but as I loved them I did try them once or twice. One time a few had been forgotten and when I found them they had produced large graceful heads with the most beautiful flowers you could imagine in colours of green, yellow and mauve. They too were added to an indoor flower arrangement, dried beautifully and lasted over a year.

In recent years, landscape gardening has been all the rage. As I survey the higgledy-piggledy of my beloved wilderness, I would have benefitted much from such advice. As we planned and planted, little heed was given to the overall effect in fifteen or twenty years time. The top half of the garden was laid out in walks, flower beds, areas of grass and shrubs with the two old holly trees right in the middle, dominating the scene. There are now two flowering cherries keeping the holly trees company. A tractor was brought in and the bottom half ploughed; potatoes were planted to clear the ground of weeds, then lifted early and grass seed sown. The grass did take a year or so to establish, but with the aid of a mower, and back-breaking pushing from Ivan, we now have a lovely sward of lawn. It has provided visitors, children and me with a lot of pleasure. Later, a hedge of privet and hawthorn was planted to divide the two areas. There, lots of tall trees - sycamores, ash and rowan and a few fir trees - were planted and they all adorn and shelter this oasis of green where children play ball games with the dogs, or roll and caper to their hearts' content while the elders lounge around watching and relaxing. Many a picnic has been enjoyed and there has been the odd garden party. One that I recall proved a great disappointment. The Young Farmers had been on a visit and everything had been set up to have tea in the garden when a downpour of rain suddenly came on and everything had to be quickly dismantled and the tea served in the barn.

A few of the shrubs and plants, like the privet and hawthorn, have been bought but the majority have been given me by friends and neighbours. I have two large rose beds. One ia a mixed bed, the other is full of yellow roses which I treasure for they were from the family, a present for our Golden Wedding anniversary. And Ena's son Robert planted a fuschia in a flower pot and presented it to me. It still produces large purple blooms even in October.

Many plants keep alive memories of places visited. Another two fuschias, which are a lovely red cascade of hanging bells in summer, bring me many lovely memories of another garden which lay near my old home in a sheltered spot at the foot of Mormond surrounding a ruined croft. The garden had been my secret place, a haven where all my joys and all my despairs were taken, a place for a quiet read or a place just to sit and dream. My two bushes originate from a tree growing there. Near them is another tree fuschia which grew from a slip off a tree growing by a wishing well in the quadrangle of Chester Cathedral. The slip came home wrapped in a piece of damp paper concealed in my toilet bag.

Still by the garden wall - or more naturally for me, the dyke - I linger. Memories come flooding back for so many people have come and gone, the dear friends of yesterday. Memory is such a wonderful thing and here in this garden there is a store of memories of things and people to cherish, a place to remember and yet a place to forget, a place for tears but a place for laughter too.

But it was not only in the garden that I enjoyed my leisure. Our French and Swiss holiday had given me a taste for travel and two holidays in particular deserve special mention. One morning, a year or so after that first trip, I was sitting at the breakfast table after the men had gone out, having a quiet read of the paper. My attention was drawn to a paragraph saying that the Reverend Alan Garrity of the South Church, Fraserburgh, was organising a trip to the Holy Land. Time stood still. I was back more than 50 years, sitting on a stool beside my dear old grandfather, listening to the kind gentle voice speak of that land. His knowledge of the bible was profound and he had a passionate concern for the wandering Jew. I remembered the words he spoke:

The birds of the air have their nests,
The foxes their lair,
Mankind his country,
Israel but the grave.

"Never mind, Granda, when I'm big, I'll tak ye there." I was an old lady of sixty remembering that conversation, till then the words, and the dream, forgotten. Slowly the dream and the desire were reborn. I got up from the table and phoned the manse. Neither Ivan nor the boys thought it was a good idea, in fact they thought I was a bit queer thinking of trucking away so far to an outlandish country, but my mind was made up. I would have three weeks in the Holy Land and I would be there at Easter time.

It was a very cold Scotland we left for the sunshine. This was my first flight but the idea of flying had never worried me. Once up above the clouds, it was beautiful. I caught a glimpse of the Alps and the outline of Italy with Sicily at its foot, like a football. It took over four and a half hours from Heathrow to Tel-Aviv. With a minimum of delay with luggage and passports at the airport, we were soon aboard an old and rickety bus on our way to Jerusalem.

Morning came and I woke early to a strange wailing noise that kept on and on. "Allah, Allah", it sounded like. I was there in Jerusalem and priests were calling the faithful to worship. Quickly slipping out of bed I drew aside the big heavy curtains. Our hotel lay high up on the slopes of Mount Scopus and I was gazing down on the indescribable beauty of Old Jerusalem all golden in the sun. It was a sheer delight and I could hardly believe it was real. There were so many mosques with domes of gold and the buildings were built with a stone not unlike our granite, but a lovely honey colour. Jerusalem is indeed the golden city as Aberdeen is the silver city.

I stood for more than half an hour trying to take it all in, and for the whole of the first week that was my daily routine. The panoramic view of the city, both old and new, lay before me and always there was something new to fascinate. Later, I was able to pick out the various buildings. Dominating the whole scene was the Dome on the Rock which I think must be one of the most beautiful buildings in the world. Away in the background was the Mount of Olives, but down below was a little, humble, family building. Early though it was, there were children playing and keeping them company were a few goats and some chickens. One morning an old Arab, dressed as in biblical times, trudged past astride a laden donkey, followed by his wife carrying a high bundle of firewood on her back. Flashing past them came a large blue Mercedes car. This was indeed a land of contrasts, covering almost everything - land, buildings and people - ancient and new all mixed together. I loved its beauty though it was strange to Western eyes. First and foremost it is the Holy Land, home of the three great faiths and home to Moslems, Jews and Christians alike with all their different sects and creeds.

On the first day we were taken to the old part of Jerusalem, but the lovely golden city I had seen early in the morning had disappeared. Built upon the Judean hills, the ground is covered with big boulders and stones. Some olive trees are grown but the soil is very poor and cultivation is carried out, as in biblical times, by women and donkeys. As I looked, the parable of the sower came to mind and I remember thinking that an awful lot of seed must have fallen on stony ground. We entered by the Damascus gate, one of the busiest, most ornate of the eight gates into the walled city. Each gate has its own history but to tell the story and describe the visit would fill a book. It is almost unbelievable that Israel has changed so little over the centuries. The Bible came alive and I think this gave a little something to my faith.

I have so many memories of those days we spent with our guide Ham. One is of an encounter with an Arab offering, at a price, rides on his camel. Some of the ladies took up the offer but I, for one, preferred to stay on the ground. Then there was the visit to The Dome on the Rock, the building which dominates all Jerusalem. Before we entered, our heads had to be covered and our shoes removed. A huge pile of shoes lay beside the door and very reluctantly I added mine - how would I ever find them again?

Inside, the beauty of the building was in contrast to the sad faces of groups of women sitting on the floor in devout prayer, their prayers seemingly giving them little contentment, joy or peace. I wondered, were they really praying or just begging? By their side lay a small bowl with some coins. Coming out, I found my shoes no bother and I needed them for we then went off on a long walk all round the Mount of Olives and visited many sites and shrines relating to the last days of Jesus.

I have fleeting memories of the room where the Last Supper took place, the church of Peter's denial and Judas's betrayal, but there were many others. Somewhere we sang '*The Lord's my Shepherd*' to the old tune of Crimond, giving us a wonderful lift. Often I longed to linger, but "Yalla! Yalla!" (Come! Come!) was Ham's constant call.

The church I liked best was the Church of Nations which stood in the garden of Gethsemane. Over the impressive entrance facade is a magnificent mosaic of Jesus on the Road of Agony and there were many lovely paintings which lent an atmosphere of tranquility and peace even though it was the scene of our Lord's agony. There were so many lovely flowers and several old and twisted olive trees which we were told could have been growing there when Jesus walked in the garden. My thoughts kept returning to our Lord on the night before he died, and I remembered too my own Gethsemane, far away on a lonely hillside in Scotland.

Another day we went to Bethlehem. I liked the outside appearance of the Church of the Nativity which is, they say, built over the stable, but once inside I felt disappointment. Never could I imagine that this was a stable and that Jesus was born within. All the brash ornaments were like idols and I longed to be outside. More real to me were the fields where, tradition says, the shepherds wandered with their flocks. Later the same day we visited Nazareth and saw the house supposed to be Mary and Joseph's.

On Good Friday we joined the parade of pilgrims up the Via Dolorosa to Calvary and thence to the Holy Sepulchre. As we travelled in the footsteps of our Lord, amongst sweet-voiced singers and black-robed priests carrying crosses, troubled thoughts came to me. I kept thinking of the hymn: "*There is a green hill far away outside the city wall*" - but where was the green hill? My heart was empty as the tomb in the Holy Sepulchre. Again there was no sense of worship, just nothing. All the candles and shining brass ornaments were, to me, graven images and to my mind came the words: "*Thou shalt have no other Gods*". Again I longed for outside; it is a great pity that those places have been built over and so commercialised. All the reality has gone.

On Easter Sunday we took part in the Easter service in the St. Andrews Presbyterian Church which lay in a secluded part of the new Jerusalem. It was an uplifting experience to go there and renew our faith.

We made excursions to many places. In Jerusalem we visited the Wailing Wall, the Holy of Holies for the Jews. We went down through the barren land of Judah and saw the place where the Dead Sea scrolls were found. We travelled on the road to Jericho and visited the pool of Siloam. There, a cherished childhood memory returned of my grandfather's voice singing one of his favourite hymns: "*By cool Siloam's shady rills*".

We entered the Jordan valley and bottles were filled with water from the river Jordan. I was given one which I later donated to the Tyrie and Aberdour churches for future baptisms. To the land we had seen before, the Jordan valley was a complete contrast: lush and fertile green hills and the sparkling blue waters of Galilee. There were whole fields of maize, corn, potatoes and other vegetables and orchards full of oranges and bananas. It was lovely to see the trees laden with fruit and whole loads of oranges going past in lorries, just like turnips here at home. We visited Caperneum twice. In Jesus' day it was bustling with life and activity, today it is desolate, almost deserted and the buidlings were in ruins, but somehow I loved it. Here Jesus had gathered his disciples and taught them the message that Drostan had carried to the shores of Aberdour. On the second day we visited a kibbutz which had been founded in 1937 as a collective settlement of about four hundred members. They had created a very pleasant, even lush, area out of desolation. We watched all its various activities and talked to the workers, some of whom were Scottish.

I must mention the shrubs and flowers of the Holy Land. What a delight they were to the eyes: their gorgeous colours, their enormous size and all growing wild. There were pokers, cyclamen, geraniums, madonna liles, to mention only a few. Then there were the children: little brown-eyed cherubs who followed you everywhere, begging for money or sweets. Last but not least, were the ever-present sellers, mostly young boys. They waited for you on the steps of your hotel, followed you around, and when you stopped for a minute they were there with their cards, their slides and beads, and trinkets of every sort, and they never gave up.

Passing through security at the airport on our way home was a nerve-wracking, nasty experience. Everything was taken out of our cases; thank goodness we were only allowed one. I had packed mine carefully, putting my dirty linen into plastic bags, but even they were thrown all over the place. While one of us was trying to gather up her things, the one in front was still valiantly trying to get hers back in her case and the one behind was pushing to get hers seen to. It was a relief to hand my case over to the airline but a further ordeal awaited. I was sent to a small cubicle where a cheeky young woman, smart in her soldier's uniform, told me in no uncertain terms to empty my handbag and get undressed. And she meant undressed - for I was left only with my small panties and my stockings down to my feet. I was spoken to as if I was already a condemned criminal, a very undignified experience for a lady nearly pension age. It was all necessary I suppose but it could have been done in a more courteous way.

A few years later, I got the chance to join a party going to Oberammergau to see the Passion Play. When I first read about this unique event, I never thought I might see it one day. We flew from Gatwick airport to Munich where we boarded a bus to Zire, a small holiday village in Austria. The weather and food were good and the people very friendly. The scenery was fantastic and a marvellous week of sight-seeing followed. We visited the ski slopes across from Berchtsegaden, Hitler's hide-out; we had a whole day in Salzburg and spent some time around Mozart's birth place; we spent a day at Innsbruck where the winter Olympics were held in 1964 and 1976 and another in Vienna, a city of spacious squares, parks and fountains and a heritage of old buildings which we were told was unrivalled in Europe. Innsbruck must be one of the most spectacular and beautiful cities in the world. From the city centre a five-minute train ride brought us to a cable car which, in another quarter of an hour, took us to the high mountains.

Part of our second week was spent in Oberammergau, very near the Austrian frontier and here, every ten years, the Passion Play is performed. The theatre buildings where the play was performed were not very impressive, giving the impression of a barn. That served its purpose, however, for the accoustics were such that every word spoken on stage could be heard even though no microphones were used. The audience of over fifteen thousand were comfortably seated under cover, but the stage was quite open to the elements and the play continued regardless of the weather. The gentle rising slopes of distant mountains and clouds scudding across the deep blue sky formed the background. The performance began at 9 am and ended at 5pm with a three-hour mid-day break. The events were taken from the four gospels and bible scenes were skilfully woven into the play. Music also played a very important part in the performance, from the opening scene with choir and orchestra to the closing scene showing the triumph and glorification of Christ over death. The play held us all enthralled the whole time. It was a wonderful experience, but all too brief.

From the fifties to the eighties I enjoyed quite a lot of holidays. I had short trips to Manchester and Edinburgh, a most delightful mini-cruise to Shetland, a week in Orkney and a visit to the Flower Festivals at Liverpool and Glasgow. Another week was spent in the North of Scotland with a party led by Ian Grimble, the historian, visiting places associated with the Clearances. I already knew the history, but visiting the deserted croft ruins brought home more vividly the almost unbelievable horror of man's inhumanity to man. I also enjoyed the peace and beauty of Iona and a week in Tighnabruaich. That was a working holiday with the Women's Guild, helping to look after old ladies in need of a holiday. I will always remember the lovely rowan trees, for although we do have rowans here, it is seldom that we see the green leaves and the red berries together.

Unfortunately, during the late sixties, Ivan was frequently in and out of hospital. I am sorry to say that he became practically house-bound and required a lot of attention. As he disliked being in hospital and dreaded going there, I would not allow him to be taken in if I was able to nurse him at home. I often found the going very difficult, however, and it would have been almost impossible to carry on without a break now and again.

Postscript

I wrote this on the twenty-fourth of May 1992. On that day sixty years ago, Ivan and I set out to build ourselves a new life together and together we were for almost fifty-five years. Over the years the changes we witnessed were almost unbelievable; I'm sure our generation has seen more than any previous one. Lots of those changes have been for the good and they have brought many comforts to my old age but today life seems to me to be just one mad rush. What I regret most is that the old values that we built on, our Christian way of life, seem to have passed away. But memory keeps returning to those other days. Youth has, perhaps, covered them in a rosy glow.

Looking back I now know I led a very sheltered life under my grandparents' roof. I had dreams and ambitions but the idea of being a cottar's or a farmer's wife never crossed my mind. Ivan's dream of a small place all his own was transferred to me. It is sad to think that anyone wishing to start as we did has no opportunity to do so now.

Our first six years were spent in cottar abodes. We had a free house, provisions of fire, meal, milk and potatoes and the almost unbelievable sum of one pound a week. We managed and were content but for many it must have been a struggle. When we moved into our own croft house at Millbrex, the thrill and wonder at the fulfillment of the dream we had cherished for so long filled our days with contentment. The seasons of the earth come and go, seed time and the fulfillment of harvest time, rearing and tending animals; our life was simple but full of delight. Most writers write now of those past days on crofts as drudgery, but to me and Ivan they were not so. We were young then, of course, and distance does lend an enchantment. Those days seem to us now some of the happiest of our life.

They lasted only four years; the winds of change came and a serpent crept into our Eden. Ivan began to hanker after better things, more independence and we became farmers at Redbriggs. Days at Redbriggs were not unhappy days; most of the time I was contented but odd times when a dark mood came over me, I felt trapped and longed to get away. The family grew and the two younger boys seemed set to be farmers so the acres at Redbriggs were not enough. When we got Bankhead our search was over. From the first moment my feet touched the ground I felt I had come home.

When Ivan died my life was torn apart; without him my life had no meaning. Sandy tried to get me out of my despondency by getting me to talk of our past life together. Then he suggested I put it down on paper and, with his encouragement, I began this book. Reliving our life together, through the book, has been a healing process that has enabled me to take up my life's burden again, giving me a feeling that, although absent in body, the Ivan I knew and loved is still with me. In my view, mine has been a good life. The simple faith I learned at my grandfather's knee has been, through it all, my guide and comfort. For a time that faith was lost, but was miraculously given back. Now, nearing 'lousing time', I am happy and content to be westering home towards my journey's end.

271

Also from Ardo Publishing

Green Heritage by John R. Allan

*A posthumous novel written in the early thirties.
A successful young London business man discovers his roots
in the North-east of Scotland.*

A Lucky Chap by Sir Maitland Mackie

*Autobiography of the former Lord Lieutenant of Aberdeen-
shire, who with his father founded what has become the
biggest farming business in Scotland. It tells of eighty years
of fun.*

Farmer's Diary by Charlie Allan

*Volumes 1, II, III & IV, the diary illustrated by Turnbull, was
first published in the Herald. It describes with humour the
efforts of Charlie and other farmers of the Discussion Group,
who meet at the Salmon Inn on a Sunday night, to make a
living off the land despite the vagaries of climate, human
nature and the EC commissioners in Brussels.*

A Desert Rat in Holburn Street
by Duncan McGregor

*A young man from the North-east, Duncan McGregor joined
up in the Second World War and soon found himself driving a
tank in the desert. After terrible experiences in the war he
built a very successful grocery business, one of the first self-
service stores, in Aberdeen's Holburn Street.*

All titles available in good bookshops throughout the
North-east or direct from Methlick.

Ardo Publishing Company Ltd.

Methlick, Aberdeenshire AB41 0HR, Tel/Fax 01651 806218